WORLD WRITING:
POETICS, ETHICS, GLOBALIZATION

Much has been said about the relationship between globalization and culture and the political implications of that relationship. There has been little effort made, however, to investigate the effect of globalization on poetics or on the ethical moment of literature. *World Writing* is therefore concerned with studying the intersection of contemporary ethics, poetics, and globalization through historical and critical readings of writing from various parts of the world.

Following an introductory chapter by Mary Gallagher, which maps this conceptual terrain, the contributors investigate how globalization inflects the necessary relationship between poetics, culture, ethics, and politics. Among the essays are Celia Britton's reading of Édouard Glissant on languages in the globalized world; Mary Gallagher's comparison of Glissant's poetics of cultural diversity with the ethics of Emmanuel Levinas; David Palumbo-Liu's exploration of the ethics of postcolonial fiction in J.M. Coetzee's work; Mary Louise Pratt's critique, based on recent Latin American writing, of the prematurely celebratory nature of globalization; and Julia Kristeva's argument for the value of poetics and the ethics of hospitality. What emerges is an intricate discussion of the elusive relationship between the realms of ethics, poetics, and politics as they intersect in our changing world.

(Cultural Spaces)

MARY GALLAGHER is an associate professor of French and Francophone Studies at University College Dublin.

EDITED BY MARY GALLAGHER

World Writing

Poetics, Ethics, Globalization

UNIVERSITY OF TORONTO PRESS
Toronto Buffalo London

© University of Toronto Press Incorporated 2008
Toronto Buffalo London
www.utppublishing.com
Printed in Canada

ISBN: 978-0-8020-9747-7 (cloth)
ISBN: 978-0-8020-9516-9 (paper)

Printed on acid-free paper

Library and Archives Canada Cataloguing in Publication

World writing : poetics, ethics, globalization / edited by Mary
Gallagher.

Includes bibliographical references.
ISBN 978-0-8020-9747-7 (bound)   ISBN 978-0-8020-9516-9 (pbk.)

1. Poetics.   2. Literature and morals.   3. Culture and globalization.
4. Politics and literature.   I. Gallagher, Mary, 1958–

PN1031.W67 2008   809   C2007-906957-6

University of Toronto Press acknowledges the financial assistance to its
publishing program of the Canada Council for the Arts and the Ontario
Arts Council.

University of Toronto Press acknowledges the financial support for its
publishing activities of the Government of Canada through the Book
Publishing Industry Development Program (BPIDP).

Contents

Acknowledgments

This book owes its existence in the first place to the material and moral support of the 'World Writing in French' research program at the Humanities Institute of University College Dublin. I would like to thank all associated with the running of that program, in particular, my colleagues Michael Brophy, Emer O'Beirne, and Douglas Smith, and the Institute's administrator, Valerie Norton. I am also very grateful to the editorial team at University of Toronto Press. The volume benefited in the crucial early stages from the encouragement, patience, and advice of Siobhan McMenemy as commissioning editor, and later on from the invaluable input of the Press's two advisory readers and from the watchful care of managing editor Frances Mundy and copy editor Ken Lewis.

MG

Editor's Note

This volume was conceived against the loud hum of higher education reform. The title of the government-sponsored research program at the Humanities Institute of University College Dublin which funded the publication is 'Identity, Memory, and Meaning in the 21st Century.' Mid-program, however, regime change in the University injected a new marginality, and consequently renewed urgency, into the terms of the project, particularly with respect to the point and place of the humanities in the new century. Internal reinvention coincided with the publication of an OECD report on education in Ireland, the global perspective of which was reinforced by the invitation extended by the University's incoming administration to the Washington Advisory Group, a private US-based, LECG-owned consultancy of 'global experts,' whose university clients appear to be, however, to date mainly domestic. The Group's brief may have indirectly included questions of identity, but not, apparently, the question of memory and certainly not the matter of meaning. The experts[1] were essentially to pronounce, and did, rather uninspiringly, pronounce, on how the University should rebrand itself to achieve local pre-eminence and global eminence. Emerging, then, against the expanding and amplifying mantra of engagement in what Zygmunt Bauman calls the 'deregulated thicket of global competitiveness,'[2] this book considers, among other related issues, the question of how various poetic, ethical, and political imperatives might thrive, or at least survive, against that droning hum.

NOTES

1 It is well worth quoting French sociologist Pierre Bourdieu on the tyranny of experts : 'il faut en finir avec la tyrannie des "experts" style Banque Mondiale ou FMI, qui imposent sans discussion les verdicts du nouveau Léviathan, et qui n'entendent pas négocier, mais "expliquer"; il faut rompre avec la nouvelle foi en l'inévitabilité historique que professent les théoriciens du libéralisme' [we must eradicate the tyranny of experts, World Bank or IMF experts, who impose without any debate the verdicts of the New Leviathan and who are not interested in discussion but rather in explanations; we have to cut our links with the new faith in historical inevitability professed by the theoreticians of liberalism] (Pierre Bourdieu, *Contre feux: propos pour servir à la résistance contre l'invasion néo-libérale* [Paris: Liber/Raisons d'agir, 1998], 31). See also Zygmunt Bauman, 'Education: Under, for, and in spite of Postmodernity,' reprinted in *The Individualist Society* (Cambridge: Polity, 2001), 123–31; Bill Readings, *University in Ruins* (Cambridge: Harvard University Press, 1996); and Imre Szeman, 'Culture and Globalization, or, The Humanities in Ruins,' *New Centennial Review* 3.2 (2003): 91–115.

2 Pierre Bourdieu is particularly exercised in *Contre feux* by the radical contemporary disjuncture between the economic and the social realms and by the prevailing view that productivity and competitivity are the sole and ultimate ends of all human activity: 'on admet que la croissance maximum, donc la productivité et la compétitivité, est la fin ultime et unique des actions humaines, ou qu'on ne peut résister aux forces économiques' [it is accepted that maximum growth, that is, maximum productivity and competitiveness, is the one and only end of human action, and that it is not possible to resist economic forces] (Bourdieu, *Contre feux*, 31). Zygmunt Bauman's analysis of global deregulation is central to all of the works cited under his name in the Bibliography, but see especially *Globalization: The Human Consequences* (London: Polity, 1998), 100–6, in relation to labour flexibility, and 68–9.

WORLD WRITING:
POETICS, ETHICS, GLOBALIZATION

1 Poetics, Ethics, and Globalization

MARY GALLAGHER

Does globalization, can globalization intersect with the work of poetics and, in particular, with the ethical moment of writing? Where and how – in writing and in reading – might the forces and gravitations of globalization be at work (or be worked upon)? What are the implications of this latter 'work' for the relation between poetics and ethics? How might the 'increasingly homogeneous brandname-driven world market'[1] for writing affect or pressure not just the creative imagination – in particular the ways in which the verbal imagination engages ethically with the world – but also the cultural, political, or ethical value of poetics? If the impetus behind this volume is partially reflected in that set of questions, a pressing concern with the relation in reverse was also in the frame. In other words, rather than seeing globalization as a phenomenon or context that might inflect poetics and ethics, might it not be possible, or even necessary, to envisage poetics and ethics as dimensions that – perhaps together, or poet(h)ically – address or even deflect, that is, modulate, divert, or resist the processes or effects of globalization, instead of merely reflecting or registering them? And, of course, a fundamental issue raised by all of the above questions concerns the nature of the relation between poetics and ethics, and indeed, upstream of that question, the matter of what poetics, ethics, and globalization are or do, and have to do with each other.

None of the four concepts central to this volume has self-evident or agreed meanings. To borrow the apt phrasing of the editor of a collection on a contiguous subject, 'none of these terms yield a stable precipitate and their interactions are correspondingly volatile.'[2] Certainly, the volume's apparently more transparent head title – 'World Writing' – although itself unstable, does signal the primary focus on writing. It suggests, indeed, that the forces and processes of globalization may lend planetary resonance to contemporary writing (all or just some of this writing, and if just some writing, then which?). Moreover, although the problematic – and still perhaps virtual? – currency of the expression 'world writing' must be distinguished both from that of 'world litera-ture,' a notion often traced back to Goethe, but invoked as well by Marx and Engels,[3] and also from that of its much more familiar contemporary homologue, 'world music,' this title does refer to these two concepts, if only sub-liminally and contrastively.

Poetics, Poiesis

Before considering the concept of 'world writing,' we need to look more closely at the primary conceptual references of the volume: poetics, eth-ics, and globalization. Of these three, poetics might be regarded as the most controversial, since its historicity and its contemporary currency are manifestly problematic. Philologically and historically speaking, poetics must be distinguished from poetry, in that, unlike the latter, it is, in generic terms, first and foremost a metadiscourse. Its theoretical, even normative, valency is clear, since in ancient and early modern use of the term in the West – in the Greek classics and later in seventeenth-century neo-classical criticism – it refers to the set of rules governing the composition of poetic works (as in Aristotle's or Horace's, Boileau's or Pope's poetics, for example). In Aristotle's lexicon, the term *poiesis* refers to the poet's making, invention, imagining, etc., of probable (rather than actual) events. However, in the post-Romantic twentieth century, as the object of the increasingly descriptive and non-normative discourse of 'poetics' spread to include all genres, 'poetics' came to refer to any gen-eral theory of literature, eventually coming to designate theories of 'lit-erariness' itself, and even the playing out of literariness. Yet, if we think of the use of the term 'poetics' by the phenomenologist Gaston Bach-elard in *La Poétique de l'espace*,[4] we see that it is mobilized in that context to suggest a semiotics, a semantics, or an imaginary of space, rather than the mediation of such a semantics or imaginary via mimesis, writing, or verbal art specifically. Notwithstanding such loose referencing, the con-temporary understanding of poetics, profoundly marked by early twen-tieth-century Russian Formalism, relates it principally to the theory of literary language, and, by extension, to theories of meaning or signifi-cation in general, even if the line between theory and application or practice is sometimes blurred.

Quite independently from the fact that the term 'poetics' suggests the tempting word-play – poet(h)ics – which points on a purely – or impurely? – ludic level towards a certain, or rather an uncertain, co-implication of ethics and poetics, it seemed appropriate in this particular project to mobilize it in preference to the word 'literature.' Firstly because its semantic resonance is – historically speaking – rather more closely focused, since Aristotle, indeed, than that of the very much younger term 'literature' on (specifically) verbal forms theoretically or speculatively envisaged in terms of their value or effects, and in particular in terms of their ethical or at least moral value or effects (for Aristotle, principally the cathartic production of affect). And secondly because of its historically recent yet tenacious – formalist/structuralist – association with what is often termed the 'linguistic turn,' with the postmodern questioning of the (unitary) subject, and with emphasis on formal patterning or systematicity, especially repetition, superimposition, etc.[5] The idea of systematicity is predictably important for some globalization commentators (notably for the proponents of 'world systems' theory), while it is subtly critiqued by others, such as Édouard Glissant.[6]

Discourse on 'poetics' is traditionally linked to broadly Western theories of representation, fiction, imagination, aesthetics, literariness, form, meaning, etc., theories that seldom, if ever, reflect on their own ethnocentricity or on their possibly (contextually) limited validity. Consequently, any contemporary appeal to the notion of poetics necessarily involves confronting the current orthodoxy of a culturalism whose respectability and quasi-monopoly are registered in the rise and prominence of 'cultural studies.' Certainly, the term 'culture' bridges the gap between an anthropological, infinitely inclusive or capacious concept of human meaning, on the one hand, so capacious in fact that the expression 'cultural difference' has become almost tautological, and, on the other, the explicitly exclusive and widely discredited, normative notion of high culture or 'civilization.' Cultural studies is a discipline whose foundation – or whose secession from literary studies – is centred on the much more commodious concept of culture: not only on culture as a factor of differentiation but also, to some extent at least,[7] on the rehabilitation if not the privileging of popular and/or mass culture as opposed to literature, poetics, or aesthetics. Assimilating rather strangely, indeed, the exclusive and the differential values of the notion of culture, Geoffrey Hartman refers to the 'fateful militancy "culture" has achieved in the world,' noting that 'there has been a shift from aesthetics – or art studies within its own institutional history, to ... "culturalism," the effort to use art to diagnose or affirm particular cultures.'[8] However, most definitions of culturalism would not stress art as the sole symptom of cultural specificity.

Mobilization of the term 'poetics' inevitably gestures towards the current debate on the disciplinary boundaries between and among cultural, literary, postcolonial, and area studies and, more especially, towards the raising of the stakes of that debate in the context of globalization, a phenomenon that particularly concerns – and indeed promotes or at least facilitates – the diffusion of mass culture even as it raises (new?) questions regarding the viability of cultural difference. In that sense, this volume challenges contemporary squeamishness towards, or disengagement from, questions of aesthetics, poetics, and literariness, or at least it confronts the perceived difficulty, even impossibility, of considering how such values or practices might intersect with what some would call the 'New World Order' (of globalization).[9] However, it also involves probing the ways in which 'globalization has disturbed the concept of culture.'[10] It is worth noting in this latter respect the theoretical pressure applied by Revathi Krishnaswamy to the construction of 'culture as the privileged locus of (global) heterogeneity, agency, and resistance.'[11] For this critic of the 'culturalist turn in critical theory,' the 'theoretical category of culture appears to have become far too overblown and overdetermined to be politically effective in the age of neoliberal globalization.'[12] However, what is particularly striking in Krishnaswamy's approach is that she uses the term 'culture' as a substitutable equivalent for, if not as a synonym of, literature. In other words, instead of distinguishing between culture and literature, she assimilates them and defines both in opposition to politically (more) effective critique of economic or material realities, and, in particular, of consumer capitalism. In complete contrast, Timothy Brennan, in an article on 'World Music,' far from conflating literary and cultural practice, points out that

> ... club or theatrical music, dance, and food – not oil painting or literature – are the cultural markers in most of the world, including in those civilizations regarded by Europe as its worthy competitors: China, India, and the Arabic world. The status of literature is itself, relatively speaking, a narrowly regional, affected, intellectual mode of cultural exchange, with exaggerated ramifications in the context of civilizations. Its priority in education in Europe and the US – a priority that cultural studies has only ineffectually challenged – is an interested one.[13]

This view is, in itself, a clear manifestation not just of globalized thinking on culture and literature (it shows one of the ways in which globalization has indeed 'disturbed the concept of culture'), but also of the perfect congruency of globalization and cultural studies.

To appeal to the notion of 'poetics' is to demur from the coerced contemporary dilution of 'literature' into 'writing' or from its relativization and despecifying conflation with all other cultural practice. It is also to question the summary dismissal of the value of the literary in favour of either the broadly 'cultural' (Brennan), or the putatively superior political traction not so much of non-literary culture as of supposedly extra-cultural political critique (Krishnaswamy). When the critic Robert Young states that 'writing is now valued as much for its depiction of representative minority experience as for its aesthetic qualities,'[14] he is suggesting that a revolution on several fronts (feminist, postcolonialist ...) has altered the relation previously supposed to obtain between aesthetics or 'the literary,' on the one hand, and political considerations, on the other. The terms 'art' and 'aesthetics' are recurrent in debates about the value of literature. They surface with particular force in this volume, too, in discussions of the thinking of Emmanuel Levinas, Maurice Blanchot, and André Malraux. More generally, however, it is fair to say that whether the value claimed for the aesthetic dimension of literature is positive or negative, it is generally construed in relation to political value and as different, or apart, from general 'cultural' value. That is, art is taken to be supremely political, or alternatively supremely non-political or a-political, or indeed supremely political precisely because it is non-political. Thus, to attempt to articulate the notion of poetics with notions of ethics and globalization is not simply to confront the 'ruse of the aesthetic' inherent in the Romantic notions of (literary) culture used to 'exercise and legitimate political domination.'[15] For, although some would argue that poetics is hopelessly compromised politically, whereas non-literary 'culture' can mediate political resistance more effectively, others would disagree and would point to the (political) 'necessity of art' (Nicholas Harrison gives indeed a very balanced account of the much-rehearsed counter-argument that the 'most literary' texts are, in fact, the 'most political').[16]

Reflecting on these questions in relation to globalization, the literary critic Chris Bongie argues that the modernist genealogy of postcolonial studies results in that discipline's foundational bias against popular culture, and notes that the term 'poetics' carries connotations of 'literary studies and the decidedly unfashionable emphasis upon hierarchies of aesthetic value that has traditionally defined [that] discipline.'[17] Moreover, he recognizes that such connotations may be seen to run counter to what he refers to as the 'insights of transnational cultural studies,' that is, the 'cultural studies project of charting the global(ized) realities of the geopolitical present (and those of popular mass culture in particular).'[18] Bongie considers, for his part, that it is vital to retain a 'measure of belief in the value of literature ... as the troubling other of contemporary (and self-evidently "progressive") disciplines such as postcolonial and cultural studies.'[19] He suggests, indeed, that 'we [literary critics] must not be afraid of (what is for us) the overwhelming truth that "literature" has a value that other texts (be they pulp fiction or manifestoes about reproductive and genetic engineering) simply do not possess, and that this value will not always, and perhaps even seldom, be compatible with the politically "oppositional" values that (we as) postcolonial and francophone critics are committed to uncovering.'[20]

Enfolded within Chris Bongie's otherwise persuasive perspective on literature and on postcolonial studies lies, however, a questionable point. The notion that literary value, the value that – presumably – distinguishes equally what Gayatri Spivak would term the 'stylistically competitive'[21] writing of the postcolonial canon (so, to reference the French/francophone canon, the writing of Assia Djebar or Édouard Glissant, for example) and/or canonical metropolitan writing (for example, the work of Paul Valéry), is often, if not usually, incompatible with 'politically oppositional value' is surely an idea that might be successfully challenged. The critical, countering thrust that Djebar's and Glissant's writing claims for itself and that some readers have claimed for the poetics of Paul Valéry's prose or for the poetics of subjectivity in the writing of Marguerite Duras, to take both modernist and postmodernist examples of twentieth-century writing in French, might be seen as answering Bongie's doubts concerning the politically oppositional potential of 'literariness.' Indeed, we might refer in this context to the work of Gayatri Spivak, who has been particularly careful to stress the politically effective value of what she terms 'literary depth' in contradistinction to (mere) 'social scientific fluency,'[22] arguing very strongly in particular for the 'power of fiction.'[23] And what is this power if not the power to challenge, to interrupt, to trouble certainties, orders, boundaries, and distinctions, not least the distinction between the political and the non-political or the a-political? The difference and the relation between literature and culture 'writ large,' between literary and cultural studies, and between 'literariness' and culture in general, including popular and mass culture, may well be, as Bongie suggests, the outstanding *impensé* of postcolonial studies. But it could equally be said that globalization, as a phenomenon that has not so much accompanied, as conditioned or even determined, the rise of both cultural studies and postcolonial studies, can often be the pretext for avoiding or under-examining not just the question of literary value, but also the historicity of the (no doubt contextually variable) definitions of art, literature, and culture, and of the relation between poetics and ethics, poetics and politics and, even more critically perhaps, the relation between ethics and politics. Indeed, several contemporary critics, such as Gayatri Spivak or Derek Attridge, draw on the ethics of Emmanuel Levinas to argue for the radically specific and potentially – though problematically – politically oppositional, value of the literary. Attridge believes that 'the *singularity* of the artwork is not simply a matter of difference from other works ... but a transformative difference, a difference, that is to say, that involves the irruption of *otherness* or *alterity* into the cultural field.'[24] For him, it is perhaps more in relation to ethics than to politics, then, that the literary presents a 'challenge to cultural norms'[25] and that it is consequently positioned both inside and outside culture.

If the pre-eminence of popular mass culture in the global context is undoubtedly the principal symptom or the chief vector of what is often represented as the irresistible levelling, if not homogenizing, process of cultural globalization, then the values of literary difference or of poetic opaqueness can surely be argued to have at least some – and perhaps some considerable – (politically and/or ethically?) resistant or contestatory potential. And indeed, although he is anxious to counter the 'instrumental attitude to literature,'[26] an attitude that would reduce the text's 'inventiveness' by assuming that its meaning or value is entirely explicable in terms of its oppositional value, Derek Attridge does nonetheless situate the 'singularity' of literature in relation to its challenge to cultural norms.

What Chris Bongie characterizes as the 'fetishistic insistence on fiction or poetry ... as the privileged metonym for culture'[27] – a viewpoint echoing Alain Badiou's complaint that philosophy in France indulges in a certain 'fétichisme de la littérature'[28] and that it is (overly) 'sutured' to the poetic dimension – does not have any bearing on the question regarding the oppositional (political and/or ethical?) value of poetics. In this volume, Douglas Smith's analysis of the poet(h)ics of Maurice

Blanchot and André Malraux underlines the context-sensitive resonance of the notions of culture, literature, and space mediated by both
writers, based as they are on a specific geographical and historical
moment of the global interplay of various political axes and forces. Is it
not entirely possible, then, that certain types of writing lend themselves
in our infant millennium to the contestation of 'empire' in the diffusely
global, totally permeating, even totalitarian sense of Michael Hardt and
Antonio Negri – that is, the global empire of the market itself?[29] Surely
the literary, contrary to what Chris Bongie suggests, can be potentially
– and because of its very mode of signification – politically defiant,
even, if not indeed especially, against the background of the new (i.e.,
global) world order? We might recall in this context the view of Jean
Ricardou, who, when writing of the *nouveau roman*, few of whose practitioners were overtly politically engaged, boldly claimed that 'the parallel between representation ... and the ideology of imperialism is so
strong that to produce anti-representational texts is itself a contestation
of imperialism.'[30] Paul Valéry and his contemporary advocates[31] would
make a similar point about the relation between a certain type of eminently intelligible and normative, representational writing, on the one
hand, and complicity with fascism, on the other. The critic Robert Pickering thus reads Paul Valéry's writing as being highly resistant on its
own terms to the very basis of the collaborationist Vichy régime in
Occupied France: 'ce genre d'écriture affirme l'indépendance de la pensée et la liberté de l'imagination créatrice, qualités qui sont particulière-
ment vulnérables dans ce contexte d'uniformisation, de résurgence et
de transformation psychologiques qui est celui de la Révolution Nationale' [this type of writing asserts the independence of thought and the
freedom of the creative imagination, qualities that are especially vulnerable in the context of standardization, revival, and psychological
transformation that is a National Revolution].[32] Pickering indeed views
the complexity of Valéry's intellectual and artistic prose as 'une attaque
en règle contre des concepts basés sur la normalisation et la totalisation'
[a formal attack on concepts based on normalization and totalization].
Indeed, linking political resistance with ethical resistance, he quotes as
an example of contestatory thinking the following statement by Valéry,
a statement that subverts the binarism upon which a certain totalizing
and very dubious moral clarity depends: 'Il y a de la victime dans le
bourreau et du bourreau dans la victime ... il y a de quoi passer de l'un
à l'autre; et c'est peut-être cette puissance de transformation qui est
l'essence même du véritable Moi' [There is something of the victim in

the butcher and something of the butcher in the victim ... there is enough to pass from one to the other and it is perhaps this transformative power that is the very essence of the true Self].[33] Even without dwelling here on the striking resonance between Valéry's words, on the one hand, and, on the other, Derek Attridge's location of the literary in the (ethical) power to transform and to 'other,' this brief reference to Valéry's writing focuses our attention squarely on the crucial, if highly problematic, distinction between literature's political and ethical dimensions. The question of the articulation of literature's aesthetic, political, and ethical facets, and the ramifications of this question in the work of Gayatri Spivak, Jacques Derrida, and Jacques Rancière, for example, have been searchingly addressed by Nicholas Harrison.[34]

The 'theoretical' or speculative dimension of poetics – its philosophical valency, so to speak – is central to many essays in this volume, even if it percolates most notably and most explicitly Julia Kristeva's essay on 'French theory' and the essays on Édouard Glissant, Maurice Blanchot, André Malraux, and Emmanuel Levinas. And this persistent focus can be seen as further evidence of what Alain Badiou regards as the unhealthy liaison between (French) philosophy and literature. Indeed, the fact that this volume dwells so predominantly, largely due to the backgrounds of the various contributors, on the very (French/ francophone) sphere of thinking that Badiou regards as hopelessly sutured to poetics, allows it to highlight what is increasingly widely regarded as a key question with regard to the relation between ethics and poetics: namely, the fact that 'the literary ... cannot be fully understood theoretically but must be engaged in its specific performance (word by word, line by line, in the unfolding text).'[35] It should be noted, of course, that Julia Kristeva's work most often consists in *reading*, very often in a reading of literary texts (of Proust and Colette, for example). The fact that she is here writing exclusively (of) theory does, however, activate and illustrate within this volume one of the deepest fault lines of poetics, namely, the line dividing poetics as a metadiscourse from poetics as verbal/aesthetic praxis. However, more 'empirical' work – that is, close readings of prose fiction or autofiction – are also crucial in many contributions, especially in those of Richard Serrrano and David Palumbo-Liu, but also in those of Mary Louise Pratt and Douglas Smith, while Rob Wilson's argument is substantially based on a reading of filmic and poetic texts. Thus, the sense of poetics that emerges from the volume is that of a feedback loop of theory and practice (i.e., writing/reading). In other words, individual readings that actualize the ethical working of specific possibilities or dimensions of writing – the ethics of literary representation, or of fictional or narrative mediation, for example – continually intersect with more wide-angle, theoretical or speculative approaches. For example, the distinction between the author and the narrator/protagonist in Moroccan francophone writing is highlighted by Richard Serrano as a locus of semantic complexity and as the basis of the literary imagination of alternative worlds or subjectivities. And the author/narrator/protagonist relation, so central to the 'power of fiction,'[36] is equally central to Douglas Smith's treatment of the ethics of the self/other relation in the fiction and other writings of Maurice Blanchot and André Malraux, as to David Palumbo-Liu's analysis of the poet(h)ics of J.M. Coetzee's novel *Elizabeth Costello*. It is interesting to note in this connection Franco Moretti's observation, in an article entitled 'Conjectures on World Literature,' that, since 'the narrator's voice' is the key variable of the novel form across 'world literature,' genuine formal analysis is, as he puts it, 'off-limits' unless one has the required linguistic competence in a huge range of languages – in 'French, English, Spanish, Russian, Japanese, Chinese, and Portuguese, just for the core of the argument.'[37] As Moretti argues, the study of 'world literature' will be, of necessity, 'second hand,' 'without a single direct textual reading,' and its ambition will be 'directly proportional to the distance from the text.' Moretti sees as a necessary corollary of this development the attenuated role, or even the disappearance, of the literary canon as such (on which the whole time-costly principle of close reading depended). However, he recalls in this connection the price of theoretical knowledge: 'reality is infinitely rich; concepts are abstract, are poor.'[38] He argues, in fact, for a bifocal approach to world literature: an approach that takes into account both geographical and historical discontinuities (the tree) and global spatio-temporal continuities (the wave), and that marries both ethno-linguistic specialisms and translinguistic or transcultural comparative approaches to criticism. These necessary tensions between the particular and the general, the empirical and the theoretical, the exemplarity and singularity of the literary text, of which (close) reading is an essential part, tensions that lie, as we have already seen, at the very heart of poetics, are visibly inscribed in the composition of this volume. It is, indeed, in order to honour the understanding that literary study or poetics, as Spivak notes, 'depends on texture'[39] and so as to respect the insight that 'a merely reasonable system, such as the kind of analogical classification envisaged by distant reading ... will not yield the singular,'[40] that this volume makes such ample room for the language of the text and aims to read it (anew). This is, again, in line with Spivak's insistence on 'learning languages, the old access to literary detail, rather than analogizing from descriptions of fractal geometry or chaos theory.'[41]

In her (here, then, purely theoretical) contribution, the 'French' writer Julia Kristeva presents poetic thinking or *poiesis* as the (best) ethics for an age of globalization. She makes a similar case to Édouard Glissant, who advocates the poetics of relation – a creative bringing-into-relation or confrontation of heterogeneous elements – as a process prophetic of, and faithful to, the global epistemology of our age. Glissant does recognize, however, that the poetics of relation is not necessarily ethical, a concession that suggests a certain divergence between Kristeva's apparent faith in the unlimited ethical and dissident potential of poetics, on the one hand, and the Martinican writer's highly qualified optimism concerning the ethico-political ramifications of poetics, on the other. Moreover, rather than specifying, as Glissant does, global relationality and cultural opaqueness as the key to both the poetic and ethico-political value of poetics, Kristeva valorizes the (essentially?) 'revolutionary' and (intrinsically?) emancipatory value of poetics; that is, the transgression of syntax and logic by trans-verbal, pre-verbal, semiotic, or poetic meaning. Arguing, moreover – in terms quite reminiscent of Paul de Man's discourse on figural language or metaphorization in *Allegories of Reading* – that 'French theory' is concerned primarily with metaphorical transfer, Kristeva identifies *poiesis* as the privileged mode of 'French theory.' The connection that she makes between the political and the poetic is based, then, on her view of the fundamentally interrogative thinking allowed or enacted by poetics, 'at the very point of emergence of language,' as she puts it. Indeed, for Kristeva, the poet, no less than the libertine, the psychoanalyst, or the revolutionary, is the main subject of this 'desire for dissidence.' Clearly, however, and notwithstanding the reservations expressed above concerning Chris Bongie's view of poetics, contestatory intent or politically subversive value may not characterize poetics either axiomatically or empirically (as conceived of or as practised through time or across the global context). Thus, a more historicized, more culturally discriminating, or less context-transcending approach might produce a quite different evaluation of the point or potential of poetics.

What is not clear, however, is whether or not what Derek Attridge terms the 'singularity' of literature is, in fact, 'universal,' whether that universality is descriptive or normative, and whether or not Gayatri

Spivak's definition of the literary, which may or may not be what she refers to as the (inherently ethical?) 'interruption' or 'othering' of intelligibility[42] – after all, she regards the imagination is the 'great inbuilt instrument of othering'[43] – but what certainly seems to be what she means by 'literary depth,'[44] can, in fact, claim universality across space and time. If, indeed, the 'singularity of the artwork is not simply a matter of difference from other works [or of] "uniqueness," but a transformative difference, a difference, that is to say, that involves the irruption of *otherness* or *alterity* into the cultural field,'[45] and if this is a statement of universal validity, then Attridge's use of the term 'singularity' acquires a new, rather ironic valency. For its would-be anti-essentialism is, in one sense at least, defeated by the implicit suggestion that literature is globally and historically singular, that its depth, power, and ethics transcend time, space, and cultural difference.

Ethics

As the twentieth century moved towards the turn-of-the-millennium, the postmodern discourse of ethics tended to be articulated less in terms of humanism, than of anti-humanism or post-humanism, a redefinition that would appear to have set off, in turn, a compensatory neo-universalist and neo-humanist reaction.[46] Coincidentally, or at least simultaneously, the promotion of difference or 'identitarianism' within literary and cultural studies began to register a certain slowdown. So, unlike the general thrust of mid to late twentieth-century global politics, the course of which was substantially determined by an inexorable, apparently irresistible movement towards decolonization and towards the claims of diversity (national, ethnic, gendered, etc.), the close of the twentieth century seems to have stabilized in a post-colonial and even post-political moment that could furthermore be regarded as inflected – some would say deflected – by an ethical turn. If late twentieth-century and early twenty-first century normative discourse tends to hold out for a pan-human counterbalance not just to nationalism but also to culturalism and to identity politics, this is because the ethical imperative, quite unlike the political imperative, has always had pretensions both to ontological primacy or priority, and also to a politically and culturally transcendent universalism. Moreover, twentieth-century discourse on ethics has tended towards an absolutism based on its disjunction from the history of moral philosophy. Prior to the ethical turn, however, twentieth-century discourse on ethics had been subordinated to political discourse; in other words, normative discourse was monopolized to a great degree by politics, for example, the politics of the colonial collapse, and of the Cold War and their respective implications and aftershocks. Then, as the millennium's final decades accelerated towards the demise of communism, the balance between ethics and politics was more or less reversed, with some philosophers such as Jacques Rancière, not surprisingly, equating this 'ethical turn' (which Rancière links, indeed, to a certain contemporary approach to aesthetics and to 'the literary'[47]) with the eclipse of politics per se.[48] Ethics has sometimes been regarded, in fact, as an anti-politics, and J. Hillis Miller claims as much when he writes that although 'the political and the ethical are always intimately intertwined, ... an ethical act that is fully determined by political considerations or responsibilities is no longer ethical. It could even in a certain sense be said to be amoral.'[49] Alisdair MacIntyre also notes the traditional separation of the two domains, stating that, historically, the distinction between ethics and politics depended 'upon there being a distinction between private and public life of such a kind that I can consider what it is best for me to do without considering in what political order it is requisite for me to live, either because I treat the political order as a given and unalterable context of private action, or because I think the political order irrelevant for some other reason.'[50] Although it would be impossible to be faithful here to the complexity of the contemporary debate (and its history) on the relationship between ethics and politics, it is, nonetheless, an unavoidable issue. As the work of some of the most influential thinkers who have engaged in this debate, including Michel Foucault and Jürgen Habermas, clearly shows, it is a most challenging, almost aporetic, question. Thus, Vincent Pecora observed at the end of the 1980s: 'Foucault's struggle with an ethics/politics articulation reiterates ... both the necessity and the difficulty the relation has posed for contemporary criticism – one which has not only been further obscured by approaches like Hillis Miller's, but remains unaddressed in the work of Laclau and Mouffe.'[51]

In his useful study on the 'ethical turn,' Pecora suggests that it is no accident that 'ethics should return to critical discourse' at a time when the 'possibility of viable adversary politics in Western Democracies (that is, more or less collective and coherent opposition to existing structures of power) has been once again reduced to mere neurotic fantasy.'[52] In the context of Pecora's article, it is clear that, for him, the new (contemporary) situation corresponds to the 'jingoist bureaucrat's "end of history,"' coinciding with the now putatively total global triumph of liberal capitalism.[53] Pecora takes politics to mean 'collective relations to existing, and in many cases traditional, exercises of power' and takes adversarial politics to 'aim not simply at what Marx called "political emancipation" – that is, a just distribution of political rights guaranteed by the state – but also an emancipation from economic and cultural domination.'[54] Ethics, on the other hand, is defined by Pecora as 'relations between an autonomous, self-determining subjectivity and a set of potentially, but never actually universalizable values – a "normative" discourse always to some extent in flux, dependent both on the inertia of tradition (an "ethos") and the appearance (at the least) of potential justification by universalizable reason.'[55] As for the relation between politics and ethics, for Pecora 'politics may or may not conceive of itself as ethically based, but it inevitably has recourse to the language of ethics in order to secure and maintain hegemony.'[56] Conversely, ethics 'will by definition claim political transcendence and will thus disavow any relation to the existing (political) exercise of power.' For Pecora, 'personal "ethics" and public "politics" [in the reduced sense of legal rights] form a paradoxical, mutually supporting dyad in Western liberal capitalism, a dyad that is itself an effect of opposition, emphasized by Marx, between civil society and the state.'[57] What is striking in this materialist approach to the relation between ethics and politics is, firstly, the anachronistic restriction of the domain of ethics to the 'autonomous, self-determining' subject (proponents of postmodern ethics would strongly contest this view of the subject); secondly, the absence from Pecora's equation (and from his conceptualization of the state in particular) of an explicit problematization of globalization; and finally, the lack of reference to discursive mediation.

The close but tense relation between ethics and politics is particularly well pointed up in the work of the Jewish philosopher Emmanuel Levinas, one of the most central and influential references of the 'ethical turn' that emerged principally out of the unspeakable damage done to the image of politics by the two totalitarianisms that disgraced the face of the first half of the twentieth century. The ethical turn could indeed be seen as a movement against the primacy of politics, as the following statement from Levinas suggests: 'Siècle qui en trente ans a connu deux guerres mondiales, les totalitarismes de droite et de gauche, hitlérisme et stalinisme, Hiroshima, le goulag, les génocides d'Auschwitz et du Cambodge. Siècle qui s'achève dans la hantise du retour de tout ce que ces noms barbares signifient. Souffrance et mal imposés de façon délibérée, mais qu'aucune raison ne limitait dans l'exaspération de la raison devenue politique et détachée de toute éthique' [A century which in thirty years has seen two world wars, totalitarianisms of the left and right, Hitlerism and Stalinism, Hiroshima, the gulags, and the genocides of Auschwitz and Cambodia. A century which is drawing to a close haunted by the return of all that these barbaric names evoke: suffering and evil deliberately imposed, but upon which no limits were imposed in the exasperation of a reason turned political and cut loose from all ethics].[58] In fact, the relation that Levinas envisages between ethics and politics mirrors the one that he sees between ethics and ontology. For it is not ontology itself, but rather its totalizing dimension or its claim to primacy, that Levinas credits ethics with disrupting.[59] Conversely, highlighting and criticizing the infinite value attributed in Levinas's thinking to the subordination of the subject (hostage not so much to the other, as to the other construed as victim), Jacques Rancière touches on one of the most tender points (and indeed Levinas would himself identify it as such) of postmodern ethics and perhaps indeed all ethics, namely, the point at which the ethical relation par excellence, the face-to-face with another person, must be (but all too often is not) articulated with justice, with the 'third person,' and politics. Writing of the 'droit absolu, extra-juridique de la victime du mal infini' [the absolute, extra-judicial rights of the victim of infinite evil] in relation to the fall-out from 9/11, Rancière notes that 'le trait le plus marquant de cette symbolisation est l'éclipse de la politique, c'est-à-dire de l'identité incluant l'altérité, de l'identité constituée par la polémique sur le commun' [the most remarkable aspect of this symbolization is the eclipse of politics, that is, of identity inclusive of otherness, of identity constituted through the polemic on commonality].[60]

It is important to note in this context that Simon Critchley, one of Levinas's most convincing commentators, insists that ethics and politics are inextricably linked for Levinas. He notes that, for Levinas, 'politics begins as ethics,'[61] 'the ethical relation always takes place within a political context, within the public realm,'[62] and 'ethics is for the sake of politics.'[63] More specifically, Critchley draws attention to Levinas's claim that 'the third party looks at me in the eyes of the Other, and therefore my ethical obligation to the Other opens onto wider questions of justice for others and for humanity as a whole.'[64] Moreover, this link is not chronological, for 'ethics is always already political,' and furthermore, in all of Levinas's invocations of a relation of diffuse solidarity with humanity, 'this relation is always mediated by the specific and concrete relation'[65] to the Other person. Going much further than Simon Critchley, another of Levinas's commentators, Colin Davis, has noted the profound impression made on the young Levinas by 'the way in which ... his thesis supervisor used the example of the Dreyfus affair to illuminate the primacy of ethics over politics.'[66]

The so-called 'ethical turn,' which, as we have seen, can be read as a turning away from politics, has made itself felt in literary studies in a number of ways. In the francophone context, for example, one of the most revealing contemporary debates around the articulation of writing and ethics sees Maurice Blanchot, Colin Davis, Leslie Hill, and Martin Crowley address – against a Levinasian perspective – the work of Robert Antelme and the complex interrelation between Antelme's writing and the work of Marguerite Duras. Robert Antelme's concentration camp memoir is entitled *L'Espèce humaine* (Douglas Smith refers to this work in his essay for this volume), and one of the most quoted passages is: 'Nous sommes obligés de dire qu'il n'y a qu'une espèce humaine. Que tout ce qui masque cette unité dans le monde, tout ce qui place les êtres dans la situation d'exploités, d'asservis, et impliquerait par là même, l'existence de variétés d'espèces, est faux et fou ... [le bourreau] peut tuer un homme, mais il ne peut pas le changer en autre chose' [We have to say that there is only one human race. And that anything that masks this unity in the world, anything that positions human beings as exploited or enslaved and that implies by this very fact the existence of varieties of species, is false and crazy ... the butcher can kill a man but he cannot change that man into something else].[67] Marguerite Duras's text *La Douleur*, written in response to *L'Espèce humaine*, seems to interrogate the limits of that statement of Antelme's, subjecting it, in a sense, to a 'poststructural politics and ethics.'[68] In the anglophone context, the critic Richard Freadman, writing of Stephen Spender and noting the 'turn to the ethical'[69] in literary studies, points to the work of figures as diverse as the classicist Martha Nussbaum, the analytical philosopher Richard Rorty, and the British novelist Iris Murdoch. Freadman astutely observes in this connection that 'postmodern theory and criticism have tended to adopt either a taken-for-granted attitude to the ethical which says that it will take care of itself if we demolish existing structures of power, or a hostile position which reposes in the belief that traditional ethical discourses or attitudes are complicit with ... those structures of power.'[70] This resolutely pragmatic position reveals the basis of much of the twentieth century's suspicion of ethics, and its subordination indeed of ethics (and often of poetics and aesthetics also) to politics, or questions of power. And yet the very pragmatism of the view cited by Freadman would seem to identify it as a position typical more of anglo-phone or anglocentric approaches than of those associated with so-called Continental philosophy.

Twentieth-century politics, dominated by issues of recognition (identity politics) as well as by issues of distribution (of power, representation, resources, etc.), is, like all politics, often, if not always, ends-oriented, whereas twentieth-century ethics typically resists instrumentalization and tends towards a certain absolutism. It is this common thread that renders Levinas's unique understanding of the relation between politics and ethics, an understanding distinguished by its singular, quasi-spiritual, or even mystical poeticity, recognizably close to that suggested by the British analytic philosopher Bertrand Russell. As Russell observes, in a remark that has serious implications for contemporary proponents of the politics of 'rational choice,' an economics-based rational approach to choice studied by David Palumbo-Liu in his reading of J.M. Coetzee's *Elizabeth Costello*, 'reason – signifies the choice of the right means to an end that you wish to achieve. It has nothing whatever to do with the choice of ends.'[71] Further on in the same text, Russell states that 'we have reached a point in human history in which for the first time, the mere continued existence of the human race has come to depend upon the extent to which human beings can learn to be swayed by ethical considerations.'[72] This anti–instrumentalist view of ethics is reflected to a certain extent in the critical theory of Jürgen Habermas. For Habermas argues that 'postconventional morality,' a social construction, 'teaches the principle that all humanity must be respected not as a means toward achieving some other goal but as an end in itself.'[73] As Simon Critchley notes, Levinas wrote approvingly of this broadly Kantian refusal to instrumentalize the human, echoing more specifically Kant's formula of the 'end in itself, which guarantees respect for persons,' recommending as it does that we act in such a way as to treat humanity both in one's own person or in the person of 'any other' never simply as a means, but always as an end. [74]

The articulation of ethics and politics is one of the principal questions that drove the work of Michel Foucault and that continues to drive the discourse ethics or communicative action theory of Habermas and the writing of Judith Butler, Ernesto Laclau, and Chantal Mouffe, without finding a conclusive answer even in Habermas's effort to envisage or found a truly transcultural or transcendent ethics. It is not surprising, then, that this question also haunts most of the contributions to this volume. Thus David Palumbo-Liu explicitly recognizes for his part a combined political and hermeneutic deficit as lying at (and undermining) the heart of the poet(h)ics of *Elizabeth Costello*, while Richard Serrano identifies an – intimately combined – ethical, political, and hermeneutic void in the globalized poetics of *Rachid O*. Moreover, the three-way articulation of ethics, poetics, and politics is precisely what is attempted in the writing analysed here in several essays (those of Rob Wilson, Douglas Smith, Mary Louise Pratt, and Mary Gallagher, in particular).

To shift our attention slightly away from the relation or intersection between ethics and politics, we might look briefly at the contemporary resonance of postmetaphysical ethics. Clearly, the importance of the connection between ethics, on the one hand, and questions of subjectivity, identity, and relation, on the other, cannot be overstated, and this is illustrated by Colin Davis's argument that, in its post-Nietzschean contemporary sense, which diverges significantly from Vincent Pecora's definition of its basis in an autonomous, self-determining subjectivity, 'ethics ... does not provide a path to knowledge of right and wrong, Good or Evil, [but is rather] a point of contact with that which challenges me most radically, and through that challenge my identity and relation with the world are thrown into question.'[75] Emmanuel Levinas, as the heir to a long tradition of phenomenological philosophy concerned to define the relation between self and other (a tradition discussed here by Celia Britton in relation to Glissant's philosophy of linguistic difference), insists particularly on 'the ethical value of the other's power to disrupt subjective categories.'[76] Although postmodern in tenor, this view of ethics as having to do primarily with self/world and self/other relations clearly resonates very meaningfully – even if it does so at a great distance – with Aristotle's conception of poetics as involving acts of identification, sympathy, or empathy, or, more precisely, our perception of resemblance with or difference from 'one like [or unlike] ourselves.'[77] For Jürgen Habermas, too, 'the conventional ethical subject is the *I for the other*. Only the subject that has first learned to reason on behalf of the other can hope to attain postconventional universals,'[78] the latter category situating the most evolved ethical level that Habermas recognizes in his discourse ethics. Likewise, Bakhtin's dialogical perspective on poetics, although it is more aesthetically and less rationally and pragmatically oriented than Habermas's perspective, also helps to conceptualize ethics in relation to questions of subjectivity: 'a dialogic definition of an ethical discourse would look to utterances that can create hybrids, that anticipate response, that can include the other within their horizon of expectation and that can keep from imposing the final word.'[79]

This concern with the importance of reception, of dialogue, of the phatic dimension of utterance, or with the position of the other (person), even if it does imply a certain lack or avoidance of semantic (fore)closure, does not at all imply the impossibility of meaning or of commonality, that is, of reading or understanding the utterances in question, or of responding to them. Indeed, refusing precisely to identify lack of closure with unreadability, Thomas Keenan links ethical responsibility with what he calls the 'de-facilitation,' difficulty, or unease, but not the impossibility, of reading (a difficulty akin to what Levinas calls the 'uncondition' of anything worthy of the name responsibility), and he notes that nothing teaches the ethical predicament better than reading.[80]

Poet(h)ics?

Insofar as this volume attempts to articulate ethics and poetics, it has to be concerned, certainly, with the problematic articulation of ethics and politics. But it must also be concerned with the historical association of poetics with notions of discursive and intellectual freedom and responsibililty (the freedom to create, to imagine, and to critique, the responsibility to respond and to critique), and with notions of complexity and excess. As we have seen above, the questions of discourse and subjectivity, meaning and responsibility, are sometimes approached in terms of the non-subordination both of the ethical imperative and of the literary imagination or of poetic language to political or, indeed, to hermeneutic imperatives. J. Hillis Miller, for example, has argued that 'the lure of intellectual mastery promised by all ... hermenuetic theories of meaning whether they are social or historical' is suspect.[81] One of the principal sparking intuitions of this project was precisely the hypothesis that the ethical and the poetic imperatives are not just compatible, but also associated, and that their mutual intrication is dependent on their shared insubordinate, or at least critical, engagement with the temptations or imperatives of closure and totalization often inherent in the plots and processes of politics and hermeneutics. Although in some of his writings, writings examined further on in this volume, Levinas would deny such an enmeshment of poetics and ethics, at least two of the approaches taken in this volume – notably the opposition established by Julia Kristeva between the ethics of hospitality or the emancipatory creativity of poetics, on the one hand, and the levelling imperium of American liberalism, on the other, and Glissant's poetics of diversity as studied further on also – tend to confirm that poet(h)ic intuition. However, they fail to silence the radically unsettling and unanswered question of the articulation of politics with that linkage. Clearly, then, it is particularly critical to bear in mind what we have termed the aporetic tensions surrounding the relation between ethics and politics.

As far as the neologism 'poet(h)ics' is concerned, it serves to consolidate the view that poetics and ethics, literature and the ethical, are intricated in ways that politics and poetics are not.[82] Michael Eskin, in his study of this question, looks at literature and ethics 'as parts of a continuum along which differences in mode and degree determine differences in ethical impetus.'[83] Noting the number of thinkers who have argued the intrication of ethics and literature, Eskin suggests that, 'depending on the given author's particular theoretical framework and approach, the ethical valence of literature (and art in general) has been located ... in what could be roughly subsumed under the heads of its relation to truth, thematics, structure and uses of language, power to effect a change in perception, inherent appeal to responsibility, or capacity of discursive subversion.'[84] Eskin's approach leans heavily on the Aristotelian understanding of poetics as non-apophantic speech. The distinction between apophantic and non-apophantic discourse is established 'on the basis of an utterance's referential relation to reality and the world.'[85] Aristotle had declared, after all, that 'it is not the poet's function to relate actual events, but the kinds of things that might occur and are possible in terms of probablitity and necessity.' According to Eskin, 'much of contemporary moral philosophy and literary criticism continues to rely on a mediated version ... of Aristotle's semiotics and poetics, taking it for granted that it is the fictional, nonapophantic, "nonserious" character of literature and its concurrent capacity to shortcircuit the universal and the particular that ultimately opens a space for the ethical closed to apophantic modes.'[86] However, Eskin holds that we need to revise Aristotle's view that literature functions as the ethical medium par excellence precisely because of its non-apophantic status (i.e., because it presents images of things, setting these outside the domain of 'actual events'). For him, one way of driving Aristotle's argument further is by recalling the contribution made by Formalist poetics to our understanding of discourse. He thus refers to the Russian Formalist, Roman Jakobson, according to whom every utterance is 'constituted by the interplay of all six linguistic functions' so that 'generic differences ... are not a matter of ontology or essence but of the degree of predominance' of these various linguistic functions. Thus, 'Jakobson's approach implicitly brings us to an "aristotelianism without essence,"' which remains entirely compatible with the 'ascription to literature of an ethically exemplary performative function.'[87] We read a text as literature (non-apophantic) on the basis of institutional convention or tradition. However, as discourses that do not emerge in the 'context of immediate verbal interaction,' ethics and literature are *both*, in Eskin's view, 'structurally "fictional."' For him, then, apophansis would be the 'fiction of certain kinds of utterance (e.g., philosophical, scientific, historical), whereas fictionality would be the "fiction" of certain other kinds of utterance, whereby "fiction" reveals itself as equivalent to "meaning" in general.'[88] However, since the specific subject of the 'fictions' of both ethics and poetics is the 'human person in all of its relations, facets, and intricacies,'[89] literature and ethics share the same central concern. Eskin goes on to argue that, because verbal language is the most semiotically 'capacious' medium, literature could be viewed as second-degree ethics, as the 'ethics of ethics or criticism of ethics, as that discourse which literally interprets ethics.' Referring to Pierce's theories of the interpretant, he suggests that literature can translate ethics into 'perhaps a more developed [more 'capacious,' more universal *and* concrete] sign.'[90]

A different idealization of literature (in more specificaly linguistic terms) is evident in Paul de Man's reading of Rousseau, which concludes that, since 'the political destiny of man is structured like and derived from a linguistic model that exists independently of nature and independently of the subject,' politics derives from a 'tension between man and his language,'[91] and so 'far from being a repression of the political, as Althusser would have it, literature is condemned to being the truly political mode of discourse.'[92] De Man implies, then, 'that the only truly "political" form of activity is the writing, reading, and discussion of literature (now defined as a special, self-conscious use of language) – a position taken up by J. Hillis Miller, who merely substitutes "ethics" for "politics."'[93] Central to this 'Enlightenment/Romantic belief in the nature and power of a *poiesis*'[94] is a view of literature held, according to Vincent Pecora, not just by de Man, but also by Jean Baudrillard. In this view, if literature is *the most political* mode of discourse, this is on account of the fact that literary language is the 'most aware of its fictionality.'[95] However, as Eskin's work suggests and as the other above-mentioned thinkers would no doubt agree, political, scientific, and ethical discourse are all fundamentally contingent, constructed, as they are, around fictional invocations. Ethics has been, indeed, historically concerned with the meaning of utterances (about rightness, wrongness, virtue, vice, etc.) and with whether or not these utterances are statements of fact. It would appear nonetheless that for others – Thomas Keenan, for example – it is not so much its (degree of) fictionality, but rather its sematic overdetermination, undecidability, or difficulty, the 'endlessness' or 'irresolution of differences,' the 'impossibility of totality,'[96] that distinguishes literary language.

The postmodern break with humanist and subjectivist paradigms as it is described by Thomas Keenan would seem, then, to reinforce the congruence of poetics and ethics: 'the experience of intolerable complexity,' writes Keenan, 'linked with the ongoing inevitability of a decision is ... *an openness to the other*, impossibility, or simply difficulty.' If, however, decision is construed as a political imperative – after all, politics is, according to Keenan, 'a matter of meaning and knowledge, of closing and fixing'[97] – then the work of politics appears simultaneously as the limit of poetics and ethics and as their end. Both politics and poet(h)ics are, in this view, however, incompatible with subjectivism: 'ethics and politics – as well as literature – are evaded when we fall back on the conceptual priority of the subject, agency, or identity as the grounds of our action.'[98] This view of poetics in relation to hermeneutics is, to a degree, consonant with that of William Connolly, who recommends in *The Augustinian Imperative* the simultaneous acknowledgment of the 'indispensability of interpretation and the limited, porous, and problematic character of any particular effort.'[99] It is also reflected in Connolly's recommendation of critical pluralism as the 'ethic' of politics.[100] But whereas Connolly would not necessarily dismiss the foundational status of 'the subject, agency, or identity,' Levinas and Keenan no doubt would. And it is worth pointing out in this connection that, when Levinas comments favourably on art as inciting a critical response in the form of commentary or discourse (and we shall see, further on, that this notion of response is indissociably linked to ethics in Levinas's thinking), it is not so much the open or the pluralistic nature of the reading, commentary, or criticism incited by art that he approves of, as the simple fact that art incites a verbal response, that it generates respons(e)ibility.[101]

Julia Kristeva recalls in this volume that, 'in a world more and more dominated by technology, freedom becomes the capacity to adapt to a cause, always exterior to the self, and which is less and less a moral cause, and more and more an economic one.' This freedom culminates, she notes, 'in the logic of globalization and of the unrestrained free market.' Kristeva emphasizes the fact that poetics posits a different kind of freedom. This other freedom, the freedom of dialogue or verbal relation, is not subordinated to any cause and is based instead on 'l'être de la parole qui se livre,' that is, the liberation of the being of language that occurs in the encounter between self and other. Kristeva links this discursive freedom to ethics, via the Greek notion of *ethos* as choice of shelter and thereby as character (the character of the species that chooses such a shelter or dwelling place rather than another). However, insofar as Aristotle, in his *Rhetoric*, defines *ethos* as the moral effect produced by the style of an orator or a work of art, we can glimpse, via notions of discourse and representation, an even stronger and more direct philological connection between ethics and poetics. Moreover, if we pursue this philological line of thought, we could also say that ethics – as a word originally meaning choice of 'dwelling' – is apparently dissonant with the idea of globalization, which implies a dynamic of displacement or of spread at odds with the stability implied by dwelling or habitus.

Certainly, in the first decade of the twenty-first century, both ethics and poetics, and *a fortiori* their conjugation, may appear terminally devalued. Both discourses may be seen as somewhat fey or otherworldly, their transcendent moralism and aestheticism respectively making them appear irresponsible, almost a distraction, in an age when the warring-twin extremes of relativism and fundamentalism both contribute to the loss of nerve already besetting political discourse. It might be possible, however, to see both poetics and ethics – both the linguistic turn and the ethical turn – as the witness or the conscience, rather than as the alibi, of twenty-first-century politics. The Slovenian philosopher Slavoj Žižek recommends, indeed, the value of 'an ethics of the political, an extrapolitical effort to protect the political,' although Thomas Keenan, for his part, dismisses this 'sealing off' of the political from politics as the quixotic fantasy of 'yet another end to ideology.'[102]

Globalization

The expression 'globalization,' one of those academic buzzwords mocked by Jean-Michel Rabaté and critiqued by Neil Larsen,[103] seems to have remained as controversial as it is, by now, hackneyed. Its vulnerability to Rabaté's derision, illustrated indeed by the suspicion expressed by the Indian intellectual Arjun Appadurai, that 'any book about globalization is a mild exercise in megalomania,'[104] stems from the rather fragile conceptual freight of what Larsen terms an 'epochal term' that is part of a 'jargon ... launched by the Right.'[105] Imre Szeman, arguing for a critical approach to the rhetorical and fictional character of globalization, notes that poetics is 'characterized by nothing other than its attention to the powerful uses (and abuses) of language in shaping and mediating our encounter with the world.'[106] As a form of cultural criticism, he suggests, the 'object of poetics ... would be the tropes and turns of language used explicitly to shape public perception.' He considers, moreover, that the critical 'possibilities that globalization opens up for poetics can be grasped only by asking the question of why capitalism needs the new rhetoric of "globalization" at this time.'

The chief conceptual coordinates of globalization are totality, identity, and difference, in that the notion turns on the implicitly teleological dynamic between a plurality of worlds, on the one hand, and the singularity and unity of the globe, on the other. However, the conceptualization of globalization – especially since its stigmatization as a contemporary by-word, if not for Americanization, then at least for late-capitalist, post-communist transnationalization or neo-imperialism – is more problematic than might at first appear, as the tenor of the recent polemical debate between the authors of *Empire*, on the one hand, and Tim Brennan, the author of *At Home in the World*, on the other, makes quite clear.[107] There is broad agreement, certainly, that globalization in its contemporary manifestation is a (primarily economic) process of increasing global permeability and displacement, but also a cultural process, the latter no doubt determined by the former, but each closely intertwined with and influenced by the other. If the predominant discourse on globalization is economic in focus, this is because the principal impetus of the phenomenon is seen to be the transnationalization of the market. But on a cultural or literary level, how does globalization manifest itself? By a homogenization or by a diversification of creativity and writing? By the elision of 'literary difference'? By a movement of deterritorialization, standardization, and virtualization, or by a (possibly compensatory) localization and particularism? While stressing that globalizing and localizing processes feed off each other, just as global homogenization and heterogenization also feed into each other, Arjun Appadurai identifies five major dimensions of global flow: ethnoscapes (founded on migration/displacement); financescapes (based on the movement of capital, currency, etc.); as well as mediascapes, technoscapes, and ideoscapes. Another way of looking at globalization, however, is to stress the globalizing dynamic itself, rather than classifying the spheres in which the dynamic is playing itself out. In his work on globalization, desire, and difference, the Polish sociologist Zygmunt Bauman suggests that global capitalism, on the one hand, elides difference in a movement of expansion and equalization, satisfying ever more (distant) desires or needs, and, on the other hand, re-establishes differences, often artificially, as the condition of its own survival. Bauman considers that 'ours is a heterophilic age. For the sensation-gatherers or experience collectors that we are, concerned (or, more exactly, forced to be concerned) with flexibility and openness rather than fixity and self-closure, difference comes at a premium.'[108] Several thinkers point, indeed, to hybrid or creole identities as a recently validated, 'new and better' type of desirable difference.[109] Thus, Stuart Hall refers to 'a new kind of difference – the difference which is not binary (either-or) but whose "*différances*" (as Jacques Derrida has put it) will not be erased, or traded.'[110] Others, however, like Zygmunt Bauman, John Hutnik, and Graham Huggan, believe that difference, especially perhaps *différance*, has, quite on the contrary, very high market value: 'hybridity, diaspora and post-coloniality are now fashionable and even marketable terms.'[111]

The conceptualization of globalization commonly manifests a Manichean split. Commentators typically present it in either utopian or apocalyptic terms, as a politically positive or negative phenomenon, as a radically new world order or as old capitalist imperialism in new garb. While there is, as mentioned above, some disagreement about the extent to which it moves or is driven by (and along) economic and political as opposed to symbolic and semiotic lines of force, it is often said that globalization represents, in all these dimensions, the continuation of a process, the principal vectors of which in past centuries were colonialism and imperialism. Paul Jay, for example, believes that globalization is not a fundamentally contemporary (postmodern) event, but rather 'has a long history.'[112] And yet a distinction is usually made between globalization, on the one hand, and, on the other, the 'modern world system,' an expression coined by the political scientist Immanuel Wallerstein to refer to a system that stemmed from the development in the late fifteenth and early sixteenth centuries of a European world-economy. As Jay observes, in such a system, as in the imperialist order, the (expanding) nation-state remained absolutely central and was certainly in no way as threatened as some claim it to be now. Moreover, the system described by Wallerstein is primarily, if not exclusively, economic. And while some postmodern theorists of globalization, such as Anthony Giddens and David Harvey, take a predominantly materialist view of the phenomenon, others, like Roland Robertson, dwell rather on symbolic exchange, arguing that the primary force driving global integration is the acceleration of global symbolic exchange.[113] We might recall in this context Fredric Jameson's often-quoted suggestion that we have been witnessing the becoming cultural of the economic and the becoming economic of the cultural.[114] Perhaps one of the most significant corollaries of this expansion of the economic is the shrinkage of the political. Thus Zygmunt Bauman, for his part, notes that the 'prime meaning conveyed by the term "economy" [today] is the area of the non-political.'[115] He supports this claim by pointing to the fact that nation-states have become mere 'executors and plenipotentiaries of forces which they have no hope of controlling politically.'[116]

Certainly, the growing link between cultural studies and globalization studies demonstrates the fact that a major strand of globalization theory is concerned with the globalization or transnationalization of culture. Even in this approach, however, there is a certain divergence of views. The ethnologist James Clifford observes, for his part, the contemporary dis-location of culture, stressing that, in an age of accelerating globalization, culture has become 'deterritorialized and diasporic.'[117] But, whereas Clifford emphasizes 'how cultures travel, become deterritorialized, and tend to hybridize under globalization,' Arjun Appadurai emphasizes, rather, the increased importance of what he calls 'culturalism,' that is, the 'conscious mobilization of cultural differences in the service of a larger national or transnational politics,'[118] a process that is, he argues, characteristic of our era of mass mediation, migration, and globalization. For Appadurai, indeed, in the global age, 'culturalist movements ... are the most general form of the work of the imagination and draw frequently on the fact or possibility of migration or secession.'[119] This view may seem to be at variance with the postcolonial orthodoxy of Clifford et al., according to which the consequence (and inverted triumph) of imperialism is the radical hybridity of culture, whereby various histories and geographies become intertwined, such intersections undermining claims to a discrete and exclusive cultural – or national – identity. In other words, insofar as it represents an 'instrumental conception of ethnicity,' allowing a 'carefully constructed group identity' to be 'naturalized' into 'something substantive, inherent, primary, or even originary,'[120] Appadurai's culturalism might seem to be at odds more generally with what Simon Critchley calls hegemonizing hybridity, as in the work of Edward Said or Homi Bhabha.[121] Yet the fetishization of the creole or hybrid culture is surely a resolutely culturalist process in effect; indeed, the residual essentialization – or even essentialism – that is so much in evidence within the Caribbean 'creoleness' movement illustrates this point perfectly.[122]

At a more subjective level, Simon Critchley's conclusions on the postmodern intellectual's 'exilic consciousness of the present'[123] echo the argument voiced by Charles Taylor that 'what is coming to the fore is the inner mobility of an individual's own life, for which coming and going, being both here and there across frontiers at the same time, has become the normal thing.'[124] But celebratory discourse on this lightness of being, on this 'inner mobility,' this 'coming and going,' could serve to distract from the darker side of contemporary displacement and dislocation. As both Rob Wilson and Mary Louise Pratt note in this volume, mobility can be seen as a choice and (hence) as a privilege from which many, in fact the majority, of global villagers are excluded, just as James Clifford's 'dwelling in displacement' is experienced by many of those directly concerned as a painful exterritorialization. As Zygmunt Bauman puts it, 'being local in a globalized world is a sign of social deprivation and degradation,' and we are witnessing a 'progressive breakdown between the increasingly global and extraterritorial elites and the ever more "localized rest."'[125]

For Arjun Appadurai, however, globalization reterritorializes rather than simply deterritorializes, and it produces not so much exclusion as inclusion.[126] Indeed, Appadurai argues that deterritorialization can be benign or empowering insofar as it disrupts centralized nation-state control over capital, people, goods, culture, and information and promotes a multiplicity of modes and systems in a 'complex transnational construction of imaginary landscapes.'[127] Appadurai seems in many ways impatient for the demise of the nation-state, since, for him, transnationalism holds out a promise of liberation. It is important, however, to bear in mind that Appadurai's view of colonialism is similarly and almost quixotically positive, for he believes that the colonized 'recover agency through the process of indigenization deployed in resisting colonialism.'[128] And while the logic of this revisionist perspective may be borne out in the local context of Appadurai's native India, it is difficult to accept without strong reservations this view of imperialism or colonialism as directly or even indirectly generative – at least, in the long term – of agency in certain other contexts: in Ireland, for example, or indeed in most parts of the former French empire, where colonialism – functioning as direct rule or as thoroughgoing assimilation respectively – resulted in various collective pathologies, both civic and political, which have long outlived decolonization. Moreover, to stress, as Appadurai does, the matter of agency is to risk reducing, ignoring, or suppressing vital questions of subjection and subjectivity that often emerge only in the articulation of the writing subject.[129] It is important, then, to recall – not just in relation to colonialism, but also in relation to globalization – Frederick Cooper's concern that the highly context-specific historical texture of power relations be kept in mind and respected as fully as possible in order to avoid specious arguments based on the theoretical monolith of what he terms 'a generic colonialism.'[130]

Ethics and Globalization

Is globalization (merely) a new, transnational, form of imperialism, then? It is often construed, after all, as a neo-imperialism. Furthermore, in the context of the demise of fascist and communist totalitarianism, what are we to make of the proclaimed movement towards the kind of planetary perspective that would seem to be implicit in the term 'globalization'? In the rather bleak perspective of the French philosopher Jean-Luc Nancy, recent years have seen a significant disjunction between knowledge, ethics, and the effort to live well together ('la convergence du savoir, de l'éthique et du bien-vivre-ensemble s'est désagrégée'), a disjunction coinciding with the hegemony of economics and technology ('la domination d'un *empire* conjoint de la puissance technique et de la raison économique pure').[131] Nancy's use of the term 'empire' in this context broadly echoes that of Michael Hardt and Antonio Negri in their millennial best-seller *Empire*. The notion of the empire of the global market is not new, of course, and was indeed explicitly referred to in the Communist Manifesto.[132] Karl Marx, who is cited in this context by Nancy, is clearly all in favour of the culturally creative and emancipatory effects of the world market. Nancy focuses, in particular, on Marx's view that an individual's relations constitute his or her chief wealth, and that it is only through this nexus of connections that individuals are emancipated from various local and national barriers, brought into contact with the production of the entire world (including, Marx notes, intellectual production), and enabled thereby to enjoy the diversity of human creativity over the whole globe. This notion of a superordinate global realm liberating individuals from the limits and strictures of the local and national chimes with Appadurai's positive evaluation of globalization. However, Jean-Luc Nancy distances himself from Marx's confusion of production and creation. For Nancy, the market-generated global dimension of today's world must be distinguished from the authentic and positive worlding-process that he terms 'mondialisation.' Indeed, the contemporary increase in 'globalité' corresponds in Nancy's view to the dissipation of the world as a place one inhabits, as the 'lieu commun d'un ensemble de lieux' [common place of a set of places],[133] as an ethos or an 'habitus,' in Pierre Bourdieu's sense of this term: that is, as 'une totalité de sens, un ensemble auquel appartient en propre une certaine teneur de sens ou un certain registre de valeur' [a semantic whole, a whole that holds a certain integrity of meaning or a certain register of value].[134] For this ethical/ semantic space has been sucked into the vortex of a spiralling globalization.[135] Nancy is here carrying out precisely an ethical, rhetorical critique of the term 'globalization,' and central to his critique is the idea that 'production' (of objects) is one of the ways in which humanity produces itself, produces the human, and that this double or reflexive process of human production constitutes an absolute value. It is, in other words, is a creative process that is free insofar as it is an end in itself and has no measure in terms of equivalence. For Nancy, in effect, the disjuncture between infinite active creativity and infinite power is the fundamental question of our age: 'la question posée par le monde se mondialisant est celle-ci: comment faire droit à l'infini en acte dont l'infinie puissance est l'exact revers?' [the question raised by the globalizing world is that of how to do justice to the infinity of action given that infinite power is its exact obverse?].[136] Globalization in this perspective is more an eviction from the world than a manner of inhabiting the world.

Many contemporary French thinkers distinguish, like Jean-Luc Nancy, between what is termed 'mondialisation' (sometimes positively viewed) and globalization (usually viewed negatively). Thus, in an article subtitled 'Postmodern Responses to Globalization and the American Empire,'[137] Paul Corey outlines Jean Baudrillard's distinction between globalization (which, for him, is nothing more than economic deregulation and its effects, with all [political] liberties fading or disappearing before the mere liberation of exchange or market freedom), on the one hand, and the positive value of what Baudrillard terms 'universality,' on the other. Jacques Derrida, for his part, denies the reality or the authenticity of the globalization allegedly taking place: rather than true global interconnectivity, we are witnessing, he believes, the mere spectacle of globalization,[138] a spectacle exposed as such by the fact that global inequalities are greater than ever,[139] and that humanity is divided as never before, riven by ethnic and religious tensions. This view is seconded in Baudrillard's observation about the global proliferation of 'singularities' resistant to Western 'universal' values. Whereas universal values were once able, in Baudrillard's view, to accommodate singularities or differences within a universal culture of difference, once universalism collapses, only globalscapes, technoscapes, mediascapes, etc., remain. Yet, although Baudrillard believes that our fragmented world cannot be shaped or unified by any transcendent system of values, of law, or of politics, other thinkers, such as Derrida (and Kristeva), would place their faith in Western Enlightenment values of universality, while still others, such as Habermas, would place theirs in the rationality of supranational constitutional, juridical, and political structures. Meanwhile, in her noted *Death of a Discipline*, Spivak has suggested 'planetarity' as an alternative to 'globalization.' Although Spivak's 'planet-thought' or 'planet-feeling' has not yet, perhaps, been fully conceptualized (Spivak is concerned to clarify that 'planetarity ... is not quite a dimension, because it cannot authorize itself over against a self-consolidating other'),[140] its potential as an alternative 'mind-set' is clear and resonates indeed in Mary Louise Pratt's contribution to this volume: 'If we imagine ourselves as planetary subjects rather than global agents, planetary creatures rather than global entities, alterity remains underived from us, it is not our dialectical negation, it contains us as much as it flings us away ...'[141]

Just as in the decentring thrust of deconstruction, subjectivity is represented as being, in the Nietzschean sense, inescapably 'enfolded in language,'[142] in a similar perspective we can ask if there is anything outside or beyond empire (in the sense in which Hardt and Negri use the term). Is poetics not outside empire? Is ethics not outside empire? Is empire not subject to ethics? If so, and even if not, (how) do contemporary poetics and their ethics register and respond to empire? The postmodern moment is characterized by its 'incredulity' (to use Jean-François Lyotard's term) towards any ontology or ideology that claims to be absolute or total, any form of knowledge aspiring to total control or mastery. Zygmunt Bauman indeed suggests that, whereas in the modern age institutions and societies sought to achieve 'universality, homogeneity, monotony, and clarity' through technology, bureaucracy, and science, the postmodern condition is, on the contrary, characterized by 'pluralism, variety, contingency, and ambivalence.'[143] As Paul Corey points out, 'the primary purpose of postmodern ethics, as formulated by Levinas and developed by Derrida, is not to undermine all politics and law'; it is, rather, to remind any political totality of its neglect of 'certain others, and of the ways in which it is inhospitable.'[144] Aligned, therefore, with the respect of difference as opposed to the universalist aspiration towards unity, and also with the critical movement of deconstruction as an attempt to demonstrate incompleteness or exclusiveness and to destabilize totalizing forces, the postmodern sensibility would seem to be antithetical with globalization. For Paul Corey, indeed, globalization smacks of 'residual modernity.' In that sense, globalization – but also culturalism, and even hybridity if this is based on some sort of hypostasized hybrid identity – and any other totalizing/totalized entity or force – provides the ideal object of critique for postmodern ethics. As we can see, then, the postmodern debate about universality, in which thinkers such as Judith Butler, Slavok Žižek, and Ernesto Laclau have taken part actively, slightly displaces the terms of the discussion in a manner that opens it up to politics without, however, excluding the ethical perspective.

The intersection of ethical and political issues in relation to globalization, and in particular to the phenomenon of extensive economic migration (and associated deterritorialization or transnationalization), has been studied by Giorgio Agamben in his writings on the status of the migrant, refugee, or asylum seeker and on the phenomenon of the internment camp. As Hannah Arendt observes, the 'conception of human rights, based upon the assumed existence of a human being as such, broke down at the very moment when those who professed to believe in it were for the first time confronted with people who had indeed lost all other qualities and specific relationships – except that they were still human.'[145] Zygmunt Bauman has noted in this connection that what the Nazi regime essentially did, was to bring (back home) to Europe 'homo sacer' as he had emerged in the extra-metropolitan colonial context. Just as Bauman writes the globalizing (colonialist) world into the meaning of the Holocaust, so one could argue that, in stripping detainees of their civil and political rights under international law[146] in Camp X-Ray and Camp Delta at Guantanamo Bay in Cuba and in various other shadowy international locations via 'extraordinary rendition,' the United States has recently been using global deterritorialization and displacement as a weapon against what it sees as a global, deterritorialized threat of terror. The questions of human-ism and human rights, and of the intersection between the ethical and the political in an age of globalization, are two of the issues tackled by the writer J.M. Coetzee – within the specific context of *poiesis* – in his novel *Elizabeth Costello*, a work probed further on in this book by David Palumbo-Liu.

Globalization and Poetics

This volume is centred on links between literature, on the one hand, and, on the other, the international and transnational processes, situa-tions, and conditions typically referred to as 'globalization' and involv-ing the putative near-universalization of cultural flow and cultural contact in the contemporary world, contact that does not always, how-ever, involve interrelation or interconnection. The project is thus in dia-logue with a number of collective volumes that have addressed the literary processing of globalization and/or the process of literary glo-balization in similar contexts. Shortly after the turn of the millennium, several major international journals devoted special issues to the inter-face between globalization and literary (or cultural) studies. The fall 2001 issue of *Comparative Literature* and the summer 2002 issue of *Dia-critics* examined respectively 'Globalization and the Humanities,' and 'Theory, Globalization, Cultural Studies, and the Remains of the Univer-sity,' while *PMLA* had looked in its first issue of 2001 at 'Globalizing Lit-erary Studies' and the *South Atlantic Quarterly* devoted its summer 2001 issue to essays on 'Anglophone Literatures and the Global.' Later on, in 2004, the *Modern Language Quarterly* devoted a special issue to 'Global-ism and Theory,' and *Comparative Literature Studies* devoted a special issue to 'Globalization and World Literature.' It is significant that the two other collective volumes that must be mentioned in this context were both commissioned as reports to the American Association for Comparative Literature. The first, edited by Charles Bernheimer, ap-peared in 1994 as *Comparative Literature in the Age of Multiculturalism*, and the second, edited by Haun Saussy, in 2006 as *Comparative Literature in an Age of Globalization*. None of these volumes had ethics as a major focus; their principal concern was rather with the disciplinary or insti-tutional implications of globalization for the humanities and for the study less of culture than of literature.

Globalization as the object of theoretical discourse and of a specific disciplinary field (globalization studies) has been prominent for about three decades, although it is said to have 'only recently migrated to the arena of cultural and literary studies.'[147] And yet, just as prolifically as in the human and social sciences or in cultural studies, critical practice in arts/letters has been taking stock over the last few decades of certain implications of the changing cultural and inter-cultural dynamics of the contemporary world, notably via an exploration of cultural displacement, flow, and contact (issues especially central to comparative literature studies and postcolonial studies). 'Waking up to the limits of its own reliance on the nation as a key organizing principle, literary studies and poetics have thus come to insist on the neeed to take into account the global character of literary production, influence, and dissemination.'[148] It would seem that scholars based in the United States, no doubt in response to that country's external politics, and – more internationally – scholars studying colonial and neo-colonial writing have been quicker off the starting-block than others in attempting to think through the implications for the imagination and for verbal art of the growing hegemony of discourse on the globalized world order. The institutional and disciplinary affiliations of the contributors to this volume certainly suggest such a headstart.[149] Moreover, certain regions of the world, the Americas, for example, and in particular the Caribbean crucible, but also the Pacific rim, have come closer to 'globalization' much earlier than others (witness Charles Carnegie's study, *Postnationalism Prefigured: Caribbean Borderlands*).[150] This epistemological advantage is also reflected in the research background of many of the contributors to this project. Thus Celia Britton and Mary Gallagher are Caribbeanists first and foremost, while Mary Louise Pratt is primarily a Latin Americanist. Moreover, a principal focus of Rob Wilson's work is Hawaiian and Pacific studies, and of David Palumbo-Liu's, Asian-American studies.

Nonetheless, whereas the longitudinal political, economic, and social impact of 'globalization' has long been recognized and continues to be exhaustively studied, the effects of this phenomenon on the textures of the creative imagination and on the ethical fabric of humanity's imaginative relation to the world have received much less sustained critical attention. The near-hegemony of comparative 'cultural studies' and of 'postcolonial' studies of one form or another in the anglophone academy at least, might suggest otherwise, yet the paradigm suggested by the term 'postcolonial' is rather unfortunate in that it is often taken to imply the generalization of some sort of 'decolonization' – not just of geopolitical dynamics, but also of discourse and of structures of knowledge more generally. And yet, as the trends and tensions of francophone literary studies clearly show, the 'deconstruction' of colonialist reflexes and structures in certain areas has been remarkably incomplete. More importantly, the quasi-stabilization of the postcolonial paradigm has given the latter a certain prescriptive, even orthodox, status in the international academy. Indeed, the notion that colonialism and imperialism belong to the past in turn seems to encourage the view that present-day political and economic oppression can be addressed either in terms of deterritorialized 'empire' (this view has been heavily criticized, particularly in the wake of the post-9/11 backlash) or in 'purely' cultural terms (in terms of resistance and subversion via hybridization, for example). Appadurai and Bhabha broadly agree on this latter model (by which the politico-economical is displaced by the cultural), suggesting most famously that subalterns are able to 'alter' the oppressors' culture. However, while the essays collected in this volume could be seen as being, on one level, symptomatic of the displacement of political questions by cultural questions – a displacement that needs to be critically questioned – they are all, at some level, simultaneously politically and/or economically critical, and concerned to relate the literary and cultural issues under consideration to political and ethical questions.

One of the assumptions underlying postcolonial studies, a field that could be said to have taken off in the 1980s, is a certain transnational frame of reference. And yet, it is probably only in English-language 'post-colonial scholarship' that the most frequently referenced text is Ashcroft et al., *The Empire Writes Back* (1989). Similarly, the most quoted luminaries of the international field of postcolonialism, such as Homi Bhabha, Gayatri Chakavorty Spivak, and Edward Said, tend to be anglophone critics. That is, they write in English, usually of an English-language context, and often have a strong institutional association with the United States. So, although postcolonial theory as an overarching discipline suggests a general applicability to all areas historically structured by 'the colonial relationship,' anglophone predominance in, or domination of, the field – especially at a theoretical, conceptual, and institutional level – is quite striking. It has often been noted, indeed, that French and francophone thinkers have been particularly slow to engage in or even with the postcolonial discourse that dominates criticism and writing in so much of the anglophone world. This reluctance is often, and perhaps not entirely unjustifiably, linked to France's persistent neo-colonial velleities – less in Africa, perhaps, than in the Caribbean and the Pacific – and to its rather quaint cultivation of what is referred to as 'la francophonie.' Yet this seems to be a rather reduction-ist reading of the complex relation linking contemporary French/fran-cophone thought, writing, and criticism, on the one hand, and the 'international brigade' of postcolonialism, on the other.

Against the context of anglophone hegemony across postcolonial studies, the critic A. James Arnold observes that 'the overall lesson of [postcolonialist] advances in criticism and theory has been to convince literary specialists that a regional model must take precedence over glo-bal models if we are to understand the functioning of literature in the colonial and postcolonial setting.'[151] In other words, the supposedly international or global, but in reality anglocentric, tenor of postcolonial studies needs to be challenged. This view – and A. James Arnold's anal-ysis in particular – seems to be contradicted, however, by Simon Dur-ing's hypothesis that 'transnational cultural studies' are eroding the 'so-called "postcolonialism" [that was] so important a feature of the late 1980s and early 1990s landscape,'[152] and also by Emily Apter's even more radical prediction of the likely 'virtualization of identity in the era of cybernetics and electronic diaspora.'[153] However, the status of these two positions – During's diagnosis and Apter's prediction – would appear to be optative rather than descriptive. In other words, we need to look closely at the 'truth-value' of the fluid, deterritorialized globe that their discourse articulates or anticipates, and one way of so doing is to test the theory, as Rob Wilson does in his essay for this vol-ume, against a consideration of particular or singular instances of both diasporic or transnational texts and of non-diasporic or less diasporic texts. As we have already seen,[154] Frederick Cooper has made a strong case for the need to examine the specificity of the power relations asso-ciated with colonialism and imperialism as realized in particular (his-torical) contexts. In other words, just as reservations have been expressed about the historiographical legitimacy of a 'generic colonial-ism,' so, too, critical noises need to be made regarding the orthodoxy of postcolonialism[155] and, *a fortiori*, regarding the new, globalization orthodoxy that has been lined up to replace it. The somewhat phago-cytic thrust of some postcolonial criticism can indeed be alarming in its failure to appreciate the local meanings and stakes of certain ideas, practices, terms, or theories. Thus, even if Gayatri Spivak's reference in a recent article on globalization to the work of Édouard Glissant[156] is welcome insofar as it demonstrates an awareness of the significance of the Martinican's work and thought, her failure to discriminate between

Glissant's work on creolization and that of a younger generation of writers who have adopted the slogan of *créolité* (translated by Spivak as creolity), along with her uninformed endorsement of a concept and a movement that have been widely criticized both locally and globally as essentialist and coercive, lends considerable weight to the warnings of A. James Arnold and of Frederick Cooper. It is ironic that Spivak, who is such an advocate of close reading and of respectful apprenticeship of and attention to the languages of others, should have so misread Glissant's work in relation to that of his younger compatriots.[157] Yet this example serves to underline the stakes of writing. For it would appear that, sometimes, even at a very high level of analysis and awareness, postcolonial orthodoxies and globalization or diaspora gospels, both strikingly anglophone in their institutional affiliation and inflection, are – perhaps in order to acquire performative value – in the process of edging the value of poetics out of the academy, if not out of the collective (globalized) mind, in favour of less resistant, less differentiated, and, thus, less opaque cultural forms, or theories ...

One is struck in this context by the extraordinary weight borne by poetics in the decolonizing struggle mounted from within the francophone colonial world. For if we consider the anti-colonial discourse of the francophone African and Caribbean colonies, this was launched largely by the *négritude* movement, a movement dominated by poets. Just as strikingly, the thinking of Édouard Glissant, one of the foremost Caribbean intellectuals writing today, has been – as we shall see further on – consistently articulated in terms of a poetics. Glissant's poetics of relation and his poetics of the 'tout-monde' articulates as such a response to globalization that is quite different to the much more strictly critical or theoretical discourse of anglophone critical thinking. It would be naïve or perverse to suggest that all appeals to poetics mean the same thing, but it would seem at the very least important to recognize that francophone thinkers often privilege poetics in a way that anglophone thinkers do not, and also that francophone thinking has not, so far anyway, signed up for postcolonialism in the way that anglophone thinking has. One could go a little bit further, indeed, and ask whether the political and cultural orthodoxy of postcolonialism is not, in fact, a dominant global discourse against which francophone poetics sounds a singular or a refractory note, if not quite a dissident blow. If such a reading of 'l'exception francophone' is very far from being unproblematic, however, this is largely because of the suture of poetics and French theory, and because of theory's global or near-global empire (its market value).

Poet(h)ics of Globalization: Imagining Others Imagining Us

Culturally speaking, globalization is, above all, a trope of (re)configuration, displacement, and circulation. To think through some of its poet(h)ical implications, we could look to the ethical and epistemological issues raised by, and considered within, the deontological discourse within contemporary ethnology. One of the principal historical functions of ethnographic discourse, a discourse highlighted later in this volume by Mary Louise Pratt, was centred on 'orientation/disorientation,' terms that are, as Edward Said exhaustively demonstrates, a relic from Europe's travel to, exploration of, and self-positioning in relation to a monolithically 'othered' 'Orient' or 'East.' Indeed, as we shall see further on, Emmanuel Levinas explicitly links the disorientation that is a function of cultural relativism to humanity's alienation from, or abandonment of, faith in transcendence. Contemporary ethnology has vigorously debated the questions associated with discourse on cultural difference and indeed with culture *per se*, and in particular the ethics of inter-cultural movement or discourse, posing the obvious normative questions such as 'How should we[158] act toward other cultures? How should they act toward us? How can other cultures take elements from us and in part become us while remaining themselves and vice versa?'[159] There is, implicit, perhaps indeed overly implicit, in these questions an assumption that 'we' and 'us' are deictic shifters, and that they refer 'purely' to discursive positions, not at all to cultural content. Moreover, we should note that contemporary ethnography is as much concerned with observing and with writing (of) the self or of one's own culture (necessarily as other?) as traditional ethnography was with writing of a culture defined as other from the writer's perspective.

In *The Predicament of Culture*, the ethnologist James Clifford asks the following set of questions: 'What processes rather than essences are involved in present experiences of cultural identity? What does it mean to write as a Palestinian? As an American? As a Papua-New Guinean? As a European? From what discrete sets of cultural resources does any modern writer construct his or her discourse? To what world audience (and in what language) are these discourses most generally addressed?'[160] Clifford seems to be taking it for granted here that national and ethnic differences, cultural identities and ethnic or national labels, still matter in what he refers to (in the same passage) as the 'literate global situation.' Certainly, Clifford's 'ethnographic modernity' is based on exponential rootlessness and mobility, and yet he questions the prevailing sense of 'local cultural breakdown' or of imminent 'cultural homogenization.'[161] He emphasizes rather, for his part, the centrality of 'conjunctures,' and of constant movement *between* cultures, arguing that in today's world the two experiences of dwelling and travel 'are less and less distinct.'[162] In fact, what Clifford describes as the 'predicament' of culture is based on his own straining towards a 'concept that can preserve culture's differentiating functions while conceiving of collective identity as a hybrid, often discontinuous inventive process. Culture is a deeply compromised idea I cannot yet do without.'[163] Instead, then, of terminally destabilizing the notion of culture or the project of culturalism, Clifford settles, like many other thinkers whose work we have been considering here, on the point that discourse always involves the vis-à-vis, and that consequently 'a sense of difference or distinctness can never be located solely in the continuity of a culture or tradition.' Nicholas Brown's deconstructive questioning of the contemporary operationality of the distinction West / Not West pushes Clifford's perspective much further, not towards the relationality of the vis-à-vis, but towards the obliteration of difference by co-option or subsumption. For Brown, 'if world literature does not spring spontaneously from a host of freely developing cultural equals, but rather represents the exploitation of geographic and cultural diversity by a limited ensemble of economic and cultural forms, we might ask to what extent "Non-Western literature" is a contradiction in terms.' He goes on then to suggest that 'what we usually call non-Western literature ... must be thought of in terms of the positions that economically, ethnically, sexually, and geographically differentiated subjects occupy within the single culture of global capitalism – a culture that has ... subsumed what was once a genuinely multicultural globe.'[164]

In *Routes*, summing up the reservations concerning the concept of culture that had been central to his first book, Clifford questions the holistic or aesthetic connotations of the notion of culture:

In *The Predicament of Culture* (1988), I worried about the concept's propensity to assert holism and aesthetic form, its tendency to privilege value, hierarchy and historical continuity in notions of common life. I argued that these inclinations neglected, and at times actively repressed, many impure, unruly processes of collective invention and survival. At the same time, concepts of culture seemed necessary if human systems of meaning and difference were to be recognized and supported. Claims to coherent identity were, in any event, inescapable in a contemporary world riven by ethnic absolutisms ... My tools for prying open the culture idea were expanded concepts of writing and collage, the former seen as interactive, open-ended, and processual, the latter as a way of making space for heterogeneity, for historical and political, not simply aesthetic, juxtapositions.[165]

This suspicious negotiation with culturalism, or at least with the aesthetic valency of the value of cultural difference or ethnic identity, contrasts with Clifford's enthusiastic embrace of poetics. In fact, poetics is to be the means both of negotiating with the notion of culture and of critiquing it. Although the discipline of cultural studies tends to avoid even mentioning poetics, it is interesting to note that Clifford, one of the pioneers of the new ethnography, highlights it. Indeed, his book *Writing Culture*, an edited volume of essays, is subtitled *The Poetics and Politics of Ethnography*.[166] Moreover, Clifford, who writes enthusiastically on the Caribbean poet Aimé Césaire in *The Predicament of Culture*, notably integrates into his ethnological reflection both an explicit interest in the epistemological potential of poetics and an anxious and highly paradoxical concern with the political implications of certain connotations of the term 'culture' (it is surprising that Clifford does not seem in the least worried about the inescapable historical associations of poetics with 'holism and aesthetic form').

The poetics and the ethics of cultural crossing or interrelation are not necessarily sutured, of course. In the first years of the twentieth century, in his *Essai sur l'exotisme* [Essay on Exoticism] – less an essay, however, than a prolegomenon, or a series of notations and reflections towards an essay on exoticism – the French writer Victor Segalen recognized empirical diversity, including (or in particular) cultural or ethnological diversity, as a prerequisite for exoticism envisioned as an aesthetics of difference. Indeed, the subtitle of his projected essay is *une esthétique du divers* [An Aesthetics of the Diverse]. Segalen was lucid enough to fear that diversity, that is, the existence of a bank of differences, this constituting the basic necessary condition for exoticism, might be under threat. Without analysing in any depth the reasons for the world's cultural contraction – imperialist commerce and the technologies of mass communication and transport, for example – Segalen does signal that diversity can no longer be taken for granted. 'Le divers décroît' [The diverse is diminishing], he warns.[167] We need to remember, however, that the value of diversity from Segalen's theoretical perspective is largely, if not wholly, aesthetic. Certainly, while recognizing that, for exoticism to function, 'une seule attitude est possible, le subjectivisme absolu' [only one attitude is possible, absolute subjectivism],[168] Segalen does open up the window onto the consciousness or subjectivity of the other by promising to explore the question concerning the effect of the exoticist's presence among his/her 'others' ('l'écho de sa présence').[169] Although this deferred concern with reciprocal impact is reminiscent of Habermas's discussion of a theory of intersubjectivity and of discourse ethics that, unlike both metaphysics and anti-metaphysical thought, 'would explain the way the object works back on the subject, or how subjects work on each other through the mediation of language,'[170] Segalen's 'theoretical' interest in this question is constructed exclusively in (the aesthetic) terms of the expansion of the subject's range of sensation, and thus betrays no concern with the ethical or political dimensions of subjectivity.

It might seem paradoxical, given the plausibility of Nicholas Brown's view that cultural diversity has indeed shrunk and that the West / Not West disjuncture does not really hold water any more, that several critics can point to the congestion of what some of them would call the 'global literary market' with works marked by 'otherness.' Crucially, these works are largely, however, fabricated for Western consumption:

> [The] attraction toward otherness has allowed for a greater circulation of art from the peripheries, above all as channeled through specific circuits. But too frequently value has been placed on art that explicitly manifests difference or that better satisfies the expectations of otherness held by neoexoticism. This attitude has stimulated the self-othering of some artists who, consciously or unconsiously, have tended toward a paradoxical self-exoticism.[171]

Studying the production of literature or culture on a global scale for 'primarily Western audiences,'[172] Simon Gikandi argues that this phenomenon 'has tremendous implications because it means that the needs and desires of Western audiences, mediated by postcolonial critics or theorists of globalization, become dominant.'[173] Gikandi notes that the African novelists who are most successful are those who are 'able to cater to the sentiments and needs of that "global" audience, because it is this "global" audience that buys books.' This is why Gikandi questions the value of literature in Africa, firstly because of the fact that, in the African context, readerships are no longer located in the writers' 'sites of reference';[174] and secondly, because, for several reasons, literature is not a dominant mode of cultural production or engagement in Africa.[175]

Globalization and the Poet(h)ics of World Writing

The notion of a poetics of globalization and, *a fortiori*, the notion of the ethical value of such a poetics, seems – on the face of it – to be a conceptual solecism. Certainly, on one level, the expression 'poetics of globalization' could evoke the specifically poetic potential or literary effects of globalization: for example, the phenomena of self-othering, and of cultural translation or distortion described by Simon Gikandi and/or the expanded possibilities within a globalized world for novel (and poetic) deterritorialization and (re)combination of diverse cultural elements. And, on a more restrictive Aristotelian level, it might suggest the production of affect by the representation of globalization in action or the representation of its effects. It remains, however, that, whereas the idea of a poetics of the local, or a poetics of place, requires little explanation – indeed, one could argue that much writing that one could classify as ethnography, travel writing, national or regional literature, etc., fundamentally articulates a poetics of the local – it would surely be much more difficult not just to define or envisage, but also to recognize and to evaluate poetically (or ethically), a poetics of the global or of globalization.[176] Insofar as globalization implies both transnational and international dynamics, the notions of World Writing and World Music might help to elucidate the national/international/transnational nexus that consitutes the globalized world (for it is clear that the world is not yet in a post-national phase), and they might also help us to envisage that world in terms of what Gilles Deleuze has termed an 'ethic of flow,' or what Édouard Glissant calls a 'poetics of relation' or a 'Whole-World poetics.'

Globalization is often accused in just such a perspective of impoverishing art and culture insofar as it is taken to bespeak a reduction of diversity. As Ulf Hannerz puts it, does globalization lead to less culture or to more?[177] If we recall Zygmunt Bauman's argument, however, we might consider that cultural capitalism requires the constant production of 'new' differences, and that cultural flow and even cultural interconnectedness itself is or becomes a source of even greater diversity, thus maintaining a poetics of relation. As Immanuel Wallerstein has written, 'the history of the world has been the very opposite of a trend towards cultural homogenization; it has rather been a trend towards cultural differentiation, or cultural elaboration, or cultural complex-ity.'[178] But the question remains: what would a poetics of the global look like? How would it relate to a poetics of the local? And how would one locate and situate its ethics? Even more perplexing questions come to mind, such as when exactly did a poetics of the global first appear?

The expression 'world writing' has a much more limited valency than its homologue, 'world music.' Perhaps this is just as well, given that the expression 'world music' is a highly ambiguous and even prob-lematic term. To judge by its classificatory use, 'world music' is typi-cally characterized by its 'ethnic diversity,' and might be credited with having made certain types of music, especially non-Western music, available far away from their places of production; available, that is, for international – but especially Western – consumption: music from the Indian subcontinent, from example, or from Africa or East Asia, in other words, music that hadn't formerly travelled so easily, or so far. Yet it is often, although not necessarily, the case, that individual examples of 'world music,' in a sort of internal meta-reference to globality, mani-fest various cultural interconnections or hybridities, combining the often very diverse styles of globally distant music. In the same way, glo-bal cuisine – Indian fusion or Chinese fusion – represents the displace-ment, mutation, adaptation, and hybridization of the cuisines in question. Perversely, however, the 'world music' rubric of the Western record store is unlikely to include Western music, except insofar as the latter has been substantially cross-fertilized by non-Western, '(alter-) ethnic' strains. This exclusion is perverse because some Western music does enjoy an almost worldwide ease of distribution. The market of Western popular music has been for some time far more global in com-pass than that of most currently termed 'world' music. Just as antholo-gies of so-called 'international' writing in previous decades usually included only writing from a variety of traditions firmly inside the Western world, so certain anthologies of global or world writing repro-duce a symmetrical, if inverse, exclusion. Thus, the volume entitled *Global Cultures: A Transnational Short Fiction Reader*,[179] although it does not include the expression 'world writing' in its title, stresses intercon-nections and intersections between various styles, worlds, traditions, cultures, etc. However, since these are virtually all non-Western, the conceptual aporia of so-called 'world music,' as it is described by Tim-othy Brennan,[180] is vividly reproduced in that volume.

What does it really mean, then, to speak of 'world writing'? Which writing, whose world? How does it relate to the 'national literatures' which do not seem to have dissolved quite yet? David Damrosch, for his part, takes 'world literature to encompass all literary works that circulate beyond their culture of origin, either in translation or in their original language ... a work only has an *effective* life as world literature whenever, and wherever it is actively present within a literary system beyond that of its original culture.'[181] A full appreciation of world writing, argues Vilashini Cooppan, would require us to see it as being at once 'locally inflected and translocally mobile.'[182] This same view (sometimes dubbed glocalism) is articulated in slightly different terms by Édouard Glissant, and it also underlies the nuanced, localized cosmopolitanism championed by Bruce Robbins: 'No one actually is or ever can be a cosmopolitan in the sense of belonging nowhere ... The interest of the term *cosmopolitanism* is located, then, not in its full theoretical extension, where it becomes a paranoid fantasy of ubiquity and omniscience, but rather (paradoxically) in its local applications.'[183] Damrosch's emphasis on the local is intended to distinguish world literature from a 'notional "global literature" that might be read solely in airline terminals, unaffected by any specific context whatever,' that is, a literature in tune with what the French anthropologist and novelist Marc Augé calls the 'non-lieu.'[184] Damrosch quotes as an example of literature read against a 'world systems' background Franco Moretti's mapping of the spread of the novel, beginning with his *Atlas of the European Novel, 1800–1900*.[185] However, Moretti's description of the difficulty of dealing directly with the masses of disparate material that a global approach should encompass and his diagnosis of the ambition of such an approach as being of necessity (as we have seen above) directly proportional *to the distance from the text*'[186] once again points to 'theory's empire' as one of the more crucial questions raised in the context of the present volume.

Composition of the Volume

The vastness and depth of the questions raised and the multiplicity of possible perspectives in which they could be approached precluded any pretension to coverage in this volume. There is no attempt, then, to identify or treat all, or even most, of the questions that arise for poetics and ethics, or for poet(h)ics, in the context of globalization. A certain balance was attempted in the mix of contributors approached, but the final gathering is inevitably eclectic. This fragmented approach has yielded, however, revealing echoes, resonances, and gravitations, as well as dissonances and discontinuities. And although this Introduction attempts a certain positioning of the contributing critics and of the principal questions that they treat, the collection remains resistant to totalization or systematization. That is indeed its ethics, and it refers back to the original decision to involve others in the consideration of the central question. While the commisioning-mode of generation risked seeming parasitical and appropriative, it was self-evident that such a big question needed to be approached dialogically. The contributors who so generously offered their work to this project are to be thanked for their patience. The silting process was a slow one and the project, engendered during the build-up to the invasion of Iraq, bears the mark of that global shudder and of its aftershocks. This conjuncture is registered, indeed, in many of the essays, quite explicitly in Mary Louise Pratt's contribution. The global importance of religion, specifically Islam, is implicit, for example, in Richard Serrano's essay, while the conflict between America and what was pejoratively labelled Old Europe underlies many of Kristeva's comments on French theory.

Despite the risks associated with the ventriloquism involved, it might be useful to note succinctly the main questions explored in the various essays. Two of these highlight the work of the Martinican writer Édouard Glissant. In 'Transnational Languages in Glissant's' "Tout-monde,"' Celia Britton analyses Glissant's notion of the 'Tout-monde' – or the world envisaged as a globalized and 'creolized' interaction of diverse cultures – asking how Glissant theorizes both the evolution of new, hybridized 'languages' and also our relationship to languages that we do not, in the conventional sense, 'understand.' This study of the Martinican thinker and poet's views on intersubjective and ethical relationships between speakers of different languages is complemented, then, by my own essay 'Relating (in Theory) in a Globalized World: Between Levinas's Ethics and Glissant's Poetics,' which studies how Glissant's poetics of cultural diversity and interrelation maps or does not map onto Emmanuel Levinas's ethics of the other person. It asks how open (or not) Levinas's ethics – centred on an 'other' humanism or on the 'other person' – is to the value of cultural difference and to the poetic, and whether these two thinkers' orientations describe, as it would at first seem, an asymptotic rather than a chiastic relationship. In her essay 'French Theory,' based on a talk given to the Humanities Institute of Ireland, Julia Kristeva, beginning by outlining her experience, as a 'French theorist,' of academic hospitality in France and in the United States and Canada, sums up her work to date as exploring four principal problems: intertextuality, semiotics, abjection, foreignness. Not only do the terms of this summary confirm the centrality of poetics in 'French Theory,' but they also locate the value of poetics (for 'French Theory'), not just metaphysically and politically, but also ethically. In the remainder of her essay, Kristeva elaborates on the ethico-political value of poetics in relation to the global conjuncture, and more specifically in relation to the place of two diametrically opposite notions of freedom epitomized respectively by the American Dream (as an economic notion of freedom) and the French/European Enlightenment (freedom as poetic resistance/ transgression and as creative connection with the sacred).

From a predominantly theoretical or speculative register, Douglas Smith's and Richard Serrano's essays move to a more archaeological mode, stressing the ethics and politics of colonization and decolonization against the specific backdrop of French colonialism in North Africa. In 'Not Your Uncle: Text, Sex, and the Globalized Moroccan Author,' Richard Serrano discusses the changing context, from colonial to globalized Morocco, of the theme of male homosexuality as a paradigm of resistance/complicity. Serrano shows how texts by two Moroccan writers, separated by almost half a century, probe the intersection of homosexuality as praxis with the historical and contemporary implication of Morocco in global economies – colonial and postcolonial, respectively – of language, exchange, and desire. Driss Chraïbi's 1958 novel, Le Passé simple, depicts a family co-opted, according to Serrano, both by French colonialism and American economic imperialism. For Serrano, one site of resistance to these forces is the specifically Arabo-Mediterranean semantics of what Westerners would call homosexuality. However, the specificity and 'opaqueness' of this semantics are central both to the construction of anti-colonial meaning/resistance in Chraïbi's text, and to the dissolution of meaning (specifically, the meaning of Moroccan 'homosexuality' and, with it, the possibilities of meaningful resistance to globalization and of ethical positionality per se) in Rachid O's postcolonial (and post-ethical?) writings.

In 'Redrawing the Hexagon: The Space of Culture in Malraux and Blanchot,' Douglas Smith studies how two influential post-war French writers view the ontological and ethical significance of culture. For Malraux, the global canon of art is configured as an imaginary museum, whereas, for Blanchot, literature operates in/as a centre-less, inappropriable and unmappable space. In both cases, the traditional Western canon is expanded: Malraux's totalized and totalizing cultural space opens up Western art to the non-West, as the art of the entire world is absorbed into the West's aesthetic tradition, whereas Blanchot's empty space hollows out Western literature from the inside. Smith shows how both reconfigurations of cultural space, both repositionings of French culture, relate to the post-war geopolitics of decolonization and the Cold war. While Malraux's deterritorialization is followed by a reterritorialization, it offers – for all its postcolonial manoeuvres (including the self's appropriation of the other, even the other's inalienable property of death) – the utopian possibility of shared global culture. Conversely, Blanchot's relatively narrow (Western) canon avoids the appropriation of other cultures, expropriating instead Western literature. The work of both writers delineates the ethically complex encounter with other cultures at a time of rejection of the collective other (the Cold War) and of assertion of the collective self in newly emergent (decolonized) nations. In a context where both self-assertion and openness to the other carry ambiguous connotations, neither rejection of the self nor assimilation of the other offers, according to Smith, an entirely adequate response to the political and ethical problem of relations between cultures. Yet their contribution to a reconfiguration of cultural space does foreshadow, Smith concludes, the complexity of late twentieth-century geopolitics and cultural ethics.

David Palumbo-Liu's essay, based on a reading of J.M. Coetzee's self-reflexive novel on the literary imagination and the ethics of fiction, *Elizabeth Costello*, takes as its starting point the deficiencies of rational choice theory, a theory which is based to a great extent on the (supposedly global) supremacy of economic culture. It then tracks the exploration in Coetzee's novel of the limits constraining our ability to imagine an 'other,' and to imagine a plausible world and matrix of interests for such an other. The value of so-called universal reason – including the Kantian *sensus communis* of aesthetics and of boundless empathy – is challenged in Coetzee's novel. But then the dissolution of the rational, of the aesthetic, and of singular being, the supposed condition for a successful poet(h)ics for a globalized age, is shown to result in a systemic meltdown, a failure due in the final analysis, according to Palumbo-Liu, to a political deficit.

For her part, in 'Planetary Longings,' Mary Louise Pratt links the limits of Western secular humanism with a crisis of ethics and epistemology. For Pratt, the neo-liberal, self-consciously global order driven by visions of futurity excludes increasingly large sections of humanity. Narratives of failed border crossings bear witness to this exclusion even as, in a process of auto-poiesis, imaginaries of alternative social, scientific, or semiotic orders emerge from zones of exclusion on the global margins. These imaginaries reject materialism, consumerism, and the failed narrative of development, constructing instead an inclusive planetary poetics. Pratt wonders whether Sylvia Wynter's vision of the 'global human' might offer a cure for the monopolism of Enlightenment metropolitan thought, a cure that would be, Pratt suggests, fundamentally and paradoxically ethnographic. Thus, what Judith Butler calls the colonial expansionist logic of Enlightenment universalism is being challenged by new forms of global desire which suggest a thinking superordinate both to Enlightenment thinking and to capitalism, a desire epitomized in the global anti-war demonstrations that opposed the US/UK invasion of Iraq. Pratt's thesis echoes, then, William Connolly's 'politics of nonterritorial democratization of global issues' and is also consonant with Masao Miyoshi's perspective in 'The Turn to the Planet: Literature, Diversity, and Totality.'[187] For Miyoshi, the global economy is not global at all, but rather exclusionist: the world is transnational and deterritorialized only for some.

In 'Reframing Global/Local Poetics in the Post-imperial Pacific: Meditations on "Displacement," Indigeneity, and the Misrecognitions of US Area Studies,' Rob Wilson argues that displacement is a prime strategic force driving (and driven by) global capitalism, but also driving cultural criticism. Noting that diaspora paradigms hold widespread currency, Wilson questions the interests behind this trend (exemplified in the displacement of frontier paradigms by borderlands paradigms in American studies). One of the key issues debated in his essay concerns how we (should) now do area studies and how we (should) situate ethnicity struggles in our global–local age. Quoting Homi Bhabha, for whom the transmission of 'national' traditions has been replaced by transnational stories of migration, Wilson cautions, however, against the failure to recognize the material context of global displacement (its frequently involuntary status), and also the ongoing geo-material realignment of power/knowledge that passes for 'globalization.' Wilson addresses three large-scale (ecological, financial, and semiotic) displacements marking the postcolonial Pacific rim and argues that these multi-layered Pacific displacements have a bearing on the field of US cultural studies, now (being) transformed by the de-sublimation of the global horizon of 'American studies.' In the context of the attendant American crisis of transnational containment both at home and abroad, minorities or ethnicities have been devalued or de-

reified. Fanned by a new transnational literacy and by the intensification of de-reifying critical attention to 'worlding' processes within and
around American studies, the local Pacific needs, according to Wilson,
to reassert its own interests and values. He argues, then, for a certain
critical suspicion of terms such as "transpacific," urging that critique of
intertextual dynamics and semiotic flows should take better account,
not just of what Deleuze and Guattari call the 'ethic of flow,' but also of
what one might call the 'economic politics of flow.'

Concluding Note

Implicit in the term 'globalization' are notions of totality and of process,
a process of becoming, by which boundaries, perimeters, and borders
are transcended, if not dissolved, in a 'becoming-global' of the world.[188]
Yet, even if we could accept that demarcations are becoming less –
rather than more – significant, just as it is difficult to imagine an a-polar
globe, a globe not subject to displacement, rotation, and gravity, or a
globe configured otherwise than in relation to the spatial coordinates of
longitude and latitude, so too it is difficult to conceive of globalization
as a dynamic innocent of axes, polarities, and gravitations. This volume
illustrates the operation of a number of such dynamics and stresses.
Some of the foremost strains or tensions informing the work presented
in this volume are between universalism and culturalism, unity and
diversity, self and other, appropriation and exclusion, West and Not-
West, the United States and France, location and dislocation, difference
and encounter, *homo economicus* and *homo poeticus*, theory and text,
empire and freedom. It is not so much the opposition of these poles that
is of interest here, however. What matters are, rather, the formulations,
the articulations, the conjugations, the mediations to which they give
rise, and especially the poetics and the ethics that emerge around the
multiple textual and discursive sites where these tensions are played or
worked out, and, of course – as one of the leitmotifs of this introductory
essay constantly stresses – the critical political stakes of that poet(h)ics.

NOTES

1 Marc Redfield, ed., 'Theory, Globalization, Cultural Studies, and the
  Remains of the University,' *Diacritics* 31.3 (Fall 2001): 3.
2 Ibid., 4.

3 See David Damrosch, *What Is World Literature?* (Princeton: Princeton University Press, 2003); and Pascale Casanova, *La République mondiale des lettres* (Paris: Seuil, 1999).

4 Gaston Bachelard, *La Poétique de l'espace* (Paris: Presses universitaires de France, 1957), and *La Poétique de la rêverie* (Paris: Presses universitaires de France, 1961).

5 Formalist poetics came to be associated with the autonomy of the sign, whose remotivation or overdetermination was held to open out onto an infinity of meanings.

6 See references below to world systems theory (note 9) and to Glissant's critique of systematic thinking (pp. 90–1).

7 See the discussion below (pp. 42–3) of Simon Gikandi's views on the relative cultural importance of literary production in Africa.

8 Geoffrey Hartman, *The Fateful Question of Culture* (New York: Columbia University Press, 1997), 1.

9 This expression is particularly associated with the work of the political scientist Immanuel Wallerstein. For a pertinent engagement with the concept of 'world system,' see Wai Chee Dimock, 'Genre as World System: Epic and Novel on Four Continents,' *Narrative* 14.1 (January 2006): 85–101; and Gayatri Spivak's reply, 'World Systems and the Creole,' *Narrative* 14.1 (January 2006): 102–12.

10 Imre Szeman, 'Culture and Globalization, or, The Humanities in Ruins,' *New Centennial Review* 3.2 (2003): 105.

11 Revathi Krishnaswamy, 'The Criticism of Culture and the Culture of Criticism: At the Intersection of Postcolonialism and Globalization Theory,' *Diacritics* 32.2 (Summer 2002): 107.

12 Ibid., 107–8.

13 Timothy Brennan, 'World Music Does Not Exist,' *Discourse: Journal for Theoretical Studies in Media and Culture* 23.1 ('Imperial Disclosures II') (Winter 2001): 48.

14 Robert Young, 'Ideologies of the Postcolonial,' *Interventions* 1.1 (1998/9): 7.

15 Szeman, 'Culture and Globalization,' 100.

16 Nicholas Harrison, 'Who Needs an Idea of the Literary,' in a special issue of *Paragraph* (July 2005), *The Idea of the Literary*, ed. N. Harrison, 1–17. Harrison is the author of *Postcolonial Criticism: History, Theory, and the Work of Fiction* (Cambridge: Polity Press, 2003).

17 Chris Bongie, 'Belated Liaisons: Writing between the Margins of Literary and Cultural Studies,' *Francophone Postcolonial Studies* 1.2 (2003): 22.

18 Ibid., 23–4.

19 Ibid., 24.

20 Ibid., 23.
21 Gayatri Spivak, 'Teaching for the Times,' in *Dangerous Liaisons: Gender, Nation, and Postcolonial Perspectives*, ed. Anne McClintock, Amir Mufti, and Ella Shohat (Minneapolis: University of Minnesota Press, 1997), 483.
22 Gayatri Spivak, *Death of a Discipline* (New York: Columbia University Press, 2003), 106. It is worth mentioning here Sangeeta Ray's cogent account of Spivak's thinking on ethics in 'Ethical Encounters: Spivak, Alexander, and Kincaid,' *Cultural Studies* 17.1 (2003): 42–55.
23 Spivak, *Death of a Discipline*, 49.
24 Derek Attridge, *The Singularity of Literature* (London and New York: Routledge, 2004), 136.
25 Ibid., 46.
26 Ibid., 7.
27 Bongie, 'Belated Liaisons,' 16. For a much fuller treatment of this question, see Chris Bongie, 'Exiles on Main Stream: Valuing the Popularity of Postcolonial Literature,' *Postmodern Culture* 14.1 (September 2003).
28 Alain Badiou, *Manifeste pour la philosophie* (Paris: Seuil, 1989), 33.
29 Michael Hardt and Antonio Negri, *Empire* (Cambridge: Harvard University Press, 2000).
30 Celia Britton, *The Nouveau roman: Fiction, Theory, and Politics* (London: Macmillan, 1992), 111. For a searching and surprisingly un-dated analysis of this question, see Fredric Jameson, 'Modernism and Its Repressed: Robbe-Grillet as Anti-colonialist,' *Diacritics* 6.2 (Summer 1976): 7–14.
31 Robert Pickering, 'Écrire sous l'occupation: les mauvaises pensées et autres de Valéry,' *Revue d'histoire littéraire de la France* 88.6 (Nov./Dec. 1988): 1090.
32 Ibid.
33 The quotation is taken from Valéry's aphoristic and significantly titled 'Mauvaises pensées' [Bad Thoughts], in Paul Valéry, *Œuvres complètes*, vol. 2, Bibliothèque de la Pléiade, (Paris: Gallimard, 1960), 862. This statement could be related to the poet(h)ic debate centred on the writing of Robert Antelme and Marguerite Duras (see below, p. 18).
34 Harrison, 'Who Needs an Idea of the Literary.'
35 Timothy Clark, commenting on Derek Attridge in 'Singularity in Criticism,' *Cambridge Quarterly* 33.4 (2004): 395. Timothy Clark is the author of *Derrida, Heidegger, Blanchot: Sources of Derrida's Notion and Practice of Literature* (Cambridge: Cambridge University Press: 1992).
36 See above, note 23.
37 Franco Moretti, 'Conjectures on World Literature,' *New Left Review* 1 (Jan.-Feb. 2000): 57.

38 Ibid. The conclusions of Moretti's book-length study, cited in the Bibliography, are built around this same set of arguments.
39 Spivak, *Death of a Discipline*, 108.
40 Spivak, 'World Systems and the Creole,' 105.
41 Ibid., 107.
42 Drawing on the thinking of Emmanuel Levinas, Spivak writes, '... it is practically persuasive that the eruption of the ethical interrupts and postpones the epistemological – the undertaking to construct the other as an object of knowledge' (Gayatri Spivak, 'Ethics and Politics in Tagore, Coetzee, and Certain Scenes of Reading,' *Diacritics* 32. 3/4 [Fall 2002]: 17).
43 Spivak, *Death of a Discipline*, 13.
44 Literary depth is opposed by Spivak to mere 'social scientific fluency' (*Death of a Discipline*, 106).
45 See above, p. 9.
46 Key references in this discussion are Martha Nussbaum with respondents, *For Love of Country: Debating the Limits of Patriotism*, ed. Joshua Cohen (Boston: Beacon Press, 1996) (Nussbaum's respondents include Immanuel Wallerstein, Charles Taylor, Elaine Scarry, Judith Butler, and Kwame Anthony Appiah); Judith Butler, Ernesto Laclau, and Slavov Žižek, *Contingency, Hegemony, Universality* (London: Verso, 2000); and Ernesto Laclau and Chantal Mouffe, *Hegemony and Socialist Strategy* (London: Verso, 2001).
47 Apart from the work cited in the next note, Rancière is the author of *La Parole muette: essai sur les contradictions de la littérature* (Paris: Hachette, 1998).
48 Jacques Rancière is concerned by the 'constitution d'une sphère indistincte où se dissolvent la spécificité des pratiques politiques ou artistiques, mais aussi ce qui faisait le coeur même de la vieille morale: la distinction entre le fait et le droit, l'être et le devoir-être' [the constitution of an indistinct sphere in which not only the specificity of political or artistic practice is dissolved, but also what was at the very heart of traditional morality: that is, the distinction between facts and rights, between what is and what should be] (Jacques Rancière, *Malaise dans l'esthétique* [Paris: Galilée, 2004], 145).
49 J. Hillis Miller, *The Ethics of Reading: Kant, de Man, Eliot, Trollope, James, and Benjamin* (New York: Columbia University Press, 1987), 4.
50 Alisdair MacIntyre, *A Short History of Ethics* (New York: Macmillan, 1966), 129.
51 Vincent P. Pecora, 'Ethics, Politics, and the Middle Voice,' *Yale French Studies* 79. ('Literature and the Ethical Question') (1991): 204.
52 Ibid., 220.
53 Ibid., 205.

54 Ibid., 204.
55 Ibid.
56 Ibid. Pecora recognizes indeed that 'after the social and intellectual upheavals of the 1960s, one might claim that it is no longer possible to pretend that "ethics" and "politics" represent distinct discourses or practices – the personal *is* the political' (ibid., 206).
57 Ibid., 205.
58 Emmanuel Levinas, *Entre nous* (Paris: Grasset & Fasquelle, 1991), 114.
59 'For Levinas ... ethics is the disruption of totalizing politics' (Simon Critchley, *The Ethics of Deconstruction: Derrida and Levinas* [Oxford: Blackwell, 1992], 221).
60 Jacques Rancière, 'Éclipse de la politique,' *Lignes* 8 (2002): 35.
61 Critchley, *Ethics of Deconstruction*, 221.
62 Ibid., 225.
63 Ibid., 220.
64 Ibid., 226.
65 Ibid., 278.
66 Colin Davis, *Levinas: An Introduction* (Cambridge: Polity Press, 1996), xvi.
67 Robert Antelme, *L'Espèce humaine* (Paris: Gallimard, 1957), 229–30.
68 Davis, *Levinas*, 178. See Colin Davis, 'Antelme, Renoir, Levinas, and the Shock of the Other,' *French Cultural Studies* 14 (2003): 41–51, and also Leslie Hill's and Martin Crowley's studies of Duras, cited in the Bibliography to this volume. All of these analyses make valuable contributions to this poet(h)ic debate.
69 Richard Freadman, 'Ethics, Autobiography and the Will: Stephen Spender's *World within World*,' in *The Ethics in Literature*, ed. Andrew Hadfield, Dominic Rainsford, and Tim Woods (London: Palgrave/Macmillan, 1999).
70 Ibid., 18.
71 Bertrand Russell, *Human Society in Ethics and Politics* (New York: Unwin Hyman, 1954), 8.
72 Ibid., 157.
73 Greg Nielsen, 'Bakhtin and Habermas: Toward a Transcultural Ethics,' *Theory and Society* 24 (1995): 815.
74 Critchley, *Ethics of Deconstruction*, 48, 58n58.
75 Davis, *Levinas*, 143.
76 Andrew Hadfield, Dominic Rainsford, and Tim Woods, eds, Introduction, in *The Ethics in Literature*, 9.
77 Aristotle, *Poetics*, trans. Stephen Halliwell (Cambridge: Harvard University Press, 1999), 1452b38 –1453a6.

78 Nielsen, 'Bakhtin and Habermas,' 815.

79 Ibid., 825.

80 Thomas Keenan, *Fables and Responsibility: Aberrations of Predicaments in Ethics and Politics* (Stanford: Stanford University Press, 1997), 175–6. See also Levinas's comments on reading and on criticism quoted below in my essay on Glissant and Levinas, pp. 108–9.

81 Hillis Miller, *Ethics of Reading*, 5.

82 'Since its appearance as a philosophical discipline on the scene of the Western intellectual and cultural tradition in Ancient Greece, ethics has been, not surprisingly, enmeshed with literature' (Michael Eskin, 'On Literature and Ethics,' *Poetics Today* 25.4 [Winter 2004]: 575).

83 Ibid.

84 Ibid., 576.

85 Ibid., 578.

86 Ibid., 580.

87 Ibid., 583.

88 Ibid., 586.

89 Ibid., 587.

90 Ibid., 587–8.

91 Paul de Man, *Allegories of Reading* (New Haven: Yale University Press, 1979), 156–7.

92 Ibid., 157.

93 Pecora, 'Ethics, Politics,' 213.

94 Ibid.

95 Ibid.

96 Keenan, *Fables*, 176.

97 Ibid., 186 (emphasis mine).

98 Ibid., 3.

99 William Connolly, *The Augustinian Imperative: A Reflection of the Politics of Morality* (London: Sage, 1993), 11.

100 Ibid., 30.

101 See above, note 80.

102 Keenan, *Fables*, 155, 186.

103 Jean-Michel Rabaté, 'Theory 911,' *PMLA* 118.2 (2003): 333–4; Neil Larsen, 'Theory-Risk: Reflections on Globalization Theory and the Crisis in Argentina,' *New Centennial Review* 3.2 (2003): 23–40.

104 Arjun Appadurai, 'Disjuncture and Difference in the Global Cultural Economy,' *Public Culture* 2.2. (1990): 18.

105 Larsen, 'Theory-Risk,' 28.

106 This quotation and the two that follow are from Imre Szeman, 'Imagining

the Future: Globalization, Postmodernism, and Criticism,' forthcoming with Palgrave in *Metaphors of Globalization: Mirrors, Magicians, and Mutinies*, ed. Markus Kornprobst et al. (pagination unavailable).

107 See Timothy Brennan's critique of the Far Left thesis of Michael Hardt and Antonio Negri in *Empire* in 'The Empire's New Clothes,' *Critical Inquiry* 29.2 (2003): 339–67, a response that was answered by Hardt and Negri's, 'The Rod of the Forest Warden: A Response to Timothy Brennan,' ibid., 368–74. This was followed, in turn, by Brennan's 'Critical Response 2:The Magician's Wand: A Rejoinder to Hardt and Negri,' ibid., 375–9. Brennan's question is how, 'at a moment of American imperial adventure almost Roman in its excess is the end of imperialism confidently announced?'

108 Zygmunt Bauman, 'The Making and Unmaking of Strangers,' in *Debating Cultural Hybridity: Multi-Cultural Identities and the Politics of Anti-Racism*, ed. Pnina Werbner and Tariq Modood (London: Zed Books, 1997), 55.

109 Graham Huggan, *The Post-Colonial Exotic: Marketing the Margins* (London: Routledge, 2001).

110 Stuart Hall, 'Whose Heritage? Un-settling "The Heritage," Re-imagining the Post-nation,' *Third Text* 49 (Winter 1999–2000): 3–13.

111 John Hutnik, 'Adorno at Womad: South Asian Crossovers and the Limits of Hybridity Talk,' in Werbner and Modood, eds., *Debating Cultural Hybridity*, 118.

112 Paul Jay, 'Beyond Discipline? Globalization and the Future of English,' *PMLA* 116.1 ('Globalizing Literary Study') (January 2001): 33.

113 Ibid., 37.

114 Fredric Jameson, 'Notes on Globalization as a Philosophical Issue,' in *The Cultures of Globalization*, ed. Fredric Jameson and Masao Miyoshi (Durham, NC: Duke University Press, 1998), 18.

115 Zygmunt Bauman, *Globalization: The Human Consequences* (New York: Columbia University Press, 1998), 66. Since economic forces are effectively transnational, they are, Bauman states, 'outside the realm of deliberative, purposeful, and potentially rational action' (ibid., 56).

116 Ibid., 65.

117 James Clifford, *The Predicament of Culture: Twentieth Century Ethnography, Literature, Art* (Cambridge: Harvard University Press, 1988), 18.

118 Arjun Appadurai, *Modernity at Large: Cultural Dimensions of Globalization* (Minneapolis: University of Minnesota Press, 1996), 18.

119 Ibid., 18.

120 Ibid., 14.

121 Simon Critchley, *Ethics, Politics, Subjectivity* (London: Verso, 1999), 134.

122 See Mary Gallagher, 'The *Créolité* Movement: Paradoxes of a French Carib-

bean Orthodoxy,' in *Creolization: History, Ethnography, Theory*, ed. Charles Stewart (Walnut Creek, CA: Left Coast Press, 2007), 220–36.

123 Critchley, *Ethics, Politics, Subjectivity*, 134.

124 Charles Taylor, *Sources of the Self: The Making of Modern Identity* (Cambridge: Cambridge University Press, 1989), 75.

125 Bauman, *Globalization*, 2, 3.

126 Appadurai, *Modernity at Large*, 31. See also Arjun Appadurai, 'Global Ethnoscapes: Notes and Queries for a Transnational Anthropology,' in *Interventions: Anthropologies of the Present*, ed. R.G. Fox (Santa Fe: School of American Research, 1991), 191–210.

127 Appadurai, *Modernity at Large,* 31.

128 Ibid., 90.

129 The imperative that weighs on writers from 'minor' cultures to write politically, well documented by Gilles Deleuze and Félix Guattari in their *Kafka: Pour une littérature mineure* (Paris: Minuit, 1975), can be imprisoning. For an exploration of this constraint in action, see Mary Gallagher, 'Contemporary French Caribbean Poetry, or the Poetics of Reference,' *Forum for Modern Language Studies* 40.4 (2004): 451–62; and 'L'Assujettissement du sujet poétique antillais,' in *Sens et présence du sujet poétique français et francophone depuis 1980*, ed. Michael Brophy and Mary Gallagher (Amsterdam and New York: Rodopi, 2006): 117–25.

130 Frederick Cooper, *Colonialism in Question: Theory, Knowledge, History* (Berkeley: University of California Press, 2005).

131 Jean-Luc Nancy, *La Création du monde ou la mondialisation* (Paris: Galilée, 2002), 15.

132 'All old-established national industries have been destroyed or are daily being destroyed. They are dislodged by new industries, whose introduction becomes a life and death question for all civilized nations, by industries that no longer work up indigenous raw material, but raw material drawn from the remotest zones; industries whose products are consumed, not only at home, but in every quarter of the globe. In place of the old wants, satisfied by the production of the country, we find new wants, requiring for their satisfaction the products of distant lands and climes. In place of the old local and national seclusion and self-sufficiency, we have intercourse in every direction, universal inter-dependence of nations. And as in material, so also in intellectual production. The intellectual creations of individual nations become common property. National one-sidedness and narrow-mindedness become more and more impossible, and from the numerous national and local literatures, there arises a world literature' (Karl Marx and Friedrich Engels, 'The Communist Manifesto [1848],' in

Karl Marx: Selected Writings, ed. David McLellan [Oxford: Oxford University Press, 1977], chapter 1).

133 Nancy, *Création*, 36.

134 Ibid., 34.

135 Nancy notes that 'ce qui nous arrive et qui déferle sous le nom de "mondialisation"' [what is happening to us and unfolding under the name of 'mondialisaton'] is in reality the exponential growth of 'globalité' (ibid., 22). And he adds that what is happening to us is a 'dissipation du monde dans le mouvement infini d'une globalisation en spirale' [dissipation of the world in the infinite movement of spiralling globalization] (ibid., 46).

136 Ibid., 30.

137 Paul Corey, 'Totality and Ambivalence: Postmodern Responses to Globalization and the American Empire,' unpublished article 2004 (Web-archived).

138 See the cult book of the Situationist Guy Debord, *La Société du spectacle* (Paris: Champ Libre, 1967).

139 As Saskia Sassen points out in *Losing Control? Sovereignty in an Age of Globalization* (New York : Columbia University Press, 1996), 107–8, 'globalization is not global. It occupies extremely structured spaces in countries.' Cf.: Misao Miyoshi: 'the global economy is not global at all, but an exclusionist economy' ('The Turn to the Planet: Literature, Diversity, and Totality,' *Comparative Literature* 3.4 ('Globalization and the Humanities' [2001]: 295).

140 Spivak, 'World Systems,' 108. (All the preceding terms in quotation marks in this sentence are Spivak's from the same source.)

141 Gayatri Spivak, *Imperatives for Re-imagining the Planet* (Vienna: Passagen, 1999), 46.

142 Taylor, *Sources of the Self*, 487.

143 Zygmunt Bauman, *Mortality, Immortality, and Other Life Strategies* (Cambridge: Polity Press, 1992), 187.

144 Corey, 'Totality and Ambivalence.'

145 Quoted in Giorgio Agamben, *Homo Sacer: Sovereign Power and Bare Life,* trans. Daniel Heller-Roazen (Stanford: Stanford University Press, 1998), 126.

146 According to a statement released by Amnesty International on 20 April 2004, 'None of the detainees was granted prisoner of war status nor brought before a competent tribunal to determine his status, as required by the Third Geneva Convention. None has been granted access to a court to be able to challenge the lawfulness of his detention, as required by the International Covenant on Civil and Political Rights (Article 9) to which the United States is a party.'

147 Jay, 'Beyond Discipline?' 34. Jay's words were published in 2001.
148 Szeman, 'Imagining the Future,' 5.
149 J. Michael Dash, 'Postcolonial Thought and the Francophone Caribbean,'
in *Francophone Postcolonial Studies: A Critical Introduction*, ed. Charles
Forsdick and David Murphy (London: Arnold, 2003) 231–41.
150 Charles V. Carnegie, *Postnationalism Prefigured: Caribbean Borderlands* (New
Brunswick, NJ: Rutgers University Press, 2002).
151 A. James Arnold, 'The Field: Regional vs Global Models,' *Francophone
Postcolonial Studies* 1.2 (Autumn/Winter 2003): 9.
152 Simon During, 'Introduction' in *The Cultural Studies Reader*, ed. Simon
During (London: Routledge, 1999), 27.
153 Emily Apter, *Continental Drift. From National Characters to Virtual Subjects*
(Chicago: University of Chicago Press, 1999), 223.
154 See above, p. 30.
155 Masao Miyoshi, 'A Borderless World? From Colonialism to Transnationalism and the Decline of the Nation-State,' *Critical Inquiry* 19 (Summer 1993):
726–51. 'The current academic preoccupation with "postcoloniality" and
multiculturalism looks suspiciously like another alibi to conceal the actu-
ality of global politics ... colonialism is even more active now in the form
of transnational corporatism' (728). 'Ours ... is not an age of *post*colonialism but of intensified colonialism' (750).
156 Spivak, 'World Systems and the Creole,' 109: 'I consulted the basic texts of
the contemporary debate on creolity. Here I will content myself with citing
Édouard Glissant, the initiator of the movement.' The point is that Glissant rejects the term and the concept of 'créolité,' which Spivak enjoins us
all to embrace: 'If we want to preserve the dignity of that strange adjective
"comparative" in comparative literature, we will embrace creolity' (110).
In fact, it would be difficult to read one of the 'basic texts' cited by Spivak
in a footnote, the manifesto of the *créolité* movement, without noting that it
diverges very significantly from Glissant's ethics, poetics, and politics.
157 See Gallagher, 'The *Créolité* Movement.'
158 Editor's note: Presumably Nielsen's 'we' refers to those of us, whoever we
are (French, Africans, Pakistanis, Americans, Iranians, etc.), who write of
cultures that are not our own.
159 Nielsen, 'Bakhtin and Habermas,' 828.
160 Clifford, *The Predicament of Culture*, 9.
161 Ibid., 10.
162 Ibid., 9.
163 Ibid., 12.
164 Nicholas Brown, 'The Eidaesthetic Itinerary: Notes on the Geopolitical

Movement of the Literary Absolute,' *South Atlantic Quarterly* 100.3 (Summer 2001): 831–2.

165 James Clifford, *Routes: Travel and Translation in the Late Twentieth Century* (Cambridge: Harvard University Press, 1997), 2.

166 James Clifford, *Writing Culture: The Poetics and Politics of Ethnography* (Berkeley: University of California Press, 1986).

167 Victor Segalen, *Essai sur l'exotisme: notes pour une esthétique du divers* (Paris: Fata Morgana, 1978).

168 Ibid., 77.

169 Ibid., 18.

170 Nielsen, 'Bakhtin and Habermas,' 813.

171 Gerardo Mosquera, 'Alien-Own / Own-Alien: Globalization and Cultural Difference,' *Boundary* 2 29.3 (2002): 165.

172 David Jefferess and Simon Gikandi, 'Postcolonialism's Ethical (Re-)Turn: An Interview with Simon Gikandi,' *Postcolonial Text* (electronic journal) 2.1 (2006): 9.

173 Ibid., 8. For a compelling comparison of the paradigms of postcolonialism and globalization, see Simon Gikandi, 'Globalization and the Claims of Postcoloniality,' *South Atlantic Quarterly* 100.3 (Summer 2001): 627–58.

174 Jeferess and Gikandi, 3.

175 Ibid.,5.

176 As Neil Larsen points out, 'globalization's reference to "totality" seems purely scholastic here, since whatever it was that universally named our "age" or our "culture" before "globalization" was presumably also a "totality."' Larsen is also justified, surely, in questioning the idea that 'we are all planetary beings in our most direct forms of spatial immediacy' (Larsen, 'Theory-Risk,' 31).

177 Ulf Hannerz, *Transnational Connections* (London: Routledge, 1996), 19.

178 Immanuel Wallerstein, *The Modern World System* (New York: Academic Press, 1974), 96.

179 *Global Cultures: A Transnational Short Fiction Reader*, ed. Elizabeth Young-Bruehl (Middletown, CT: Wesleyan University Press, 1994).

180 See the reference to Timothy Brennan above, p. 6.

181 Damrosch, *What Is World Literature?* 4.

182 Vilashini Cooppan, 'World Literature and Global Theory: Comparative Literature for the New Millennium,' *Symploke* 9.1–2 (2001): 33.

183 Bruce Robbins, 'Comparative Cosmopolitanisms,' in *Cosmopolitics: Thinking and Feeling beyond the Nation*, ed. P. Cheah and B. Robbins (Minneapolis and London: University of Minnesota Press), 260.

184 Marc Augé, *Non-Lieux: introduction à une anthropologie de la surmodernité* (Paris: Seuil, 1992).

185 Franco Moretti, *Atlas of the European Novel, 1800–1900* (London and New York: Verso, 1998).

186 Moretti, 'Conjectures on World Literature,' 57.

187 See above, note 139.

188 See Charles Carnegie's book on postnationalism and Caribbean borderlands (note 150, above), and also his article 'Reaching for the Border,' *Small Axe* 10.2 (March 2006): v–ix.

2 Transnational Languages in Glissant's 'Tout-monde'

CELIA BRITTON

It is widely accepted that Édouard Glissant's work undergoes a dramatic change of perspective and of mood in the late 1980s and 1990s, between *Le Discours antillais* (1981), on the one hand, and *Poétique de la Relation* (1990), *Tout-monde* (1993), *Introduction à une poétique du divers* (1996), and *Traité du Tout-monde* (1997) on the other.[1] *Le Discours antillais* was, as its title suggests, exclusively concerned with the French Antilles, and in fact mainly with Glissant's own home island, Martinique, and it gave an extremely pessimistic evaluation of Martinique as a 'morbid,' politically stagnant, alienated, and isolated society. The major texts of the 1990s, in striking contrast, expand their focus to encompass the whole world, and are dominated by a far more up-beat, exuberant celebration of hybridity and cross-cultural contact. The emphasis here is on dynamism and change; Glissant takes the Caribbean phenomenon of creolization and – in a move that is emblematic of his whole shift of perspective – reworks it on a global level, as a force capable of endlessly generating new forms of culture and experience. Creolization becomes a supercharged, generative version of hybridity: 'le métissage sans limites, dont les éléments sont démultipliés, les résultantes imprévisibles' [hybridity without limits, hybridity whose elements are multiplied, and whose end-results are impossible to foresee] (*PR*, 46). This new position is encapsulated in the concept of the 'Tout-monde'; that is, the world envisaged as a multiplicity of communities, all interacting and all aware of each other's existence: 'Pour la première fois, les cultures humaines en leur semi-totalité sont entièrement et simultanément mises en contact et en effervescence de réaction les unes avec les autres' [For the first time, the semi-totality of human cultures are wholly and simultaneously placed in contact and in effervescent reaction with one another] (*TTM*, 23).

The 'Tout-monde' thus comes to stand as a kind of shorthand for a 'good' version of globalization: contact which not only preserves diversity but creates new forms of it. Globalization in the negative sense of 'the reign of the multinationals, standardization, the unchecked ultra-liberalism of world markets'[2] cannot be resisted from a purely local standpoint. The first chapter of the *Traité du Tout-monde*, entitled 'Le Cri du monde' [The Cry of the World], argues eloquently that, while it is necessary and important to fight to preserve one's own particular community, this must not preclude a more general awareness of, and solidarity with, other struggles across the world: 'nous acceptons maintenant d'écouter ensemble le cri du monde, sachant aussi que, l'écoutant, nous concevons que *tous l'entendent désormais*' [we are now willing to listen to the cry of the world, and in listening to it, we understand that *from now on everyone hears it*]. (*TTM*, 17). An important aspect of the 'Tout-monde' is thus communication, and therefore language. Globalization has, paradoxically, created the conditions both for much greater contact between different language communities as a result of migration and hybridization, and at the same time for the increasing dominance of the major world languages at the expense of those spoken by smaller and economically weaker communities. How, then, does the 'Tout-monde' resituate languages in this context of generalized hybridity and creolization?

The texts of the 1990s are full of references to language, and languages; but so, equally, are Glissant's earlier works. In fact, it is arguably Glissant's position on language that changes most dramatically in the work of the '90s. In the earlier texts there is a strong emphasis on the lack of any language adequate to the needs of the Antillean speaker, and indeed writer. In *L'Intention poétique*, for instance, he writes:

Et c'est à cette absence ce silence et ce rentrement que je noue
dans la gorge mon langage, qui ainsi débute par un manque:
Et mon langage, raide et obscur ou vivant ou crispé, est ce manque
d'abord, ensuite volonté de muer le cri en parole devant la mer.

[And it is to this absence this silence and this withdrawal that I knot my
language up in my throat; my language which thus starts out with something
lacking; and my language, stiff and obscure or living or clenched, is

this lack first of all; then the will to transform the cry into words by the sea.] (*IP*, 44)

Le Discours antillais concentrates in particular on the tension between French and Creole, arguing that neither of these, for different reasons, can provide a ready-made idiom which will unproblematically fulfil the expressive needs of the subject, who is therefore marooned in the 'muteness' which Glissant sees as the legacy of 'the implacably silent world of slavery' (*CD*, 161) in which 'self-expression is not only forbidden, but impossible to envisage' (*CD*, 122). In *Tout-monde*, however, this scarcity of language is replaced by a 'chaotic' super-abundance of languages of all kinds, all apparently available to the speaker. Whereas in the earlier work language is sometimes imaged as the painfully thin trickle of water in a dried-up river-bed, in *Tout-monde* it is described as huge crashing waves; and the Antilleans, from hardly having one language at their disposal, are now seen as exuberantly 'surfing' a whole number of different languages: 'Alors encore vous entendez ces langages du monde qui se rencontrent sur la vague le mont, toutes ces langues qui fracassent l'une dans l'autre comme des crêtes de vagues en furie et vous entreprenez, tout un chacun applaudit, de bondir d'une langue dans l'autre ...' [So again you hear the world's languages meeting each other on the mountainous wave, all these languages crashing into each other like the crests of raging waves, and you set about leaping – everyone applauds – from one language into another ...] (*TM*, 20). The contrast between the two positions is immediately striking. However, there is also a less obvious level on which one finds a surprising degree of continuity in Glissant's view of language. In fact, I am going to argue here that *Tout-monde*'s vision of multilingual 'surfing' can be fully understood only if it is seen as developing *out of* the model of language and subjectivity which underlies not just earlier texts such *Le Discours antillais* – but also the even earlier *L'Intention poétique*, the collection of essays published in 1969, which in some ways has more in common with *Tout-monde*. Rereading *L'Intention poétique* today, one is struck by how presciently it already imagines a globalized and hybridized future of a kind that very few other writers were envisaging in the 1960s.

One of the key phrases of *Tout-monde*, much repeated throughout, is 'Mélanger les langues' [Mix(ing) up the languages]. At times this acts as an exhortation, at times as a factual description of the existing situation. In its most obvious sense, it refers to individuals speaking more than one language and switching fluently from one to another – the kind of 'surfing' of languages implied in the fragment quoted above – and the book has various examples of fictional characters doing precisely this.[3] But 'mixing up' languages also has implications which extend beyond this switching and surfing, two sets of implications, in fact, that I want to explore in the rest of this essay. The first set is ethical and the second structural; both are somewhat problematic, but both also offer the possibility of an original and far-reaching theorization of how globalization in the positive sense of the 'Tout-monde' impacts on questions of language and language use.

'J'écris en présence de toutes les langues du monde' [I write in the presence of all the world's languages] is a formula that recurs insistently in *Tout-monde, Introduction à une poétique du divers,* and *Traité du Tout-monde.* It relates in the first place to Glissant's concern to save minority languages from being obliterated by the domination of American English and, to a lesser extent, standard French. He insists that this has to be done on the basis of the equal importance of all languages – '... on ne sauvera pas une langue en laissant périr les autres' [we will not save one language by letting the others perish] (*TTM*, 85) – because the battle cannot be fought purely on a local level without lapsing into the kind of linguistic sectarianism that he criticizes in some of the promoters of French-Caribbean Creole.[4] Thus Anestor, one of the characters in *Tout-monde*, argues:

> Comment ferez-vous accepter à tous ces gens de se lever pour défendre ou sauver une langue créole ou une langue quéchoua ou une langue islandaise, si vous ne commencez pas par changer toutes leurs idées sur les langues? S'ils ne consentent pas enfin que toutes les langues sont également importantes pour notre vie secrète ou publique?

> [How will you get all these people to agree to rise up to defend or rescue a Creole language or a Quechua language or an Icelandic language, if you don't start by changing all their ideas about languages in general? If they don't accept that all languages are equally important for our secret or public lives?] (*TM*, 469)

So far, this is a familiar argument, based on an analogy with the notion of *biodiversity*: all languages must be preserved because different languages incarnate different visions of the world, and so offer unique and valuable insights that are not accessible other than through the language itself : 'Car avec toute langue qui disparaît s'efface à jamais une part de l'imaginaire humain' [For with each language that disappears a part of the human imagination is forever obliterated] (*TTM*, 85). But the biodiversity analogy, as usually formulated, has quite serious limitations. It relies upon the vision of reality incarnated in a particular language being untranslateable, because otherwise there is no argument for the need to preserve the language itself. Therefore, whereas the medicinal value, for instance, of a particular plant in the Amazon rain forest can in principle be made available to people all over the world, the philosophical value of a particular language's articulation of reality is only available to the speakers of that language and those who are prepared to learn it. And, since all languages are equally valuable, the only gain lies in speaking more than one, and preferably as many as possible. Simply preserving a language does not enable anyone other than its speakers to share in and benefit from its vision of reality.

Glissant avoids this problem by realizing that insistence on inclusivity means that the claim for the value of every language cannot be based on its being intelligible to us, and shifting his argument away from the problem of *understanding* foreign languages, at least in the ordinary sense of the word.[5] In *Traité du Tout-monde* he admits that 'il est vain d'essayer d'en connaître le plus grand nombre possible; le multilinguisme n'est pas quantitatif' [it is futile to try to know as many of [the world's languages] as possible; multilingualism is not a matter of quantity] (*TTM*, 26). Instead he outlines a different, less concrete and more global kind of 'multilingual' awareness of them. 'Writing in the presence of all the world's languages' means that my text is 'inflected' by other languages, not because it incorporates lexical borrowings, for instance, but in the more negative sense that it is haunted by the knowledge that other languages, offering a vision of reality that lies beyond the scope of my own, are endangered. The act of writing *a* text in *a* particular language is experienced almost as an act of homage to all the other languages that are necessarily excluded from it, and that are perhaps destined to disappear, but whose spectral presence nevertheless makes an ethical demand on the writer. As he rephrases it in *Traité du Tout-monde*, 'J'écris désormais en présence de toutes les langues du monde, dans la nostalgie poignante de leur devenir menacé' [From now on I write in the presence of all the world's languages, in the poignant nostalgia of their threatened future existence] (*TTM*, 26).

This situation, in turn, alters my perception of my own language. Even if it is the only one I know, I can no longer inhabit it with the unreflexive confidence that normally characterizes the monolingual native speaker; it no longer appears to me as complete and self-sufficient, but as existing only in its conflictual and fluctuating relations – and the connection with Glissant's central concept of 'Relation' is very evident here – to all other languages:

> Je ne peux plus écrire de manière monolingue. C'est-à-dire que ma langue, je la déporte et la bouscule non pas dans des synthèses, mais dans des ouvertures linguistiques qui me permettent de concevoir les rapports des langues entre elles aujourd'hui sur la surface de la terre – rapports de domination, de connivence, d'absorption, d'oppression, d'érosion, de tangence, etc. –, comme le fait d'un immense *drama*, d'une immense tragédie dont ma propre langue ne peut pas être exempte et sauve. Et par conséquent je ne peux pas écrire ma langue de manière monolingue; je l'écris en présence de cette tragédie, en présence de ce drame.

> [I can no longer write monolingually. In other words, I displace and shake up my language, not through syntheses but through the linguistic openings which enable me to conceive the interconnections between languages on the earth's surface today – relations of domination, complicity, absorption, erosion, tangency, etc. – as evidence of a huge *drama*, a huge tragedy from which my own language cannot remain safely exempt. And the result is that I cannot write my language monolingually: I write it in the presence of this tragedy, in the presence of this drama.] (*IPD*, 40)[6]

This multilingual awareness has, however, a further dimension. It can be seen as one form of Glissant's long-standing fascination with the phenomenon of *not understanding a language*. This has its roots in his childhood, when he used to witness the effect that unintelligible fragments of African languages surviving in the oral culture of Martinique had on those listening (*IPD*, 115). He claims that this experience informs his concept of opacity, as he goes on to state: 'j'ai subi l'influence de cette présence non élucidée de langues ou de formules dont on n'a pas le sens et qui agissent quand même sur vous, et il est peut-être possible que toute une part de mes théories sur les nécessaires opacités de langage proviennent de là' [I experienced the influence of this unelucidated presence of language or phrases whose meaning we do not possess and which neverthless act on us, and it is perhaps possible that a whole area of my theories on the necessary opacities of language stems from this] (*IPD*, 116). Thus one of the central ideas of Glissant's theoretical work is intimately connected with a very naïve, life-long affective engagement with foreign languages. Glissant's pervasive interest in exploring the kinds of relationship and communication we can have with individuals or texts whose language we do not understand is evident throughout his writing. In *L'Intention poétique*, for instance, he refers to 'the conscious, fruitful nostalgia for the languages that [he] *will not understand*,' and illustrates this with his experience of trying to read Hölderlin without speaking German: 'nous avons rêvé (ceux qui ne connaissent pas l'allemand) devant le texte du Rhin de Hölderlin, tâchant à vif, aidés des diverses traductions, d'entrer dans la masse de ce texte' [we have dreamt (those of us who do not speak German) in the presence of Hölderlin's *The Rhine*, trying desperately, with the help of various translations, to penetrate the mass of this text] (*IP*, 47) – and the 'consciousness of a lack' which results from this.[7] Similarly, the much more recent *Traité du Tout-monde* laments the fact that his inability to speak Arabic prevents him from appreciating the ways in which the Palestinian poet Mahmoud Darwich expands and reworks the language (224–5).

In other words, 'writing in the presence of the world's languages' is an ethical commitment to the equal importance of all languages and the need to defend their existence; and it is also a particular sensitivity to a mode of intersubjective and/or intertextual contact that does not depend on ordinary linguistic comprehension. What is less clear, however, is whether writing in this way is intended to make a difference which will be perceptible to the *reader*; and if so, what exactly such a difference might consist of. Is there something about the way in which Glissant writes French that makes us realize he is not writing it 'monolingually'?

In a rather indirect way, we can perhaps find a clue to what this might be in the description of one of the characters in *Tout-monde*: an Italian woman called Amina who tells the narrator, Mathieu, that she can predict what will happen to him in the future. Mathieu guesses that Amina is a gypsy; and from the fact that she speaks French with no trace of an Italian accent he further guesses (without any actual evidence) that she also speaks a number of different languages that are unknown to him: 'Si elle était gitane, elle était capable de parler toutes les langues du monde' [If she was a gypsy, she was capable of speaking all the world's languages] (*TM*, 44). Amina is therefore an example of the fascination with 'secret' unknown languages; and she is also an example of an individual subject whose identity is not bound up with any one language: 'Elle était bien gitane, puisqu'elle ne se fixait dans aucun idiome privilégié ni dominant' [She really was a gypsy, since she was not fixed in any one preferred language] (*TM*, 45). But what is given most emphasis in the text is Amina's 'multilingual' way of speaking Italian; and this is not, as we might have expected, that her Italian is mixed up with fragments of other languages, but that she speaks it with a particular kind of 'hésitation légère au bord des mots' [slight hesitation on the edges of words] (*TM*, 45). Rather than being solidly installed in a language that she takes for granted, it is as though her Italian is shadowed by the ghostly presence of all the other languages that she might have chosen to speak instead, and as though she is surprised to find herself in this language rather than another one:

> Amina par exemple, qui était bien italienne ... avait une manière étonnée de commencer ses phrases, comme si l'usage de cette langue italienne lui était difficile, en sorte qu'on pouvait se demander si elle n'avait pas grandi dans les échos d'une autre langue qui pour l'instant dormait ailleurs, dans un lieu imaginaire d'où elle ne pourrait jamais la faire rejaillir.

> [Amina for example, who was certainly Italian ... had a way of starting her sentences with a kind of surprise, as though the use of this Italian language did not come easily to her, so that one might have wondered whether she had not grown up among the echoes of another language which for the time being lay sleeping somewhere else, in an imaginary place from where she would never be able to bring it out into the open.] (*TM*, 45)

But it is only from the way in which she speaks Italian, which he does understand, that Mathieu guesses she is multilingual; and this suggests that there is a way of using a language which makes it clear to one's listener that one does not identify exclusively with it, but that one is rather tentatively and provisionally choosing it among a number of possible other languages. Extrapolating from this example, one could perhaps conclude that this is also the impression that the *monolingual* writer who nevertheless writes 'in the presence of all the world's languages' creates in his or her readers; that is, Mathieu's relationship to Amina acts as a parallel to and an example of what Glissant hopes will be the *reader*'s relationship to the text written 'in the presence of the world's languages.'

'Mixing up languages,' however, also has a second major implication: that the greatly increased contact between languages changes not just the behaviour of the speakers who 'surf' from one to another, but also the structures of the languages themselves – and perhaps even the way in which we define 'a language' in general. Glissant's presentation of the 'interchange des langues écrites et parlées' [interchange of written and spoken languages] (*TTM*, 112) makes it clear that the mixing he envisages goes beyond the ordinary and unproblematic phenomenon of lexical borrowing. So, for instance, when he describes the way in which French-Caribbean writers write a kind of French that is 'inflected' by their knowledge of Creole, he emphasizes that he is not talking about the simple incorporation of isolated words and phrases of Creole – which he considers merely 'le côté exotique de la question' [the exotic aspect of the question] (*IPD* 121) – but about the importation into French of the large-scale discursive 'structures' that are typical, for instance, of the Caribbean folktale (*IPD*, 121). It is only these, he argues, that will produce in the French reader the recognition of opacity – the experience of not understanding – which alone challenges the monolingual self-sufficiency that obliterates the 'presence of all the world's languages.' Faced with a new picturesque word, the French reader will simply be amused and intrigued by its exoticism; 'mais la poétique, la structure du langage, la refonte de la structure des langages lui paraîtront purement et simplement obscures' [but the poetics, the structure of the language, the reworking of the structure of the languages, will seem purely and simply obscure to him] (*IPD*, 121).

The linguistic structures in question here are those of a 'poetics': the examples that Glissant gives are those of repetition, circularity, and lists. In other words, they are stylistic and discursive rather than grammatical. Glissant does not here refer explicitly to *syntactic* structures, although the logic of his overall commitment to 'mixing up languages' would imply that ultimately it has to engage with these as well. His vision of languages morphing into one another is simply incompatible with the traditional conception of a language as a discrete structure defined by a finite set of grammatical rules. This conception originates historically with Saussure's notion of the *language-system*; in fact, the whole thrust of Saussure's innovation in linguistics was to construct, out of a heterogeneous amalgam of 'faits de langage' [facts of language], a distinct, clearly defined structure, amenable to scientific analysis, that he calls 'langue' as opposed to 'langage,' and that has the characteristics of forming a coherent whole, all of whose elements are held together by their relations to other elements in the system and are, by virtue of this, clearly separated from all other language systems. Saussure defines 'langue' as follows:

> It is a well-defined object in the midst of the heterogeneous collection of facts of *langage* ... It is the social part of language, external to the individual, who can neither create or modify it on his own; it exists solely by virtue of a kind of contract agreed by the members of the community ... Not only can the science of the *langue* do without the other elements of *langage*, but it is possible only on the condition that these other elements are not mixed up with it.[8]

Saussure's 'langue,' in other words, is constituted in such a way as to exclude the possibility of its being 'mixed up' with other languages. Glissant, in contrast, is asking us to consider what it would mean to conceive of a language which lacks definite, impermeable boundaries, and this would seem in the first place to mean a language which is not a 'language-system.'

There is in Glissant's recent thought a prominent antipathy towards any kind of thought that relies upon the notion of a system; in *Tout-monde*, systems in general are characterized as oppressive and destructive, and as being opposed to poetic thought. He writes, for example: 'systematic thought [la pensée du système] on the other hand is dead and deadly, the systematic thought which has so dominated us, we must get rid of systematic thought' (*TM*, 237). The Saussurean language-system could thus be taken as just one example of 'la pensée du système,' and in the same text we find Glissant also celebrating uses of language that transgress grammar or even bypass it completely. The character Mahmoud, for instance, an eleven-year-old tourist guide in Egypt, is introduced as someone who speaks 'à peu près bien quatre langues à touristes. Il a appris auprès des gens de passage, qu'il pilote depuis bien longtemps. *Il parle par halètements et cris, n'ayant pas besoin d'une syntaxe suivie'* [four tourist languages pretty well. He has learnt them from the visitors he has been showing around for a long time now. *He speaks in gasps and shouts, not needing a consistent syntax*] (*TM*, 532). But the idea of a language, specifically, that does not have or need a grammatical system, can also be traced back much further in Glissant's work, albeit in a somewhat different sense. The texts that he wrote in the 1960s and 1970s are dominated by an explicit anti-colonial emphasis that is largely superseded by the concept of the 'Tout-monde.'[9] Language plays an important role in these works, and *L'Intention poétique* includes a critique of linguistics which, like Glissant's more recent attacks on the idea of system *per se*, may well refer to Saussure:

> La linguistique, en tant qu'elle formule des constantes et des règles, se trouve déjà en retard sur ce vagabondage de langues et de parlers qui en chaque être (collectif) manifestera la présence de l'être au monde. Elle devra passer de l'analyse statique aux profils dynamiques, si elle veut englober cette condition; faute de quoi elle n'ira qu'à confirmer un anach-ronisme et se rendre solidaire des plus aveugles accommodements académiques.

> [Linguistics, insofar as it formulates invariants and rules, has already been overtaken by this vagrancy of the languages and ways of speaking that in each (collective) being manifests that being's presence in the world. It will have to move on from static analysis to dynamic profiling, if it aims to cover this condition; otherwise it will do nothing more than reinforce an anachronism and align itself with the most short-sighted kind of academic expediency.] (*IP*, 46)

But this remarkably modern perspective, in which linguistics is said to have been overtaken by the realities of a newly creolized world, is less typical of the early texts than a narrower focus on the situation of the colonized subject in relation to the colonial language; and here, Glis-sant's critique is not in fact aimed at the 'scientific' descriptive notion of Saussure, but at a more old-fashioned prescriptive, normative grammar which he links with nationalism and colonial domination. Teaching and learning French grammar, in other words, is one major aspect of the oppressive imposition of metropolitan norms of correctness on colonized subjects. In this context, grammatical structure has political implications; the language-system is a hostile force which Glissant calls on the colonized subject to attack or subvert. This is the basis for the important concept of 'counter-poetics' elaborated in *Le Discours antil-lais*, but also occurring as early as *L'Intention poétique*, where linguistic correctness is defined as a kind of purity with racial overtones – 'L'ère des langues orgueilleuses dans leur pureté doit finir pour l'homme' [The era of languages taking pride in their purity must come to an end for humanity] (*IP*, 47) – and where the concern to promote such purity is equated with aggressive nineteenth-century nationalism:

Autrement dit, toute nation hier encore se parfaisait dans la projection unique et souvent exclusive, agressive, de son parler. Mais je n'hérite pas de cette unicité, n'ayant pas même à réagir contre elle. Les épurations académiques de la langue ne me concernent pas (ne me satisfont, ne m'indignent ni ne me font sourire); me passionne par contre ... mon affrontement à sa loi.

[In other words, until recently every nation achieved its perfect definition in the projection, always singular and often exclusive and aggressive, of its speech. But this uniqueness is not my inheritance, and I do not even have to react against it. Academic purifications of language do not concern me (do not satisfy me, irritate me or amuse me); on the other hand ... I am fascinated by my confrontation with its law.] (*IP,* 45)

However, both the prescriptive notion of correctness and the Saussurean concept of systematicity have in common the basic criteria of purity and uniqueness, whether these are seen as an obstacle to the free 'mixing up' of languages or as a manifestation of cultural domination, and Glissant's hostility to both presents some problems for other aspects of his ethical commitment to the notion of linguistic 'biodiversity.' Every language, he claims, is precious and worth saving because it contributes something different: 'Car avec toute langue qui disparaît s'efface à jamais une part de l'imaginaire humain' [For with each language that disappears a part of the human imagination is forever obliterated] (*TTM,* 85). Glissant is careful to stress that 'mixing' languages does not erase their distinctive characteristics; he evokes, for instance, 'a country in which words are mixed up without merging together [se mélangent sans se confondre] or vanishing, all the world's languages, known and unknown' (*TM,* 278). But these unique features must surely include the syntactic peculiarities of a given language as well as the lexical items that he has characterized as more superficial and 'exotic.' The particular vision of the world that is embodied in a language is expressed, one might think, more powerfully by its system of tenses, or by how many gender distinctions it makes between nouns, for instance, than by the presence or absence of certain items of vocabulary. But it is difficult to see how the general syntactic structures that operate on the level of the language as a whole could survive a process in which the language is broken up and mixed with others. Is it possible, in other words, to conceive of syntax, not as a single global system which, in Saussurean fashion, holds together by virtue of the necessary interrelatedness of all its parts, but as a more flexible and decentred phenomenon whose component elements could be *interchangeable* with structures taken from other languages?

The group of languages which, at least in some analyses, come much closer to this pattern than standard French or English are of course the different varieties of Creole, on which Glissant has written a great deal both in *Le Discours antillais* and subsequent texts. In the former work, it was at the forefront of his concerns in the narrower context of anti-colonial resistance, and in the context of the difficult relation between French and Creole that, I have argued, is at the root of his transgressive attitude towards French.[10] Later, just as the wider cultural phenomenon of creolization becomes a pattern for developments across the 'Tout-monde,' so the Creole language itself also provides a model for the way in which all languages are, or ought to be, developing – 'Je crois que toute langue à son origine est une langue créole' [I believe that every language is a creole language at its origin] (*IPD*, 28) – insofar as it can be seen as providing an example of precisely the kind of fluid, non-totalizing syntax that Glissant's position requires. He subscribes, in other words, to what used to be a widespread view (although it has been contested by some linguists) that Creole is a language whose structure is *mixed* in its very foundations: 'une langue créole joue à partir de "zones" linguistiques différenciées, pour en tirer sa matière inédite' [a creole language takes as its starting point differentiated linguistic 'zones,' drawing on them for its new substance] (*TTM*, 25). Specifically, it is said to combine French vocabulary with 'African' syntax: 'c'est un vocabulaire des marins bretons et normands du xviie siècle "accordé" 'à une synatxe qui n'a plus rien à voir avec; probablement une synthèse des syntaxes de la côte ouest de l'Afrique noire' [it is the vocabulary of seventeenth-century Breton and Normandy sailors 'fitted together' [accordé] with a syntax that has nothing to do with it; probably a synthesis of the syntaxes of the west coast of sub-Saharan Africa] (*IPD*, 52). At the same time, it is a language which has never been subjected to the efforts of prescriptive grammarians to establish norms of correctness, and so allows a considerable amount of free variation in its syntactic use.[11] Glissant's promotion of 'mixing up languages' thus leads him to a new conception of the very principles of language structure – a conception in which Creole, no longer a marginalized exception to the rule, acquires exemplary status as a language which retains a concept of syntactic structures as distinctive, but as no longer necessarily bound to one particular total system.

However, even if we accept that this creolization of languages is a general ongoing process, the question still remains of what kind of *agency* it involves. How, concretely, do different separate languages become mixed up with each other, recombined in new hybrid configurations? Glissant's descriptions of the process tend to be lyrical rather than analytical; but it is possible to construct a more substantial account of this new phenomenon by relating it to an idea that has been an important emphasis in his thought for much longer, from *L'Intention poétique* onwards, but that has undergone some significant modifications. This is his concept of 'langage,' and its relationship to 'langue.'[12] Glissant's use of these terms is entirely different from that of Saussure. In his formulation, *langage* denotes the speaking subject's relation or attitude to the *langue* – French, English, Creole, etc. – that he or she uses, as that attitude is materialized in a particular practice of the *langue*. In *Le Discours antillais,* he defines it as 'a shared attitude, in a given community, of confidence or mistrust in the *langue* or *langues* it uses' (*CD,* 120). In the case of the Martinican community during the period that Glissant is writing about in *Le Discours antillais*, this attitude is determined by the tension inhabiting the colonized subjects' use of the colonial language: they speak French, but in a particular way that expresses their conflictual relationship with it.[13] It is a conscious, willed struggle for expression – the Caribbean speaker has to 'frayer à travers la langue vers un langage, qui n'est peut-être pas dans la logique interne de cette langue' [wend his or her way through the *langue* towards a *langage* that may not correspond to the internal logic of that *langue*] (*DA,* 237) – and, as such, reflects the problems and the scarcity of language that characterize Glissant's representation of Martinique in this period.

But the distinction between *langue* and *langage* exists in all language communities; according to Glissant, one does not just 'speak French,' or any other *langue*. Rather, one speaks one's *langage*, which is a personalized variant of the *langue*: 'Dans toute langue autorisée, tu bâtiras ton langage' [In every official *langue*, you will build your *langage*] (*IP,* 45). And, as the verb 'bâtiras' suggests, this activity is both intentional and creative. Glissant's *langage* has interesting similarities with the phenomenological notion of the 'parole parlante' developed by Maurice Merleau-Ponty, and, although Glissant does not refer to Merleau-Ponty, and has not been directly influenced by him, a comparison of the two concepts will help to illuminate the relation between *langue* and *langage*.[14] For Merleau-Ponty, linguistic meaning is possible only on the basis of the pre-reflexive intentionality of one's embodied presence in the world; and speech, as distinct from language, emerges directly from this primary expressivity: 'speech takes flight from where it rolls in the wave of speechless communication' (*Signs*, 17). The act of speaking – like Glissant's *langage* – precedes the existence of a constituted *langue*, which is formed by a gradual process of 'sedimentation' of multiple acts of 'parole parlante'; and, again like *langage*, it is 'creative' in a way that established language – which Merleau-Ponty also calls 'empirical language,' because it is the object of the empiricist philosophies of language that he is critiquing – is not:

> The empirical use of already established language should be distinguished from its creative use. Empirical language can only be the result of creative language. Speech in the sense of empirical language – that is, the opportune recollection of a pre-established sign – is not speech in respect to an authentic language. (*Signs*, 44)

One particular passage in *L'Intention poétique* is strikingly close to Merleau-Ponty's insistence on the primacy of speech – or in Glissant's terms, *langage* – over *langue*. *Langage* is defined here not only as the way in which the subject inhabits one *langue* but also as a very basic mode of expressivity, comparable to Merleau-Ponty's 'parole parlante': that is, as a disposition towards language in general that precedes the use of any particular *langue*. Therefore, in the multilingual situation that, according to Glissant's prediction, will become generalized in the future, *langage* also provides a means of relating one *langue* to another:

> On devra tenir compte de ce que l'être de demain parlera *naturellement* plusieurs langues; que chaque langage (chaque choix du dire) courra d'une de ces langues aux autres ... que par conséquent l'analyse de chaque langage devra intégrer l'étude non pas seulement des langues intéressées mais encore de *leur réaction conjuguée dans l'être*. Définir un langage, ce sera définir l'attitude générale de l'être face aux mots dont il use, oui; mais aussi approcher le principe (en l'être) d'une symbiose élocutoire qui signifiera une des modalités de sa liaison à la totalité du monde.

> [One will have to take account of the fact that the human being of the future will *naturally* speak several *langues*; that each *langage* (each choice of a way of saying things) will run from one of these *langues* to the others ... that as a result the analysis of each *langage* will have to include not only the study of the *langues* concerned, but also that of their *combined reaction in the*

person. Defining a *langage* will of course involve defining the person's general attitude towards the words he or she uses; but also trying to elucidate the principle (in the person) governing a symbiosis of speech which expresses one of the modalities of his or her connection with the world as a whole.] (*IP*, 46)

It is this aspect of *langage* that is developed much further in the writings of the 1990s in the context of the 'Tout-monde.' Here, in other words, its most significant role becomes that of acting as a bridge between *langues* and thus making possible the process of 'mixing them up.' In the section of *Introduction à une poétique du divers* entitled 'Langues et langages' (33-57), for instance, Glissant argues that 'la construction d'un langage dans la langue dont on use permet la visée vers le chaos-monde: parce que cela établit des relations entre des langues possibles du monde' [the construction of a *langage* in the *langue* that one uses opens up an orientation towards the chaos-world: because it sets up relations between the possible *langues* of the world] (*IPD*, 42). He claims that the writers of the Caribbean have a common *langage* that 'weaves' or mediates between the *langues* – English, French, Spanish, and Creole – that they use (42-3). *Tout-monde*, similarly, returns again and again to 'la question des langues qu'on utilise, de la manière dont on les pratique, de la licence qu'on exerce à les mettre en relation avec d'autres langues, c'est-à-dire à en faire un langage (*TM*, 316) [the question of the *langues* one uses, the way in which one puts them into practice, the freedom one exercises in relating them to other *langues*, that is, in transforming them into a *langage*] (*TM*, 316). Here the mobile, dynamic quality of *langage* is stressed by presenting it as a 'journey' which traverses and hence weaves together different *langues*: 'Le langage est un voyage et voyez qu'il n'a pas de fin. Les langues sont des étapes' [*Langage* is a journey, and you see it has no end. The *langues* are stages on the way] (*TM*, 316). Finally, this in turn impacts on the *langues* themselves: it is *langage* which remixes them and relativizes the boundaries between them: 'le langage importe ici, qui dévie les limites des langues utilisées' [*langage* is what counts here, as it deflects the boundaries of the *langues* used] (*TTM*, 76).

One major type of activity that involves putting languages in relation with each other is of course translation, and Glissant brings *langage* into play here too, to produce a theory of translation which makes of it a prime example of anti-systemic thought. In *Traité du Tout-monde* he describes it as an elusive, creative activity based on 'l'esquive' [dodging or sidestepping] and 'la trace' [the trace], as opposed to the system:

L'art de traduire nous apprend la pensée de l'esquive, la pratique de la trace qui, contre les pensées de système, nous indique l'incertain, le menacé, lesquels convergent et nous renforcent. Oui, la traduction, art de l'approche et de l'effleurement, est une fréquentation de la trace.

[The art of translation teaches us to think in terms of evasion, to practise the art of the trace, which, as opposed to systematic thought, points us towards what is uncertain, what is under threat, as these come together and strengthen us. Translation, the art of coming close to something, just brushing against it, does indeed move in the realm of the trace.] (*TTM*, 28)

Translation, in other words, is not simply a mechanical process of replacing one *langue* with another. It can work only through the invention of a new *langage* that bridges the two *langues*, but also produces something new and different from either of them: translation is thus by definition unpredictable – 'Le langage du traducteur opère comme la créolisation et comme la Relation dans le monde, c'est-à-dire que ce langage produit de l'imprévisible' [The translator's *langage* operates in the same way as creolization and Relation in the world, which is to say that this *langage* produces the unpredictable] (*IPD*, 45) – and will always contain an element of opacity (*TTM*, 29). When Anestor, in *Tout-monde*, asks his friend from the Ivory Coast to translate into his own language a fragment of French, he tells him: 'n'essaie pas de comprendre, seulement la machine à traduire, mais à traduire vraiment, hein, tout en poésie, tu brodes tant que tu veux' [don't try to understand, you're not just a translating machine, try to really translate, you know what I mean, like poetry, you can embroider it as much as you like] (*TM*, 470). The work of the translator is as creative as that of the poet, and both work by exploiting the capacity of *langage* to transform and regenerate the *langue*: 'Une langue se rehausse de permettre que nous y tracions notre langage: la poétique de notre rapport aux mots' [A *langue* enhances itself by allowing us to trace our *langage* in it – the poetics of our relation to its words] (*TTM*, 86).[15]

The concept of *langage* thus underpins both the early and the more recent stages of Glissant's theorization of language. Despite the apparently radical break between the difficulty and scarcity of language in *Le Discours antillais* and its ease and proliferation in *Tout-monde*, both positions, and the transition between them, are made possible by the distinction between a fully constituted, 'sedimented' *langue* and the primary subjective force of *langage*. Originally developed in response to the pressures placed on the colonized subject by the dominance of the French language and the resulting constraints placed upon any possibility of self-expression, *langage* recurs with equal prominence in the freer and much expanded environment of the 'Tout-monde,' where one of its main functions becomes that of relating one *langue* to another, breaking down their boundaries and so enabling them to be 'mixed up.' In this context, it acts on the *structural* features of language: by its position, as it were *between* the speaking subject and the *langue* (in the sense that I do not speak French, rather I speak my *langage*, which draws on the resources of French), it redefines *langue* as a resource or reservoir of materials, rather than a structure; this, in turn, enables the subject to move between different *langues* and mix them up, and both of these factors have the effect of changing the *langue* itself, pushing at its boundaries.

The concern with language that is so central to *Tout-monde* and to Glissant's recent theoretical texts also has the ethical dimension discussed in the first part of this essay, under the slogan 'I write in the presence of all the world's languages.' I want now to return to this aspect, to argue that *langage* has an equally important role to play in the question of our ethical relationship to other languages that we do not know. It is *langage*, in other words, that can enable us to 'understand' people speaking or writing in a language that we do not 'understand'; and that therefore acts as a bridge in this sense, too, between what I have identified as the ethical and the structural strands of Glissant's thought on language.

In the first place, *langage* allows Glissant to resituate the relation between language and identity. He has almost from the start rejected the idea that personal identity involves the kind of straightforward identification with a *langue* that is in any case not accessible to colonized communities. This point is forcefully restated in the later work: in *Traité du Tout-monde*, for instance, Glissant writes: 'La langue n'est plus le miroir d'aucun être' [The *langue* is no longer the mirror of any being] (85). But now it is because, rather than defining ourselves within one *langue*, we 'surf' them all – 'et vous entreprenez ... de bondir d'une langue à une autre' [you set about leaping ... from one *langue* into another] (*TM*, 20) – and we are able to do this, as we have seen, through the agency of *langage*. It is *langage* that embodies the speaker's subjective relationship to the *langue* that s/he is using; so *langage* is, in a sense, an aspect of the speaker's identity, defined, however, not as a fixed separate entity, but as an open-ended, multiple, and mobile relation to others: 'la langue, c'est le creuset toujours bouleversé de mon unité. Le langage, ce serait le champ ouvert de ma Relation' [*langue* is the constantly disrupted crucible of my unity. *Langage* is the open field of my Relation] (*TTM*, 112).[16]

The Relation to other people includes, most crucially, other people whose languages we do not know; *Poétique de la Relation* insists that 'understanding,' at least in the conventional sense, is unnecessary and even harmful to the proper exercise of Relation, which is ethically bound to respect the other's opacity.[17] But Glissant is able to develop this idea further by linking it specifically to *langage*: *langage*, that is, also opens up the possibility of a different mode of understanding the other's speech, a mode that does not depend either upon the reductive transparency that Glissant is opposing, or upon ordinary linguistic knowledge. Here again the phenomenological resonances of *langage* are very evident. Merleau-Ponty's definition of speech, as we have seen, places it in direct continuity with the primary 'intercorporeal communication' (*Signs*, 19) that is a basic given of one's situatedness in the world. One major implication of this is that the meanings of words are not mechanically encoded as discrete units of language; rather, 'their conceptual meaning must be found by a kind of deduction from a *gestural meaning* which is immanent in speech' (*Phenomenology of Perception*, 179). And, just as in Glissant's view understanding is not an introspective process but a relational openness to the other's speech which does not try to exclude opacity, so Merleau-Ponty argues that 'to understand [speech], we do not have to consult some inner lexicon which gives us the pure thoughts covered up by the words or forms we are perceiving; we only have to lend ourselves to its life, to its movement of differentiation and articulation, and to its eloquent gestures. There is thus an opaqueness of language' (*Signs*, 42). Moreover, understanding someone else is not a passive process of reception, but a matter of making their 'significative intentions' converge with my own – as the translator of *Signs* puts it in his introduction:

> Every spoken word appears to me as a visible trace of the invisible significative intention which is constituting it, and I comprehend and respond to it by means of my own significative intentions. In my dialogue with other speaking men, expression and communication are polarized about significative intentions which converge through reciprocal encroachments in spoken words. (xxi)

Therefore, also, 'men whose languages are different are able to communicate because they find within themselves a speaking power which lets them pass into the style of another language which encroaches on their own' (xxii). Thus, when Glissant claims that in his attempts to read Faulkner's novels in English, he can 'gain direct access to the structure of Faulkner's work before having access to the letter of that work' (*IPD*, 116), or that when faced with a Haitian speaking an unfamiliar variety of Creole, you spontaneously translate it into your own variety – 'you hear his Creole with your ear' (*TM*, 386) – he is, I suggest, invoking something very close to the phenomenological concept of 'significative intentions.' But he himself locates this ability (to understand a language we do not understand) precisely in *langage*, which thus assumes the role of the phenomenological primary expressivity of one's situatedness in the world, which precedes any *langue* and transcends the barriers between *langues*. Or, as he puts it:

> La barrière de la langue tombe; dans une telle fonction c'est le langage qui opère ... Chaque langage: sillon, faisceau de rapports par-dessus (et dans) les diverses langues et leurs obstacles ... Autrement dit: je te parle dans ta langue et c'est dans mon langage que je te comprends.

> [The barrier of the *langue* falls; in this situation it is *langage* that takes over ... Each *langage* is a furrow, a collection of links across (and in) the various *langues* and their obstacles ... In other words, I speak to you in your *langue*, and I understand you in my *langage*.] (*IP*, 53)

I have tried to show how Glissant's engagement with the subject of globalized multilingualism revolves around two main issues, neither of which is definitively resolved, but both of which are explored in fruitful and illuminating ways. Firstly, how should we respond to the presence all around us of languages which we do not 'understand,' in the normal sense of the word? Secondly, how does the existence of 'mixed,' structurally heterogeneous languages, without fixed structural boundaries separating them, alter our conception of what 'a language' is? I have argued that both these questions need to be interpreted in the light of the distinction between *langue* and *langage* – a distinction which in fact goes back a long way before Glissant's more recent work, which is more explicitly focused on multilingualism. *Langage* is a central and richly multi-faceted concept; it implies an extremely active, creative relationship to established languages – both those that we speak and those that we do not – and it is thus ultimately a major dimension of our 'Relation' to the 'Tout-monde.'

NOTES

1 *Le Discours antillais* (Paris: Seuil, 1981) (*DA*); *Poétique de la Relation* (Paris: Gallimard,1990) (*PR*); *Tout-monde* (Paris: Gallimard,1993 [Folio edition]) (*TM*); *Introduction à une poétique du divers* (Paris: Gallimard, 1996) (*IPD*), and *Traité du Tout-monde* (Paris: Gallimard, 1997) (*TTM*). I shall also be referring to Glissant's 1969 collection of essays, *L'Intention poétique* (Paris: Seuil, 1969) (*IP*). I shall use the above-noted abbreviations of these titles in references (*DA, PR, TM, IPD, TTM, IP*). Translations from these texts are my own except in the case of those sections of *Le Discours antillais* that have been translated by Michael Dash as *Caribbean Discourse: Selected Essays* (Charlotteville: University Press of Virginia, 1989), which I identify as '*CD*' rather than '*DA*.' The term 'Tout-monde' is roughly equivalent to the English 'Whole-world,' but given the very special connotations that Glissant attaches to it, I have preferred to leave it in French throughout. I distinguish typographically between the text *Tout-monde* and the concept 'Tout-monde.'
2 'Édouard Glissant avec *Les Périphériques vous parlent,*' *Les Périphériques vous parlent*, November 2002, p. 1.
3 The Caribbean migrants who are described as 'the salt of Diversity,' for instance: 'they have crossed limits and frontiers, they mix up languages, they relocate languages, they shift things around, they fall into the madness of the world' (*TM*, 407).
4 The implicit criticism here is directed at the 'créolité' group of writers (Patrick Chamoiseau, Raphaël Confiant, and Jean Bernabé), with whom Glissant has a somewhat ambivalent relationship. In *Introduction à une poétique du divers,* he writes: 'Certains défenseurs du créole sont complètement fermés à cette problématique. Ils entendent défendre le créole de manière monolingue, à la manière de ceux qui les ont opprimés linguistiquement. Ils héritent de ce monolinguisme sectaire et ils défendent leur langue à mon avis d'une mauvaise manière' [Some of the defenders of Creole are completely blind to this problematic. They are intent on defending Creole monolingually, in exactly the same way as those who used to oppress them linguistically. They have inherited this sectarian monolingualism, and they defend their language in the wrong way, in my opinion] (*IPD*, 113).

5 This is not the case in *L'Intention poétique*, where he is still assuming that multilingualism in the ordinary sense will become the norm in the future; it is already the case, he argues, in large parts of the world, and 'on devra tenir compte de ce que l'être de demain parlera *naturellement* plusieurs langues' [one will have to take account of the fact that the human being of the future will *naturally* speak several languages] (45).

6 Glissant's use of 'monolingual' here has something in common with Derrida's argument in *Le Monolinguisme de l'autre* that even if I only speak one language, it is not 'mine,' because of 'a sort of originary "alienation" which institutes every language as the other's language: language, the impossible property [l'impossible propriété d'une langue]' (*Le Monolinguisme de l'autre, ou la prothèse de l'origine* [Paris: Galilée, 1996], 121). It is worth remembering that this book originated in a conference that Glissant organized at the University of Louisiana in Baton Rouge in 1992.

7 His second novel, *Le Quatrième Siècle* (Paris: Seuil, 1964), contains an important scene in which a Maroon, Longoué, meets, in the forest, the plantation owner from whom he escaped ten years previously; rather than speaking to each other in Creole, each chooses to use his mother tongue – respectively, the African language which Longoué has not used for years, and standard French – so that they cannot in fact understand what the other is saying but choose to remain 'respectueux de cette paix et, à l'extrême, de cette incompréhension mutuelle dans laquelle ils se retrouvaient solidaires' [respectful of this peace, and, to an extreme degree, of this mutual incomprehension within which they found themselves in solidarity with each other] (111).

8 Ferdinand de Saussure, *Cours de linguistique générale* (Paris: Payot 1968), 31.

9 See, for example, Peter Hallward's analysis of this in 'Edouard Glissant between the Singular and the Specific,' *Yale Journal of Criticism* 11. 2 (1998): 441–62.

10 See my *Edouard Glissant and Postcolonial Theory: Strategies of Language and Resistance* (Charlotteville and London: University Press of Virginia, 1999), 25–30, 140–8, for a more detailed consideration of the place of Creole in Martinican society and in Glissant's writing.

11 Derek Bickerton's schema of 'levels' of Creole has been influential in francophone conceptualizations of Creole, such as the work of Jean Bernabé and the GEREC group at the Université des Antilles-Guyane. Bickerton analyses Creole as a continuum going from a 'basilect' through a 'mesolect' to an 'acrolect' which shades off into the standard language; in other words, exactly the model of unfixed, permeable frontiers that Glissant is also putting forward. See Derek Bickerton, *Dynamics of Creole System* (Cambridge: Cambridge University Press, 1975); Jean Bernabé, *Fondal-Natal:*

grammaire basilectale approchée des créoles guadeloupéens et martiniquais (Paris: L'Harmattan, 1983).

12 Since the English term 'language' covers both of these and does not allow one to make the distinction between them, I am retaining the French terms in my discussion of them.

13 *Langage* thus acts as the basis for the concept of counter-poetics, which results from the struggle Antillean speakers have in constructing for themselves a means of expression that simultaneously *uses* and *contests* the existing languages that are in theory available to them – Creole, but more particularly standard metropolitan French. 'Counter-poetics' both reflects and resolves the tension with which, as postcolonial subjects, they relate to the colonizer's language. I discuss this more fully in *Edouard Glissant and Postcolonial Theory*, 30–4.

14 Maurice Merleau-Ponty: *Phenomenology of Perception*, trans. Colin Smith (New York: Humanities Press, 1962); and *Signs*, trans. Richard McCleary (Evanston: Northwestern University Press, 1964).

15 A little later in *Traité du Tout-monde*, Glissant elaborates on the poet's relation to *langue* and *langage* to emphasize even more clearly the *creative* force of the latter: 'The poet, going beyond the *langue* that he uses, but in a mysterious way in the *langue* itself, on the level of the *langue* [à même la langue] and in its margins, is a builder of *langage*' (122).

16 It is significant in this context that in *L'Intention poétique* and *Le Discours antillais*, *langage* is seen as a collective phenomenon, while in the later work individuals create their own particular *langage*. This is especially true of individuals whose lives are marked by displacement and migration; a striking example is the character of Stepan Stepanovitch in *Tout-monde*, who responds to the devastation of war by creating his own 'secret' *langage*: 'Stepan Stepanovitch, d'au milieu de cette misère apocalyptique de la guerre, dans des pays aussi absolument ravagés, avait commencé de fabriquer autre chose, une absolue exigence d'autre chose, pays arbitraire ou langage secret' [Stepan Stepanovitch, out of the midst of the apocalyptic destitution of the war, in countries so completely ravaged, had begun to make something else, an absolute demand for something else, an arbitrary country or a secret *langage*] (*TM*, 403).

17 In the section entitled 'Pour l'opacité,' he contrasts opacity with the 'transparency' that reduces the other to its own norms and preconceptions: 'Si nous examinons le processus de la "compréhension" des êtres et des idées dans la perspective de la pensée occidentale, nous retrouvons à son principe l'exigence de cette transparence. Pour pouvoir te "comprendre" et donc t'accepter, il me faut ramener ton épaisseur à ce barême idéel qui me fournit

motif à comparaisons et peut-être à jugements. Il me faut réduire' [If we look at the process of 'understanding' beings and ideas as it operates in Western society, we find that it is founded on an insistence on this kind of transparency. In order to 'understand' and therefore accept you, I must relate your density to this scale of conceptual measurement which gives me a basis for comparisons and perhaps for judgments. I must reduce] (*PR*, 204).

3 Relating (in Theory) in a Globalized World: Between Levinas's Ethics and Glissant's Poetics

MARY GALLAGHER

As a reflection on the tangency of ethics and poetics in a globalized world, this essay confronts the poetics of cultural diversity and inter-relation envisioned by the Caribbean thinker and poet Édouard Glissant with the writings of Emmanuel Levinas, the Jewish philosopher of Lithuanian origin, famous for stressing the primacy and the priority of ethics over ontology and, indeed, over poetics.[1] That is, it treats the question of how Glissant's view of globalization – his vision of the emergent '*tout-monde*' articulated as a poetics of diversity – relates to Levinas's ethics. More specifically, how might Glissant's idea of the 'world as a whole,'[2] this 'global' vision of diversity and relationality, map onto Levinas's thinking about 'the other' (l'autre) or about 'the other person' (autrui), and more especially onto Levinas's critique of totality in, for example, *Totalité et infini*? Can Glissant's poetics of globalization – perhaps through its emphasis on opaqueness, complexity, multiplicity, 'unencompassability,' or resistance – accommodate an ethics of responsibility for the other (culture)? And conversely, how open is Levinas's ethics to the value of the poetic and to the possibilities of poetics? In considering such questions, we might approach – in theory at least – a better understanding of the creative and ethical potential, implications, and limitations of the movement towards globalization.

Édouard Glissant on the Imperative of Cultural Diversity

From the oustet of the intellectual trajectory charted in his writing (essays, fiction, poetry, and drama), a fundamental imperative of cultural diversity or plurality has driven the work of the contemporary

Martinican writer and intellectual Édouard Glissant, widely recognized as being one of the most compelling postcolonial poets/thinkers writing in French today.[3] Glissant situates the value of cultural diversity not just poetically, but also both existentially and phenomenologically, and he considers, moreover, that this value both depends on – and itself promotes – a certain decentring or decolonizing of world consciousness. Glissant does not, however, make extravagant claims for the ethical effectiveness of the diversity imperative, although he does argue strongly, as we shall see, for its ethical potential. For him, the mid-twentieth-century fracture of the singular, monopolistic, historical narrative articulated by the West opened up the salutary horizon of a non-hierarchical totality of diverse experience, values, and narratives. Already, throughout the 1960s and 1970s, in the essays published in 1969 under the title *L'Intention poétique* [The Poetic Intention] and in 1981 under the title *Le Discours antillais* [*Caribbean Discourse*],[4] Glissant was writing about the emergence of a previously unimaginable pan-cultural integrality, a nascent 'world imaginary,' which he emphatically envisioned, however, as a development entirely compatible with respect for diversity. For Glissant, this ever-increasingly global cultural ecology translates an interruption of the primacy of Being in favour of the primacy of 'beings.' It effects, in other words, a rupture of the supremacy of ontology over existence. Glissant considers that the lone singularity that is a feature of the sameness or self-identity of Being is incapable of revealing or recording diversity. True diversity can only be registered, he argues, in the multiplicity, variety, and interrelationality of all peoples and communities.[5] The totality that Glissant has in mind here runs counter, then, to essentialism and idealism, more specifically to 'cette Idée que l'on place derrière les choses pour en ramener la diversité à l'idéal confortable de l'unitaire' [this Idea that we trace behind things in order to reduce the diversity of these things to the comfortable ideal of the unitary] (*IP*, 88). Indeed, as early as the 1960s, Glissant was an advocate for an emerging global totality – or better said – a holism that is not just existential rather than ontological, but that is also relational and processual rather than summative in tenor: 'Il y a tant de terres: la totalité résulte (bien plus que de leur somme) de leur relation à venir' [There are so many earths: the totality results not so much from their sum as from their as-yet-to-be-realized relationality] (*IP*, 90). What Glissant is envisioning here, then, is a combinative or connective mesh, a poetics – not a politics – of diversity. He is imagining the world as a labile network of irreducible relations, as a holistic dynamic of interconnections that is, crucially, resistant to the reductive reflexes of idealism, abstraction, or universalism.

Glissant explicitly distinguishes the poetic value of a given people's or a given culture's emergence as an entity within the world imaginary – what he calls 'l'appel poétique de surgissement au monde' or the poetic call to emergence within the world – on the one hand, from the collective, political (decolonizing), and existential struggle for a recognized place or position in the world – 'la lutte collective d'établissement dans le monde' (*IP*, 149), on the other. Even if the two emergences – poetic and political – are connected, they are not, in Glissant's view, coterminous. Difference, and especially the freedom to exist (as different) – undoubtedly a political matter – is certainly represented as a core value: 'Le Divers renaît quand les hommes se diversifient concrètement dans leurs libertés différentes' [The Diverse re-emerges whenever people diversify concretely according to their various liberties] (*IP*, 101). Yet, crucially, Glissant goes much further than this positive evaluation of the – political and existential – freedom to differ. What is for him of supreme value are the lines of 'adventitious' relation connecting diverse elements, connections that are conditional on prior differentiation and diversity: 'Ce qu'il faut ... c'est une communication possible ... entre des opacités mutuellement libérées, des différences, des langages' [what is required ... is some sort of communication ... between mutually liberated opaquenesses, differences, or languages] (*IP*, 51). The significance within this formulation of the term 'opacités' cannot, as we shall see further on, be overemphasized.[6] Moreover, if it is, in Glissant's view, crucial to be opaque, this is because, in a circular argument, he considers not just that relations can only be established between opaque, resistant, or visible entities, but also that an entity owes its particular consistency – or its resistance to reduction – to its constitutive or constitutional relationality. Moreover, at a very obvious level, opaqueness or density counters transparency and ensures that the invisible, those who have been overlooked or looked through, become visible, that they are seen, if not recognized.

The Poetics of Globalization

Observing that the whole contemporary world, or what he calls the 'totalité monde,' is stage to a convulsive and spectacular encounter of diverse and even opposed cultures (which he defines as intellectual, spiritual, and moral entities),[7] the author of the novel *Tout-monde* and of the parallel theoretical treatise *Traité du tout-monde* stresses the globality of this phenomenon of cultural contact:

> Pour la première fois, les cultures humaines en leur semi-totalité sont entièrement et simultanément mises en contact et en effervescence[8] de réaction les unes avec les autres. (Mais il est encore des lieux clos et des *temps* différents.) La globalité, ou totalité, du phénomène en dessine la caractéristique.

> [For the first time, human cultures in their semi-totality are entirely and simultaneously in contact and in effervescent reaction with each other. (But there are still closed places and different *timescales*.) The globality or totality of this phenomenon is what characterizes it principally.] (*TTM*, 23)

However, what is crucial in the current conjuncture for Glissant is not alone the quasi[9] worldwide scale of the encounters, but also the fact that this highly global relationality is taking place on a clearly self-conscious level. He repeatedly stresses the importance of awareness and of mediation in this matter: 'Pour la première fois aussi, les peuples ont totalement conscience de l'échange. La télévision de toutes choses exaspère cette sorte de rapports-là' [For the first time too, the peoples in question are completely aware of the exchange. The fact that everything is now televized exaggerates this type of connection] (*TTM*, 23). Saturated consciousness of the scale of this cultural exchange and its (virtual and virtually) worldwide mediation[10] are, then, the factors that distinguish our age.

Glissant's primary focus as a writer is on the poetic charge attaching to the world-scale dimension of inter-cultural encounter, and on the relational and transformative quotient of that charge. For not only are innumerable minorities or minority cultures that had previously been veiled or hidden by monolithic or monological thinking now surfacing and imposing themselves as such upon the world stage, but they are also beginning to regroup and to reconfigure themselves there, in the eyes of others as well as for themselves.[11] Glissant often describes this recombination in terms of creolization, expanding the reference of the latter term to include the current situation of the world as a whole.[12] In other words, for him, the mutually transformative and unpredictable effect of the (new) phenomenon of exponential cultural contiguity

within a functional, worldwide totality operates as a process of creolization, or what he calls a 'poetics of relation.' He is thus quick to
claim that laboratories of cultural contact – such as the Caribbean and
the Americas more generally – have prophetically revealed the widespread and grand-scale creolization now taking place right throughout
the world.[13] Significantly, Glissant's 1990 volume of essays is entitled
Poétique de la Relation – The Poetics of Relation – and it was followed in
1996 and 1997 by collections entitled *Introduction à une poétique du divers*
[Introduction to a Poetics of Diversity] and *Traité du tout-monde* [Treatise
on the Whole-World]. Thus, from *L'Intention poétique* of 1969 through
Caribbean Discourse (1981, 1992) to the latest three volumes of essays, his
work indicates a constant preoccupation with poetics, as well as a consistent but accelerating movement outwards and beyond the local Caribbean synecdoche, to reflect upon more general levels of (global)
diversity and relationality. Indeed, Glissant gave the new editions of his
1956, 1969, and 1990 essays new subtitles: Poétique I, II, and III respectively. *Traité du tout-monde* appeared in 1997 with the subtitle 'Poétique
IV,' and *La Cohée du Lamentin* in 2005, subtitled 'Poétique V.' However,
the subsequent collection of essays, published in October 2006, *Une
nouvelle région du monde*, is subtitled 'Esthétique.I.'

In Glissant's account of it, the poetic charge of the 'tout-monde' is
activated by the creation of force-fields between and around the heterogeneous constituent elements of the totality, elements that have been
or are being creolized. As in Surrealist poetics, the poetic charge is
taken to be proportionate to the gap between elements being brought
into alignment. And since, in the global poetics of culture, the cultural
elements that are confronted with one another (or creolized) are often
extremely distant and heterogeneous, the (poetic) outcome of their
encounter is exponentially unpredictable. For Glissant, linguistic creolization is the contemporary paradigm of (all) culture: 'rien ne donne
mieux l'image de ce qui se passe dans le monde que cette réalisation
imprévisible à partir d'éléments hétérogènes' [nothing gives a better
picture of what is going on in the world than this unpredictable construction based on heterogeneous elements] (*TTM*, 37). In order to
emphasize the non-systematic, unforeseeable, non-teleological, and
incommensurate nature of this global poetics – a dynamic rather than a
state of being – Glissant characterizes it as a 'système déterministe erratique à variables multiples' (*IPD*, 84), that is, as an erratic system
involving multiple variables. The poetics of creolization or globalization is thus a baroque poetics rather than a classical one, and chaos

rather than order, incommensurability rather than measure or predictability, are its defining principles: 'Ce qui était un rêve unitaire ou universalisant chez le poète traditionnel devient pour nous une plongée difficile dans un chaos-monde' [What was for the traditional poet a universalizing dream has become for us a difficult immersion in a chaos-world] (*IPD* 37). Since this poetics is also remarkably anti-teleological,[14] humanity is beginning to accept that we are 'en perpétuel processus' [in perpetual process] and that we are not 'de l'être, mais de l'étant, et que comme tout étant, [on] change' [being as such but rather *a being* or *beings* in constant flux] (*IPD*, 37). By analogy with creolization, a crucial dimension of globalization, then, is the elusiveness of the cultural relations and reactions that it allows, as is the resistance of these processes to closure. With respect to this 'globalité insaississable du Chaos-Monde' [elusive globality of World-Chaos], Glissant argues that it is a fundamental aspect of contemporary inter-cultural reality: hence his conviction that 'les systèmes de pensée ou les pensées de système ne procurent plus le contact avec le réel, ne donnent plus la compréhension ni la mesure de ce qui se passe réellement dans les contacts et les conflits de culture' [systems of thought or thought about systems no longer afford contact with the real, nor indeed do they allow us to understand or measure what is really taking place in cultural contact and cultural conflict] (*IPD*, 87).

The (Ethical) Value of the Poetics of Diversity

For Glissant, as for most writers, the term 'poetics' refers primarily to the creative potential of literary use of language and of other (secondary) signifying 'systems.' The aesthetic basis of Glissant's thinking – or its articulation as a poetics – is underlined, indeed, by the intertextual reference from his *Introduction à une poétique du divers* to Victor Segalen's definition of exoticism as 'une esthétique du divers.'[15] However, in the shift from Segalen's aesthetic to Glissant's poetics, there is a significant change in ethical valency, since Glissant's view of creativity – that is, his understanding of poetics – is, unlike that of Segalen, intimately linked to an ethics, more specifically an ethics of global diversity. Clearly, poetics is an absolute value for Glissant. For him, poetics, in contrast to theory, provides a unique insight into the fundamentally existential operations of relation and relativity. However, rather than signalling a renunciation of knowledge or a turning away from epistemology (we shall return to this question at the end of this essay), poetics is valued by Glissant as intimation. Moreover, to his mind, only poetics – insofar as it offers an alternative to systematic thinking – can give us a sense of the ethical imperative, and it does this by realizing a relational totality. It is precisely the exemplary poetic modelling of relationality that suggests a response to the (fundamentally ethical) question of the encounter with another or with the other: 'Comment être soi sans se fermer à l'autre, et comment consentir à l'autre, à tous les autres sans renoncer à soi?' [How can one be oneself without shutting oneself off from the other, and how can one consent to the other, to all others, without renouncing oneself?] (*IPD*, 37).[16] In other words, what is original about Glissant's thinking is that he considers the imaginary or poetic plane as (the only) one capable of intimating how the non-reductive integration of specificities within a unified (yet non-closed), relational yet non-systematic world might work. In his view, literariness or poetics, as a non-sytematic mode of unbounded thinking, allows us to conceive of an ethics of relation incommensurate with conceptual or systematic thinking, and with the coercive or at least reductive side-effects of such thinking. Thus:

> ... une intention poétique peut me permettre de concevoir que dans ma   ·
> relation à l'autre, aux autres, à tous les autres, à la totalité-monde, je me
> change en m'échangeant, en demeurant moi-même, sans me renier, sans
> me diluer, et il faut toute une poétique pour concevoir ces impossibles-là.
> C'est pour cela que je pense que la pensée poétique aujourd'hui est au
> principe du rapport au monde.
>
> [... poetic intention allows me to understand that in my relation to the
> other, to others, to all others and to the world-totality, I change by both
> exchanging and remaining myself, without denying or diluting myself; a
> whole poetics is required in order to conceive of these impossibilities. That
> is why I think that poetic thought is today at the very heart of relation to
> the world.] (*IPD*, 102)

It is, above all, literature or writing, as the discovery or revelation of the 'tout-monde,' that accomplishes, in Glissant's view, the work of poetics.[17] The 'tout-monde' is actualized insofar as literature throughout the world is in the process of being creolized or globalized ('mondialisation de la littérature'): 'L'écrivain contemporain ... n'est pas monolingue, même s'il ne connaît qu'une langue, parce qu'il écrit en présence de toutes les langues du monde' [The contemporary writer ... is not monolingual, even if he only knows one language, because he is writing in the presence of all the languages of the world] (*IPD*, 27). In a specifically literary context, then, there is, according to Glissant, widespread artistic and cultural understanding of the fact that 'les cultures en contact multiplié [or what he elsewhere terms 'la multi-relation'] produisent ce bouleversement qui refait nos imaginaires' [cultures in exponential contact produce this overturning that renews our imaginations] (*TTM*, 248). For literature constitutes, fundamentally, the revelation of a mode of non-systematic, non-coercive thinking that is simultaneously an approach to complexity: it is a mode of thinking that is 'ni dominateur, ni systématique, ni imposant' [neither dominating, nor systematic, nor imposing] but rather 'intuitif, fragile, ambigu, qui conviendra le mieux à l'extraordinaire complexité et à l'extraordinaire dimension de multiplicité du monde dans lequel nous vivons' [intuitive, fragile, ambiguous – most in keeping with the extraordinary complexity and the extraordinary multiplicity of the world in which we live] (*IPD*, 25).

Not only, then, does Glissant argue that exposure to new cultural concatenations, synergies, and reactions changes our imaginations, but he claims that it also serves a revelatory, epistemological role that has a deep ethical consequence. For it allows us (human beings) to understand that we do not abdicate our identities when we open ourselves up to other human beings.[18] Although Glissant highlights the ethical potential of such a configuration, he does explicitly acknowledge that 'la Relation n'est pas vertueuse ni "morale" et qu'une poétique de la Relation ne suppose pas immédiatement et de manière harmonieuse la fin des dominations' [Relation is neither virtuous nor 'moral' and a poetics of Relation does not necessarily mean the immediate and harmonious end of domination] (*IPD*, 106). In other words, a poetics of diversity or even a poetics of relation does not in itself offer a solution to the kinds of annihilation of the other that have been attempted in Rwanda or Yugoslavia, since mentalities will have to change radically in the direction indicated by Glissant's poetics if they are to accommodate the notion of 'identité rhizome' instead of 'identité racine unique' (rhizomed identity as opposed to an identity founded on a single root).[19] However, Glissant points out that 'on ne peut pas se sacrifier pour la créolisation, alors qu'on peut se sacrifier pour son identité; pour son identité-racine unique, etc. On peut être assassin, meurtrier, bourreau pour son identité-racine unique. On peut faire la guerre pour son identité-racine unique' [one cannot sacrifice oneself for creolization as one can for one's identity, one's single-rooted identity. One can turn assassin, murderer, butcher for one's single-rooted identity. One can wage war on behalf of one's single-rooted identity] (*IPD*, 99). In Glissant's view, then, creolization potentially inoculates humanity against genocide.

   Glissant's own writing, his own poetics, is in keeping with his faith in the epistemological and ethical efficacy of the 'entrelacements du "Tout-monde"' [the intertwinings of the Global World] (*IPD*, 7) enabled, revealed, or enacted by the exercise of the imagination ('l'exercice de l'imaginaire'), as opposed to tyrannically and reductively systematic or merely empirical thinking: 'L'objet de ces quatre conférences apparaîtra complexe et erratique, et il est probable qu'au cours des exposés je reviendrai sur des thèmes qui s'entrelaceront, qui se reprendront: c'est ma manière de travailler' [The object of these four lectures will appear complex and erratic, and it is probable that during these presentations I will return to themes that will thus criss-cross or embroider each other: that is how I work] (*IPD*, 11).The value of indissoluble, relational complexity is, moreover, realized in the poetic language that Glissant mobilizes, not just in his novels and poetry, but also in his essays and indeed in his writing in, around, and between these genres. It is a language whose relational density sometimes places it at the very edge of what is readable. It has often been noted, indeed, that Glissant's writing (across all genres) is thick with memory and landscape. And it is precisely because of this poetic thickening of the theory in the writing that Glissant's poetic intention does not remain a pure intention or aspiration.

The Global Moment of Glissant's Poet(h)ics of Relation

As we have just noted, Glissant acknowledges that global cultural contact does not always take place in a climate of mutual acceptance and appreciation. On the contrary, he admits that 'les échanges entre les cultures sont sans nuance, les adoptions et les rejets sauvages' [exchanges between cultures are without nuance, adoptions and rejections are savage] (*TTM*, 23). And yet, despite the continued eruption of merciless warfare, he believes that certain global developments in awareness suggest that the exclusive model of identity may be on the wane.[20] It is in the process of inter-cultural contact, and especially of consequential change and exchange, that the world is, in Glissant's view at least, in the process of abandoning a notion of identity based on exclusion of the other in favour of a relational notion of identity, and it is this opening that constitutes, for Glissant, the ethical moment of globalization.

Place or locality has a crucial role to play in the ethical balance of the poetics of the *tout-monde*, in that writing usually emerges in or from a particular place. But in today's world, 'l'œuvre littéraire convient d'autant mieux au lieu, qu'elle établit relation entre ce lieu et la totalité-monde' [the literary work is all the more attuned to a specific location in that it establishes a relation between that location and the global totality] (*IPD*, 34). Glissant recognizes, then, that one belongs to the (whole) world via one's attachment to some patch of earth – 'quelque carré de terre' (*SC*, 70). Without this attachment, he argues, the world vanishes in the smoke of an absolute disorder that it has itself provoked: 'le monde s'évanouit dans les fumées d'un absolu dérèglement qu'il a lui-même suscité' (*SC*, 70). For Glissant, it is primarily in and through literature that a (self-) emancipatory movement from local consciousness to global consciousness can take place: 'C'est par la littérature que s'illustre ce mouvement désentravant, qui mène de notre lieu à la pensée du monde' [It is through literature that this movement of freeing-up is illuminated, a movement that leads from our particular place to thought of the world] (*SC*, 71). Thus, the poetics of the 'tout-monde' moves beyond simple toleration of diversity towards the embracing of relation as a mutual, contextualizing process of liberation, openness, and integration. In articulating his view of la *pensée-monde* in which the term 'world' is both subject and object, he sees no contradiction between the role of literature as an expression of a 'communauté ... reconnue dans sa spécificité,' a community that, through the literary imagination, states 'son entour, son pays' [its surrounds, its land], on the one hand, and, on the other hand, its role as an expression of 'l'Autre, le monde' (*IPD*, 92). He does repeat, however, that 'le lieu est incontournable. Il n'y a pas de mondialisation à partir d'une série de dilutions dans l'air' [Place cannot be ignored. Globalization cannot happen from a series of dilutions in the air] (*IPD*, 92).

Glissant explicitly rejects standardization as a reduction of diversity and is open to the suggestion that the prominence of virtual realities in the contemporary world corresponds to an effort to escape the world's relational operation, or the 'complexité trop angoissante du Tout-monde' [excessively anguishing complexity of the globalized world]. He emphasizes, however, the need to 'combattre réellement les uniformités, les dominances, les standards' [fight with reality against uniformities, dominances, standardizations] (*TTM*, 225). In his *Traité du Tout-*

monde (192), he indeed argues for a critical version of globalization, which he calls 'mondialisation,' based on a non-totalitarian totality, that is, on the recognition of the infinite detail of the diversity of the world in all its reality, and not on reduction, dilution, virtualization, or standardization to the sort of 'non-lieu' criticized by Jean-Luc Nancy as a factor of 'démondialisation.'[21] For Glissant, the aim is to develop a 'theory of specific opaquenesses' (*DA*, 245),[22] and it is perhaps surprising that, despite his opposition to abstract universals (dismissed as 'cet idéalisme de l'Un'), he is so confident of the value of abstractions such as totality, humanity, and diversity. His conviction is, perhaps, explained by his view that the 'healthy' or 'poetic' variant of totality, which he terms 'le rapport aux autres' [connection with others] (*IP*, 53), is immunized against the temptation or threat of reduction by its anchorage in iterativeness and by its immanence to relational organicity. In other words, its inscription in place and time, and also in the dynamic density of a hyper-relativized/relational reality protects it against reduction, abstraction, or synthesis. It is very important to recognize that Glissant's 'tout-monde' is based on a rejection of ideal globalism in favour of a real, itemized globalism, concrete and multiply located. The West 'crut vivre la vie du monde là ou il ne fit souvent que réduire le monde et en induire une globalité idéelle' [thought it was living the life of the world, whereas it was often simply reducing the world to an ideal globality] (*IP*, 27). Termed 'réelle' in order to distinguish it from 'une globalité idéelle,' Glissant's 'totalité' is synonymous with the inexhaustible vigilance of a poetics of diversity. He seems well aware of the ethical pitfalls involved in positive approaches to wholeness or totality: 'Écrire, c'est dire le monde. Le monde comme totalité, qui est si dangereusement proche du totalitaire' [To write is to speak the world. To speak it as a totality, which is so dangerously close to the totalitarian] (*TTM*, 119). Yet he insists quite vigorously that 'la totalité n'est pas ce qu'on a dit être l'universel. Elle est la quantité finie et réalisée de l'infini détail du réel. Et qui, d'être au détail, n'est pas totalitaire' [totality is not what we said the universal was. It is the finite and realized quantity of the infinite detail of the real. And which, because it is spelled out in its infinite detail and particularity, is not totalitarian] (*TTM*, 192). It is precisely by contesting Western cultural hegemony that other cultures can, in their unique detail, in their poetic 'thickness' or density (and here, the German word 'Dichtung,' meaning poetry, but also 'a becoming dense' is helpful), 'relativize' the West, thus bringing it into relation with the rest of the world or, indeed, with the whole world:

'à contester la prédominance de l'Occident, du même coup, [on] intègre celui-ci au monde' [by contesting the West's predominance, we integrate it into the world] (*IP*, 28). This is a movement of reciprocal relativization, then, since to emerge into world consciousness means, for Glissant, finding one's own voice, allowing one's own specificity to surface, thus imposing relativity on others or at least making an essential contribution to a truly relativized world, and, thereby, to the accomplishment of 'the human.'

Levinas: Indifference to Cultural Difference?

Édouard Glissant's vision of global totality, or what he calls the *tout-monde*, and his apologia for world consciousness are, as we have seen, founded in a defence of the poetics of diversity and interrelationality. The totality that he argues for is an infinitely 'itemized' or 'iterative' totality. This fidelity to the value of irreducible diversity has always been at the very heart of Glissant's poetics, but it also lies at the heart of the divergence of that vision from Emmanuel Levinas's ethics. Espousing an ethics that is more akin to a spirituality or a mysticism than to an epistemology or a hermeneutics, Levinas is firm in his rejection of all identification, classification, or naming of *the difference of the other (person)*. Indeed, he anathematizes the thematization or exegesis of the other because of the totalizing perspective that he deems inseparable from the transitive act of knowledge. For Levinas, the ethical relation consists precisely in the suspension of the totalizing perspective on the other person.[23] The ethical moment is synonymous for him with the interruption of comprehension, with the avoidance or refusal of cognition or intellectual grasp. For it is when one focuses on difference as a theme or content that one reduces the other person, cancelling his/her strangeness and reducing everything that is irreducible and inalienable about him/her. The only viable plurality for Levinas is strictly incompatible, then, with the respectively heuristic or hermeneutic impulse of understanding or interpretation, and *a fortiori* with an integrating or totalizing perspective.

Of the many significant and indeed problematic questions raised by the writings of Levinas, one could cite their apparently sovereign disregard for cultural difference (or identity). For Levinas situates ethics, to which he accords priority over ontology, far above and beyond the cultural density of composite and relational 'wholes.' He considers, indeed, that 'les normes de la morale ne sont pas embarquées dans l'histoire et la culture' [the norms of morality are not involved with history and culture] (*HAH* 61), and that the standpoint of ethics consists in considering the other person in the 'nudité de son visage'[nudity of his face]: that is, as an abstract human being, 'dégagé de toute culture' [cleared of all culture] (*HAH*, 60). This approach would seem to betoken an overt and sovereign indifference to cultural, racial, and political difference, an indifference or a non-differentiation intended as a defence of the 'humanisme de l'autre homme' [humanism of the other man], where 'autre' is taken to mean 'any other' and is not (necessarily) a synonym of 'different.' Is it the case, then, that Levinas's ethics cannot offer any defence or resistance to the elimination or reduction of cultures?

Levinas on Planetary Civilization

Far from being blind to the conjunctural climate of the day, Levinas explicitly recognizes the reality of globalization when he asserts that mankind is currently 'imbriqué dans une civilisation et une économie devenues planétaires' [involved in a civilization and an economy that have become planetary] (*HAH*, 96). In a poetic turn of phrase, he describes this new globality of civilization and economy as a 'mutation de la lumière du monde' [mutation of the world's light] (*HAH*, 9). That term, 'lumière,' with its resonances of 'enlightenment,' is not, in my view, a neutral one. And, indeed, Levinas goes on to outline the contemporary evolution of the new relativist, even planetary episteme. He declares that there has been a paradigm shift linked to a new rejection of the preachiness of Western humanism, a proselytizing movement that has been shown, despite its so-called enlightenment, to have, in the final analysis, little or no purchase on the reality of violence and exploitation committed within its ambit and sometimes even in its name. Hence, the widespread

> aversion pour une certaine prédication où tomba – malgré sa science et ses audaces d'antan – l'humanisme occidental établissant dans l'ambiguïté remarquable des belles lettres, de 'belles âmes,' sans prise sur le réel de violences et d'exploitation.

> [aversion towards a certain preachiness into which Western humanism fell despite its former knowledge and boldness, as it established within the remarkable ambiguity of literature or 'bellettrisme,' a spirituality of beau-

tiful souls without any purchase on a reality brimming with violence and exploitation.] (*HAH*, 96)

Levinas seems to be suggesting here a complicity between aesthetics or 'bellelettrisme,' on the one hand, and the fey ineffectuality of spiritual-ity and aesthetics equally, on the other. In *Noms propres*, certainly, Levi-nas shows himself aware of mankind's contemporary alienation from Western humanism and from the latter's pretensions to universality: 'l'aliénation de l'homme par cette universalité même qui, dès l'aube de notre civilisation, devait garantir l'humanité de l'homme' [the alien-ation of man by that selfsame universality that, since the dawn of our civilization, was supposed to guarantee man's humanity] (*NP*, 133). And yet, in an essay on the Holocaust entitled 'Sans nom,' Levinas appears to acknowledge that the contemporary 'one world' phenome-non – a universalism that constitutes the acceptable face of globaliza-tion? – at least gives (cold?) comfort to the victims of the ongoing oppression of nations and individuals, who, in contrast to the victims of the Holocaust, now 'know where to turn,' even if that 'where' couldn't or wouldn't save the victims of genocide in Rwanda or of ethnic cleans-ing in former Yugoslavia (*NP*, 141).[24] On the face of it, then, globaliza-tion is credited by Levinas with the positive consequence of explicitly universalizing what is identified as right and wrong or good and evil – via 'one world' notions such as human rights or war crimes.[25]

Levinas would situate the aforementioned benefits of universalism as pertaining to ethics and as being located, therefore, beyond ontology, beyond difference. But to what extent is Levinas's universalism, as Ber-nadette Cailler has suggested, residually ethnocentric? Cailler is cer-tainly correct in claiming that there is no trace in Levinas's work of what Martin Bernal has termed 'Black Athens' and that, apart from the occasional reference to 'Lévy-Bruhl et Lévi-Strauss' there is no trace either of 'une interférence ou d'un questionnement, avec ou sur les cul-tures africaines, amérindiennes, ou autres, même si l'humanisme de l'autre homme est partout, par lui, reconnu' [a crossover with, or a questioning of African or Amerindian or other cultures, even if he everywhere accepts the humanism of the other man].[26] Levinas is, in fact, quite open sometimes about his own cultural bias and often speci-fies, for example, that his comments refer exclusively to European thought and to Europe. Even his most lucid and supportive critics, such as Simon Critchley, are uneasy about the suspicion of both Eurocentri-cism and Zionism hanging over Levinas's thinking.[27] It remains that he has, however, directly and explicitly addressed the questions of cultural diversity and relativism.

Cultural Relativism as Disorientation

In *L'Humanisme de l'autre homme*, Levinas notes the significant coincidence of cultural and economic globalization, on the one hand, and the formalist/structuralist dethroning of the subject, on the other. He is, moreover, openly critical of the de-subjectivization common to the approaches of formalist and structuralist thought, whose hallmark it is, he suggests, to privilege mathematical identities that can be identified (objectified, classified, and de-singularized, as it were) from outside.[28] In a highly significant passage, he establishes a link between the political movement of decolonization, the structuralist undermining of subjectivity, and the cultural relativism informing contemporary ethnography.[29] He further observes, however, using a language that – given the religious spirituality that underpins his whole worldview – suggests his disapproval or, at least, his own profound ambivalence on the question of cultural relativism, that this newly recognized 'multivocité du sens de l'être – cette essentielle désorientation – est, peut-être, l'expression moderne de l'athéisme' [plurivalence of the meaning of being – an essential disorientation – is, perhaps, the modern expression of atheism] (*HAH*, 34). In this diagnosis, Levinas identifies the new meaning ascribed to ontology, now relativized according to multiple cultural differences, as the modern expression of atheism. It does not, in other words, allow for any transcendent meaning, which for Levinas would be ethics; instead, it recognizes only a multiplicity of variable, equally valid, culturally sensitive meanings and values. And yet, for Levinas, the acknowledgment of the meaning of being as culturally relative, historically determined, or context-sensitive, is *itself* a culturally conditioned position. It is based, moreover, on the problematic, fundamentally self-contradictory extension of an unequivocally transcendent orientation that is ethical in nature, according to Levinas. In other words, cultural relativism has been developed and articulated, in particular, in and by the West, and it is based on (what Levinas would regard as) a paradoxical and dangerous extension of ethical respect for human beings to ethical respect for the latters' cultures.

Cultural Penetrability and the Transcendence of Ethics

In a quasi-Habermasian moment, Levinas refers to the dominant contemporary perception that cultures are reciprocally penetrable, interpretable, comprehensible (in other words, are not opaque to one another, to use Glissant's language), and he observes that this communicability is commonly taken to found the unity of Being and also, indeed, contemporary universality.[30] In the absence of some sort of esperanto that would translate culturally or linguistically specific meanings, this mutual comprehensibility of cultures and languages that allows us to 'pénétrer une culture à partir d'une autre, comme on apprend une langue à partir de sa langue maternelle' [penetrate one culture coming from another, as we learn another language coming from our native language] (*HAH*, 59), no doubt means that one can be multicultural just as one can be multilingual, that one can move among and between cultures, just as one can move from one language to another. For Levinas, such lateral translatability or mobility is perfectly consistent with the notion of a superordinate meaning prior to culture, and, for him, this transcendent meaning is ethics: 'Nous dirons ... qu'avant la Culture et l'Esthétique, la signification se situe dans l'Éthique, présupposé de toute Culture et de toute signification. La morale n'appartient pas à la Culture : elle permet de la juger' [We might say that before being mediated by culture and aesthetics, meaning is located in ethics, which is presupposed by every culture and every system of meaning, just as meaning precedes signification. Ethics doesn't belong to culture. Rather it allows us to evaluate that culture] (*HAH*, 58). Levinas emphasizes, then, 'l'antériorité du sens par rapport aux signes culturels' [that cultural signs are posterior to meaning] (*HAH*, 58). In other words, the very notions of relation, communication, and meaning are for Levinas pre-eminently and originally ethical in nature and are presupposed by all individual signifying systems, just as he claims priority for saying over what is said (for *le dire* over *le dit*) and for ethics over ontology. Levinas repudiates, then, any notion of cultural equivalence that fails to recognize that each and every culture is itself produced by, and can be judged and measured by, 'une orientation et [d']un sens sans équivoque où l'humanité se tient' [an orientation and an unequivocal meaning upon which humanity stands] (*HAH*, 22). He also criticizes the view that attributes to cultural plurality a de-historicized positive value, or that sees it as a benefit of decolonization:

> On raisonne comme si la multiplicité des cultures plongeaient, de tous temps, leurs racines dans l'ère de la décolonisation, comme si l'incompréhension, la guerre et la conquête ne découlaient pas tout aussi naturellement du voisinage des multiples expressions de l'être ...

[We reason as though cultural diversity has always been grounded in the era of decolonization, and as though misunderstanding, war, and conquest did not flow just as naturally from the close proximity of the multiple expressions of Being ...] (*HAH*, 39)

Levinas is here making a point also made by Glissant, namely, that both the existence and the recognition of cultural diversity are, in fact, ethically neutral. In other words, the promotion of diversity or multiculturalism, the recognition and even the valuing of difference, are not, in themselves, ethical. Indeed, Levinas goes much further in this sense than Glissant, in that he is much more reluctant to accord to cultural diversity even the minimal ethical potential with which it is vested by Glissant. He considers, rather, that the 'postcolonial' discovery and/or valorization of cultural diversity is disorienting:

Mais la sarabande des cultures innombrables et équivalentes, chacune se justifiant dans son propre contexte, crée un monde, certes, dés-occidentalisé, mais aussi un monde désorienté.

[But the round of countless equivalent cultures, each one of which justifies itself within its own context, creates a world that while it may be de-westernized, is also dis-oriented.] (*HAH*, 60)

Given its alignment with the term 'de-westernized' (apparently a neutral or even positive development, in Levinas's eyes), the parallel use of the term 'dis-oriented' may look like a pun in rather poor taste. And yet the negative connotations (of confusion, loss of direction, purpose, meaning, etc.) associated with the notion of disorientation that Levinas is evoking here bespeak a much more radical absence or loss of meaning than the merely ethnocentric loss of the West's major 'orienting' Other, the Orient, and therewith the West's loss of (privileged, oriented) meaning. It corresponds, rather, to the loss of the notion of meaning itself. Not the loss of a merely dialectical, or vectorized, ethnocentric meaning dependent on an 'orienting' Other; rather, the loss of all 'sens' – all direction as well as all meaning – because this (i.e., 'sens' in the sense of 'directionality' as itself the basis of meaning) is what, according to Levinas, precedes and is presupposed by all signification and all culture.[31]

Levinas acknowledges the idealism of his own thinking, but he also blows the anti-Platonic cover of the relativizing, ethnological rejection of colonialism by showing the return of the Platonic repressed[32] in the générosité même de la pensée occidentale qui, apercevant l'homme abstrait dans les hommes, a proclamé la valeur absolue de la personne et a englobé dans le respect qu'elle lui porte jusqu'aux cultures où ces personnes se tiennent et où elles s'expriment.

[the generosity of Western thought which, seeing the abstract human in all human beings, has proclaimed the absolute value of the person and includes within the respect that it affords the latter, respect for the cultures that situate those persons and in relation to which they express themselves.] (*HAH*, 60)

The complicated nature of Levinas's idealism and universalism surfaces, then, in connection with his view of the contemporary Western extension of respect for the absolute value of the human person to the person's culture. For Levinas, this generosity is misguided, and its relativist blank cheque is potentially disastrous, partly because cultures are not equivalent, but rather variable in their ethical quotient. He thus seems to consider that the West, having first failed to recognize that the hegemony of (Western) culture was itself culturally and historically conditioned, and having identified its own culture with the unchanging truth, then went on to throw the baby out with the bathwater, rejecting out of hand the idealist universalism and the humanism that had indeed stood by or even behind the violence and exploitation of colonization. For Levinas, however, humanity went too far after decolonization in rejecting the very concept of transcendent measure, specifically that of ethics as a universal standard against which all cultures can be judged in the name of 'l'humanisme de l'autre homme.'

On the False Transcendence of Economic Value

Given that the Western ethnocentric notion of 'civilization' has had to be jettisoned, the only belief, meaning, or value allowed to be transcendent in the contemporary globalized world is that of economics (synonymous for Levinas with technical and scientific value).[33] For Levinas, however, this view of the centrality or transcendence of economic value is both ethnocentric and deluded. Not only does he regard the predominance of a technical/scientific/mathematical understanding of the universe as being itself culturally conditioned, but he notes that it is not resistant to heterocultural challenge: 'La désignation technique de l'univers, est, elle-même, une modalité de la culture' [the technical désignation of the universe is itself a cultural disposition] (*HAH*, 35). More-over, its fragile hegemony frequently comes under attack from other needs such as nationalism or other forms of particularism and funda-mentalism (Levinas could not have foreseen the torpedoing of the World Trade Center, precisely one such offensive):

> Il n'est pas certain d'ailleurs que la signification scientifique et technique du monde puisse 'dissoudre' la multiplicité des significations culturelles. On peut en douter, en effet, lorsqu'on constate les menaces que font peser sur l'unité de la nouvelle société internationale placée sous le signe du développement scientifique et industriel moderne et du regroupement de l'humanité autour des impératifs univoques du matérialisme, les particu-larismes nationaux, comme si ces particularismes répondaient eux-mêmes à des besoins.

> [It is not clear indeed that the techno-scientific meaning of the world can dissolve the multiplicity of cultural meanings. That would seem all the more unlikely when one sees the threats bearing down on the new inter-national society governed both by modern scientific and industrial devel-opment and by its organization around the single imperative of materialism – threats emanating from national fundamentalisms, as though such particularisms were themselves answering certain human needs.] (*HAH*, 35)

Levinas on Aesthet(h)ics and Poetry

Levinas's views on poetics are difficult to summarize, partly because they are so dispersed, partly because they are so self-contradictory, and partly because they are so extremely vague.[34] As one commentator points out, 'Levinas's writings are rich in comments and reflections on ... the relations between poetry and ethical theory,' but 'unfortunately, Levinas never engaged these matters in any sustained or systematic way, and certainly never without confusion.'[35] For example, whereas Levinas does sometimes associate or even confuse art or aesthetics and poetics or poetry, he quite often distinguishes and even opposes them. However, despite the difficulties associated with such tangles, and despite the inconsistencies in Levinas's views, certain key points do emerge from the dispersed pronouncements on poetry and poetics, especially those communicated in the studies on writers and poets such as Blanchot, Proust, Leiris, and Celan.

In the lines that he devotes to the problematic intersection of ethics and aesthetics, Levinas has quite a lot to say about visual art – the image, in particular – whereas his discourse on poetics is, in a sense, more diffuse, partly because of his tendency to write quite poetically himself. He seems to recognize that visual art is a type of expression, and writes that (in general) expression is what makes signification possible, and that it involves as such integration into, or the formation of, a whole: 'Ramasser en un ensemble, c'est-à-dire exprimer, c'est-à-dire encore rendre la signification possible – voilà la fonction de l' "objet" – œuvre ou geste culturel' [To gather up into a whole (un ensemble), that is to express, that is to make meaning possible, that is the function of the cultural object, work, or gesture] (*HAH*, 26). Levinas denies that the opening-up of meaning or thought can take place prior to, or independently of, the 'ensemble,' or, indeed, of the system of signification that renders such 'ensembles' significant. In other words, he stresses that meaning cannot be seen as autonomous with respect to the medium, or to the linguistic or cultural system which precedes it: 'prise au niveau de l' "objet" culturel, l'expression n'est plus guidée par une pensée préalable. Le sujet s'aventure par la parole effective ou par le geste manuel dans l'épaisseur de la langue et du monde culturel pré-existants' [taken at the level of the cultural object or subject, expression is no longer guided by thinking that precedes it. Rather the subject wanders through word or action into the thickness of a language or a cultural world that precede it] (*HAH*, 26). This notion of the prior existence of both cultural and linguistic systems is important. Levinas acknowledges that these systems have a density, or a thickness (an 'épaisseur'), which precedes the subject's intervention. In this sense, each specific instance of thinking and of expression 's'insère dans la Culture à travers le geste verbal du corps qui la précède et la dépasse' [inserts itself into Culture through the verbal gesture of the body that both precedes and transcends Culture] (*HAH*, 26). In *De l'existence à l'existant*,[36] in a comment that applies at least as much to poetry as to art in general, Levinas further observes that in the experience of the image or of rhythm, the subject is caught up, taken in, and carried away, while art, via the image, provides us with the 'essential projection of a mere shadow.'[37] Levinas's reservations regarding these two aspects of poetry at least partly explain Blanchot's assertion in *L'Entretien infini* that 'Levinas mistrusts poems and poetic activity.'[38] Certainly, the magic of the image and the 'enchantment' of rhythm are not positively viewed by Levinas. After all, the author of *Totalité et infini* renders 'Rimbaud a figure for the poet in general, whose "imagination" is incapable of recognizing ethical transcendence.'[39] Indeed, his denunciation of image and of rhythm, and also of rhetoric, is reminiscent – as Jill Robbins notes – of 'Plato's criticism of mimesis and of his rejection of poetry in the *Republic* and elsewhere.'[40]

And yet, it is undoubtedly the case that Levinas would be no more sympathetic to Aristotle's attempt to 'find a place for poetry in his organon ... by reconceptualizing it as a species of cognition (mimesis) and as a kind of consecutive reasoning (plot),'[41] since cognitive mastery is, as we have seen above, antithetical to the ethical relation as Levinas envisages it. Indeed, it sometimes seems as though the manner in which art (more specifically, rhythm) evicts the ego from its sovereign position, that is, the manner in which art disables rather than enables the relation of knowing, reminds Levinas of the disposession fundamental to the ethical relation. In this way, for Levinas, poetry both 'does and does not give access to the ethical.'[42]

Gerald Bruns has noted the hyperbolic nature of Levinas's language or discourse, basing this characterization on Paul Ricoeur's definition of hyperbole as the systematic practice of excess in philosophical argumentation.[43] Indeed, for Bruns, 'in Levinas, the materiality of language as Blanchot understands it comes to the fore not as a theme but as an increasingly dominant and controversial dimension of his own writing.' Here, if anywhere, Bruns submits, is where poetry and the ethical 'draw near one another.'[44] Levinas's own, quasi-mystical writing could, then, be characterized as poetically charged (even if it is difficult to locate precisely its poetic valency). However, his commentary on poetics is somewhat reductive, principally because of its (discursive) inattention to the linguistic, semantic, and formal specificity of poetry. There are exceptions to this inattention, of course. For example, at one point in *Noms propres*, Levinas directly evokes literary excess or semantic overdetermination when he wonders, 'Mais qu'est-ce donc la littérature, sinon cette disproportion entre l'écriture et l'œuvre, sinon ce "langage porteur de sens" venant se superposer au sens que "l'auteur a cru mettre dans les mots"?' [But what is literature, then, if not this discrepancy between writing and the work, if not this 'meaning-laden language,' a meaning that is superimposed on the meaning that the 'author intended his words to have'?] (*NP*, 107).

In a further example of Levinas's more focused consideration of literary difference, he sometimes invokes a hierarchy of literary values reminiscent of that suggested by Sartre. Poetry, according to Sartre, insofar as it operates outside of, or beyond, language as it functions in prose discourse, and insofar as it functions in the domain, rather, of rhythm, charm, incantation, and image, is set outside of moral or political engagement, while the prose writer uses language as an instrument for engaging with the world. Sartre's view of the distinction between poetry and prose is not dissimilar to Roman Jakobson's (more ethically neutral) contention that, whereas prose is 'transparent,' carrying us into the domain described in the words, poetry focuses our attention on the medium itself. For Jakobson, the poetic function of language renders words themselves obtrusive.[45] Levinas, while adopting Sartre's hierarchy, bases it on a quite distinctive (and rather negative) view of poetic language as interrupting the (dia)logical movement of signification, thereby opening up a dimension of exteriority or worldlessness. He claims more importantly that poetry's reduced phatic function places it more in the realm of the (ontologically driven) 'dit' than of the (ethically pregnant) 'dire.' On this basis, Levinas has, on occasion, distinguished between prosaic and poetic language as respectively emblematic and destructive of the ethical relation. As Jill Robbins notes, Levinas favours prose as 'nothing other than the sobriety, the gravity of ethical language.'[46]

It would seem, however, that for Levinas it is in particular a certain type (or dimension) of poetics, specifically poetic signification centred on the play of the *signifiant*, that 'contradicts' ethics, or that aligns itself with the 'dit' and away from the 'dire' or the 'face-to-face' with another person. The primary reason, indeed, for his general suspicion towards art and poetry is related to what Jill Robbins calls 'the necessary indirection of a work's mode of signification.'[47] That is, the fact that the work is not directed towards 'autrui' in the way that the act of saying (*le dire*) is. The term 'indirection' suggests a very Levinasian play on the French word 'sens,' which designates, as we have already seen, both 'meaning' and 'direction.' In contrast, poetry conceived as a verbal gesture towards the other, as a *dire* – or as Paul Celan suggests in an image entirely consonant with Levinas's thought – the poem as a handshake, has a clear ethical value for the thinker of *Otherwise than Being*. Levinas is thus explicitly drawn towards Celan's Buberian poetics, a poetics centred on the I-Thou relation or face-to-face, which he contrasts with the non-dialogical or anti-dialogical poetics of Celan's Parisian contemporaries. For Levinas, the value of Celan's poetics lies in its 'interruption de l'ordre ludique ... du jeu des concepts et du jeu du Monde' [interruption of the ludic order ... of the play of concepts and of the play of the World] and in its 'interrogation et recherche de l'Autre, recherche se dédiant en poème à l'autre' [questioning of and search for the Other, a quest dedicating itself as a poem to the other] (*NP*, 55–6). For Levinas attaches immensely positive, ethical value to what he terms the 'signifiance de la signification' [significance of signification] (*NP*, 54). In this (itself ludic) formula, 'signifiance' is the supremely positive term, with mere 'signification' referring to the 'ordre ludique' of work accomplished on or by the 'signifiant.' It is in Celan's writing, in fact, that Levinas glimpses the poetic as a 'modalité inouïe de l'autrement qu'être' [unheard of mode of the otherwise than being] (*NP*, 55), in other words, as an ethical manifestation. And it is this insight that allows Gerald Bruns to refer to Levinas's view of 'poetry and the ethical as analogous forms of transcendence in the special sense that Levinas gives to this term.'[48]

Jill Robbins highlights the phonocentrism of Levinas's view of language and poetics. And indeed in *Hors sujet*, in a text entitled 'La transcendance des mots: à propos de *Biffures*,' about a text by Michel Leiris, Levinas writes: 'Il y a en effet dans le son – et dans la conscience comprise comme audition – une rupture du monde toujours achevé de la vision et de l'art' [In sound, and in consciousness as hearing, there is in effect a rupturing of the always-entire, self-sufficient world of vision and art] (*HS*, 219). This comment can be related to one of the rhetorical questions posed in *Noms propres*, where Levinas asks whether language is 'manifestation et dévoilement ou communciation et proximité du prochain et événement éthique irréductible au dévoilement'? [is language demonstration and revelation, or communication and proximity of the neighbour and thus an ethical event irreducible to revelation?] (*NP*, 108). As Gerald Bruns notes, for Levinas, 'the ethical and the poetic are evidently species of saying (le Dire) in contrast to the propositional character of the said (le Dit), yet neither one is translatable onto the other and in fact they are in some sense at odds with one another.'[49] However, in some of his writings on art and poetry, Levinas associates poetics and ethics very closely by displacing the ethical valency of art onto the response that it elicits from the reader or the public: 'Ce besoin d'entrer en relation avec quelqu'un, malgré et par-dessus l'achèvement et la paix du beau – nous l'appelons besoin de critique' [As for this need to enter into relationship with somebody, despite and beyond the completeness and tranquility of the beautiful, we call this the need to comment/critique] (*HS*, 219). Here, once again, Levinas seems to be rescuing art from closure and self-sufficiency. He goes on to note:

Le langage de la critique nous fait sortir des rêves – dont le langage artistique fait intégralement partie. Certes, sous sa forme écrite, il appelle toujours des critiques nouvelles. Les livres appellent des livres ... mais cette prolifération d'écrits s'arrête ou culmine au moment où la parole vivante s'y insère, où la critique s'épanouit en enseignement.

[The language of criticism takes us out of the world of dreams, a world to which artistic language completely belongs. Of course, in its written form, criticism calls for more criticism. Books call for more books ... but this proliferation of writing stops or culminates the moment that the living word takes its place therein, the moment that criticism blossoms into teaching.] (*HS*, 220)

What Levinas has in mind when he refers to 'la parole vivante' is 'expression':

L'expression comporte une impossibilité d'être en soi, de garder sa pensée 'pour soi,' et par conséquent une insuffisance de la position du sujet où le moi dispose d'un monde dominé. Parler, c'est interrompre mon existence de sujet et de maître.

[Expression involves the impossibility of staying within oneself, of keeping one's thought 'to onself,' and consequently it injects a certain inadequacy into the position of the subject where the self has at its disposal a world that it dominates. To speak is to interrupt my existence as a master subject.] (*HS*, 221)

On a rather different note, however, Levinas sometimes (again discursively, rather than through the tenor of his style) articulates an even more unequivocal defence of the solidarity of poetics and ethics, contrasting ontology, which he sees as inhering in the dissipation of opaqueness, with poetry, which is, on the contrary, a thickening, temporalization, or desynchronizing of essence that occurs alongside the ethical, if not in advance of it, as 'an unheard-of modality of the otherwise than being.' Without spelling out how poetry, in accordance with the meaning of the word that names it in German ('Dichtung,' which means thickening or densification), achieves this opaqueness, or this thickening, Levinas implicitly links this latter understanding of poetic language with Mallarmé's poetics, which promotes a certain materiality of language: 'dans les poèmes, les vocables – matériaux du Dit – ne s'effacent plus devant ce qu'ils évoquent, mais chantent de leurs pouvoirs évocateurs et de leurs façons d'évoquer, de leurs étymologies' [in poems, the words – the material of the Said – no longer disappear behind that which they evoke, but rather sing of their evocative power and of their manner of evocation, of their etymologies].[50] Certainly, it is clear that Mallarmé's poetry does not function as a form of mediation that brings something other than itself into view (i.e., the poem does not function as allegory or symbol), and that in Mallarmé's poetics, the materiality of poetic language seems to obliterate rather than consecrate the world of objects and events. Levinas captures very well this reflexivity of poetics, suggesting that 'l'écriture sur l'écriture serait la poésie même' [poetry could be defined as writing on writing][51].

Writing on Proust, Levinas again situates the value of poetics not so much in its being a 'mode of ethics,' but rather – as in his writing on Blanchot and Mallarmé – in the specificity of its operation as such a mode. He is thus prepared to recognize that, for poets, 'il ne s'agit pas d'exprimer mais de créer l'objet' [it is not a question of expressing the object but rather of creating it] (NP, 123), and he acknowledges that the specificity of the poetic effect inheres in 'le scintillement de possibles que la définition n'a pas éteints' [the sparkling of possibilities that definition has not extinguished] (NP,119) and in the creation of a 'monde jamais définitif où la réalisation ne sacrifie pas de possibles' [never-definitive world where actualization does not mean the sacrifice of possibilities] (NP,119). It is in this sense, indeed, that Levinas distinguishes between the painter and the poet, between the portraitist of a social world and Proust as a 'poète du social' (NP, 121). Thus, very occasionally, one is tempted to say exceptionally, it is the specificity of poetics, its overdetermination of meaning, in other words, the specificity of its transcendental dimension, that acts as a reminder for Levinas of the infinity opened up by the ethical relation.

Between Poetics and Ethics? Glissant's Opaqueness, Levinas's Nudity

Clearly, Levinas wants to resist the flattening force of theory or ontology in much the same way that Glissant wants to resist the reductions of systems (and) theory. Levinas's ethics is fundamentally, after all, a critique of ontology:

> À la théorie, comme intelligence des êtres, convient le titre général d'ontologie. L'ontologie qui reamène l'Autre au Même, promeut la liberté qu'est l'identification du Même, qui ne se laisse pas aliéner par l'Autre.

[The word 'ontology' applies to theory as the understanding of beings. Ontology, in reducing the Other to the Same, promotes the freedom inherent in the self-identification of the Same, which does not allow itself to be alienated by the Other.] (*TI*, 13)

Moreover, Levinas defends – precisely against theory – 'le primat de l'éthique, c'est-à-dire, de la relation d'homme à homme' [the primacy of ethics, that is, of the relation of one human to another] (*TrI*, 51). His view that 'la relation avec l'être, qui se joue comme ontologie, consiste à neutraliser l'étant pour le comprendre ou pour le saisir' [the relation with being, which is played out as an ontology, consists in neutralizing a being by understanding or grasping him/her, or it] (*TI*, 16) resonates with Glissant's call for the development 'contre un humanisme universalisant et réducteur' [in order to counter a reductive and universalizing humanism] of a defence or a 'théorie des opacités particulières. Dans le monde de la Relation, qui prend le relais du système unifiant de l'Etre, consentir à l'opacité, c'est-à-dire à la densité irréductible de l'autre, c'est accomplir, véritablement, à travers le divers, l'humain' [theory of specific opaquenesses. In the world of Relation, which is taking over from the unifying system of Being, to consent to opaqueness, that is to the irreducible density of the other, is truly to accomplish the human through diversity] (*DA*, 245). Despite his use of the term 'theory' here, Glissant's critique of theory has been consistently articulated throughout all his writings.

Yet, although Levinas's ethics, especially in its lyrical defence of the non-synthesizable infinity of the other, would seem, then, to manifest certain unmistakable similarities with Glissant's poetics of diversity (for example, both thinkers denounce the traps of idealism and universalism, operations through which the irreducible plurality of beings is inevitably reduced), this shared concern with a non-reductive relationality belies profound divergences in their thinking. Thus, for Levinas it is mainly nudity, or detachment from all culture, that guarantees the sovereign irreplaceable value of the human person (he refers, for example, to 'la nudité du visage' [the nudity of the face] and to its 'dépouillement sans aucun ornement culturel' [bareness, stripped of all cultural ornament] as an absolution, and claims that this nakedness transpierces, or punctures, the order of the world). Glissant, on the other hand, embraces as the supreme value that opaqueness by which 'on s'oppose à la généralisation neutralisante' [one opposes neutralizing generalization]. For him, this quality of density or thickness, closely linked to values of opaqueness, resistance, and embeddedness, is a function of relational expansion, extension, and composition or layering, as much as of compaction. One becomes opaque, even for oneself, through a certain concentration or sedimentation of relations, and also through a multiplication and interpenetration of relations: to one's own plurality, to several histories, to (several) landscape(s) and language(s). 'Comment assumer la relation à l'Autre quand on n'a pas (encore) d'opacité savante à lui proposer?' [How can we take on a relation to the Other if we don't (yet) have a knowing opaqueness to offer?] (*IP*, 51).

It would be foolish to deny, however, that Glissant's 'intention poétique' has a certain cognitive or epistemological thrust. After all, he compares the poetics of relation to a non-scientific science. An epistemological plot, a trajectory towards knowledge or understanding, whether or not this plot is ultimately 'dénouée' (or untangled), remains the central, if confused, orientation of Glissant's poetics. His highly ambiguous discourse on this question reveals, indeed, a profound tension. He thus argues that 'l'opacité est fondamentale du dévoilement' [opaqueness is fundamental to revelation] (*IP*, 182) and that 'l'opacité, la résistance de l'autre est fondamentale de sa connaissance' [the opaqueness or the resistance of the other is fundamental to knowledge of it], and he stresses, moreover, that it is only 'dans l'opacité (le particulier) que l'autre se trouve connaissable' [in its opaqueness (its specificity) that the other is knowable], even referring at times to 'l'éclairante opacité' [clarifying opaqueness] (*IP*, 23).

If Glissant's thinking seems incompatible with that of Levinas, it is not, then, because he inscribes it in aesthetics or praxis (political activity). Because for Levinas, as we have just seen, poetic writing does indeed have ethical possibilities, just as political constraints do weigh on ethics. Nor is it simply because Levinas inhabits principally the utopian and optative dimensions of being. Rather it is because Glissant considers as the condition of an enduring diversity what Levinas stigmatizes, for his part, as the apotheosis of reduction: namely, the acceptance and understanding of difference in a relational context envisaged as a totality.

Other divergences also bespeak a chasm between the two thinkers. For example, Levinas in *Totalité et infini* states that 'l'Autre en tant qu'autre est autrui' [the Other as other is the other person] (*TI*, 42–3), whereas in *L'Intention poétique*, Glissant affirms the exact opposite. He claims, indeed, that 'l'autre n'est pas autrui mais ma différence consentie' [the Other is not the other person but rather my difference accepted or consented to] (*IP*, 84). He goes on to state that 'autrui n'est que de morale; en l'Autre est toute poétique' [the other person is only a matter of morality; all poetics lies in the Other] (*IP*, 84). Glissant's concern is with the density that protects difference, rather than with the other person. It is not so much that Glissant privileges poetics over ethics as that he considers that poetics points towards ethics, that it is poetics that best points to how the ethical relation works. For him, 'naître au monde, c'est concevoir (vivre) enfin le monde comme relation: comme nécessité composée, relation consentie, poétique (et non morale) d'altérité' [to be born to the world is to conceive of and experience the world at last as a relation: as a composite necessity, as a relation by consent, as a poetics (and not a morality) of otherness] (*IP*, 20). It would seem, then, that the 'Other' in Glissant's thinking *is* different; it is not so much 'another I,' not so much a 'tu,' or someone who is other by simple virtue of his/her position opposite me, but rather a locus of fundamental, nameable, content-laden difference. For Glissant, then, poetics depends on difference and diversity. In other words, in his poetics, difference is crucial because it precedes and enables the relations that can be established between 'des opacités sauves et intégrées' (*IP*, 41), relations that, instead of threatening distinctions, affirm them while integrating them in the web of a generous and organic totality. This poetics is not an ethics, but it points the way to ethics.

To sum up, then, the fundamental gap between Levinas's 'nudité' and Glissant's 'opacité,' between the former's ethics and the latter's poetics, we could say that, for Levinas, 'la thématisation et la conceptualisation, d'ailleurs inséparables, ne sont pas paix avec l'Autre, mais suppression ou possession de l'Autre' [the linked processes of thematization and conceptualization do not bring peace with the Other but amount rather to the supression or possession of the other] (*TI*, 16), whereas, for Glissant, 'La Relation ne peut se tramer qu'entre des entités persistantes. La totalité monde ... n'est pas le totalitaire mais son contraire en diversité [Relation cannot be created between entities that are not persistent. The totality of the world is not totalitarian but rather the opposite of totalitarianism in diversity] (*IP*, 105). 'Comment façonner nos contraires tremblements,' Glissant goes on to ask, '– sinon par la relation qui n'est pas tout court l'impact ni le contact, mais plus loin l'implication d'opacités sauves et intégrées?' [How can we give shape to our respective and opposed tremblings if not by a type of relation which is neither impact or contact, but a much more far-reaching co-implication of protected and integrated opaquenesses?] (*IP*, 41). Making the same point even more forcefully, he states further on in the same volume that si l'humanité se dessine non pas comme une sorte d'indivis où il faudra tout ramener à une essence, mais comme la relation approfondie du même à l'autre, du divers au semblable, obligation y sera faite à chacun d'être soi, intègre, et intégré (mais non assimilé à l'autre) dans la totalité.

[if humanity presents itself not as a sort of indivisible in which everything must be brought back to an essence, but as the deepened relation of the same to the other, of the diverse to the similar, then there will be an obligation on everyone to be themselves, integral and integrated (but not merged) with the other within a totality.] (*IP*, 48)

And yet, because the divergence betweeen these two optics, or rather between Glissant's optic and Levinas's ethos, is a delicate one, it would be wrong to conclude without recalling, one last time, their convergence. Glissant's totality, his 'totalité monde,' is always poetic, always 'à venir,' or virtual: it is never more than an infinite or impossible integrality of all possible contacts and relations. Moreover, Glissant's praise of opaqueness betokens an unambiguous recognition of the value of difference as resistance and impenetrability. Thus, however equivocal his pronouncements on the epistemological value of (cultural) opaqueness or impenetrability may be, the poetics of opaqueness defended by Glissant resonates with Levinas's rejection of 'une relation avec ce qu'on égale et englobe, avec ce dont on suspend l'altérité, avec ce qui devient immanent, parce que c'est à ma mesure et à mon échelle' [a relation with what we are equal to and with what we encompass, suspending its otherness, with what becomes immanent because I have the measure of it and because it is on my scale] (*EI*, 52). What, then, is the value of such insistent intimations of a consonance between the thinking of the philosopher of ethics and that of the poet of relation? What are we to make of the convergence suggested by their common sensitivity to the primacy of beings over Being and by their shared hostility to the reflex of generalization which, in the words of Glissant, renders the other indistinguishable from the same (*DA*, 196)? Is it simply the case that the whole point of the *rapprochement* between ethics and poetics is that there can be no 'final analysis'? And are we forced to conclude, or at least suspend our exploration, by suggesting that the thinking of Levinas and Glissant traces an asymptotic relation rather than a tangency, much less an intersection? Is this as close as we can come to imagining what an ethics of poetics, or a poetics of ethics, in other words, a poet(h)ics, might look like?

NOTES

1 For two alternative approaches to the questions studied in this chapter, see Bernadette Cailler, 'Totalité et infini, altérité et relation: d'Emmanuel Levinas à Edouard Glissant,' in *Poétiques d'Edouard Glissant*, ed. Jacques Chevrier (Paris: Presses de l'université de Paris-Sorbonne, 1999), 112–31; and Peter Hallward's penetrating 1998 study of Glissant, as revised in *Absolutely Postcolonial: Writing between the Singular and the Specific* (Manchester: Manchester University Press, 2001).

2 Glissant's novel *Tout-monde* (Paris: Gallimard, 1993) expresses in fiction many of the theories outlined in the sister-text, *Traité du tout-monde* (Paris: Gallimard, 1997) (*TTM*).

3 See Celia Britton, *Edouard Glissant and Postcolonial Theory: Strategies of Language and Resistance* (Charlottesville and London: University Press of Virginia, 1999).

4 Neither the *Traité du tout-monde* nor *L'Intention poétique* (Paris: Seuil, 1969) (*IP*) has been translated into English; *Caribbean Discourse: Selected Essays* (*CD*) is the English translation by J. Michael Dash of selected parts of *Le Discours antillais* (Paris: Seuil, 1981) (*DA*), and was published in 1992 by University of Virginia Press. *Introduction à une poétique du divers* (*IPD*) (Paris: Gallimard, 1996) and *Soleil de la conscience* (*SC*) (Paris: Seuil, 1956) have not been translated into English either. References to these works, identified by the abbreviations *IP*, etc., as indicated above, will be given in the text in parentheses. Translations are my own unless otherwise indicated.

5 '... s'il était loisible que le Même se révélât dans la solitude de l'Etre, il demeure impérieux que le Divers "passe" par la totalité des peuples et des communautés' [if it was legitimate that the Same should have manifested itself in the solitude of Being, it is imperative that the Diverse be mediated by the totality of people and of communities] (*DA*, 191).

6 Celia Britton examines this question in some detail in the present volume, more specifically in relation to language.

7 '... le culturel manifeste l'angoisse et la convulsion des entités intellectuelles, spirituelles ou morales mises spectaculairement en relation avec d'autres, divergentes ou opposées, dans ce qui est désormais pour nous la totalité monde' [the cultural realm demonstrates the convulsive anxiety of those intellectual, spiritual, or moral entities brought into spectacular relation with others from which they diverge or to which they are opposed in what is henceforth for us world totality] (*TTM*, 247).

8 Note Douglas Smith's reference in this volume to the idea of 'effervescence' (pp. 155–6).

9 The parenthetical qualification is not insignificant. The reference to these exceptional or supplementary spaces means that Glissant's *tout-monde* avoids claims to the closure of a bounded, complete, or exhaustive totality.

10 The reference here to television emphasizes the technologically 'specular' nature of the phenomenon.

11 'La Diversité s'élargit de toutes les apparitions inattendues, minorités hier encore insoupçonnées et accablées sous la chape d'une pensée mono-lithique, manifestations fractales des sensibilités qui se reforment et se regroupent de manière inédite' [Diversity is widening to include the unexpected appearance of heretofore unsuspected minorities which had been crushed beneath the mantle of monolithic thinking, now become fractal manifestations of sensibilities that are refashioning themselves and assembling in previously unknown ways] (*IPD*, 25).

12 '... où une totalité terre enfin réalisée permet qu'à l'intérieur de cette totalité (où il n'est plus aucune autorité organique et où tout est archipel) les éléments culturels les plus éloignés et les plus hétéroclites s'il se trouve puissent être mis en relation' [where the ultimate realization of a totalized world makes it possible for the most heterogeneous and distant cultural elements to be, as it were, brought into relation within this totality (where there is no longer any organic authority and where the archipelago is all)] (*IPD*, 22).

13 'Ces microclimats culturels et linguistiques que crée la créolisation dans les Amériques sont décisifs parce que ce sont les signes mêmes de ce qui se passe réellement dans le monde, c'est qu'il s'y crée des micro- et des macro-climats d'interpénétration culturelle et linguistique' [These cultural and linguistic micro-climates created by creolization in the Americas are crucial because they signify what is happening in reality the whole world over. That is, the creation of micro- and macro-climates of cultural and linguistic interpenetration] (*IPD*, 19).

14 'Est-ce que ce processus – car la créolisation est un processus – parviendrait à un état, à une phase finale? Je ne le crois pas parce que c'est la conscience qui réactive le processus et c'st la non-science, la non-connaissance, qui le stabiliserait en une identité définie' [Could this process – for creolization is indeed a process – reach a final state or phase? I do not believe that it could, since it is consciousness that reactivates the process each time, and it is non-knowledge or non-consciousness that would stabilize it into a definite identity] (*IPD*, 37).

15 Victor Segalen, *Essai sur l'exotisme: notes pour une esthétique du divers* (Paris: Fata Morgana, 1978).

16 '... c'est seulement une poétique de la Relation, c'est-à-dire un imaginaire,

qui nous permettra de "comprendre" ces phases et ces implications des situations des peuples dans le monde d'aujourd'hui, qui nous autorisera s'il
se trouve à essayer de sortir de l'enfermement auquel nous sommes réduits
... entrer dans la difficile complexion d'une identité relation, d'une identité
qui comporte une ouverture à l'autre, sans danger de dilution' [... it is only
a poetics of Relation, an imaginary, that is, that will allow us to 'understand' the various phases and implications of the situation of the various
peoples of the world today, and that will authorize us perhaps to try to
break out of the imprisonment to which we are reduced ... to enter into the
difficult, complex construction of an identity-relation, of an identity which
entails openness to the other, without any danger of dilution] (*IPD*, 24).

17 'Je rêve une nouvelle approche, une nouvelle appéciation de la littérature,
de la littérature comme découverte du monde, comme découverte du Tout-
monde' [I dream of a new approach, or a new assessment of literature as
discovery of the world or of the Whole-World] (*IPD*, 91).

18 'Nous n'abdiquons pas nos identités quand nous nous ouvrons à l'Autre,
quand nous réalisons notre être comme participant d'un rhizome étince-
lant, fragile et menacé mais vivace et obstiné, qui n'est pas un rassemblement totalitaire, où tout se confondrait dans tout, mais un système non
systématique de relation, où nous devinons l'imprévisible du monde' [We
do not abdicate our identities when we open ourselves up to the Other,
when we realize our being as part of a dazzling, fragile, and threatened rhizome that is vigourous and obstinate, that is not a totalitarian collection in
which everything gets mixed up with everything else, but rather a non-systematic system of relationship that allows us to intuit the unforeseeability
of the world] (*TTM*, 248).

19 'Le tout-monde est une démesure et si nous ne prenons pas la mesure de
cette démesure nous risquons – c'est l'un des repères de ma poétique ... les
intolérances, les massacres et les génocides' [The global world is excess and
if we do not take the measure of this lack of measure we risk – and this is
one of the touchstones of my poetics ... intolerance, massacres, and geno-
cides] (*IPD*, 91).

20 'des avancées de conscience et d'espoir qui permettent de dire – sans qu'on
soit utopiste, ou plutôt, en acceptant de l'être – que les humanités
d'aujourd'hui abandonnent difficilement quelque chose à quoi elles s'obsti-
naient depuis longtemps, à savoir que l'identité d'un être n'est valable et
reconnaissable que si elle est exclusive de l'identité de tous les autres êtres
possibles' [advances in awareness and hope that allow one to say, without
being uptopian or at least accepting to be utopian, that today's humanities
are abandoning with difficulty something to which they had been clinging

for a long time, namely the thought that a being's identity is neither valid nor recognizable as such unless it excludes the identity of all other possible beings] (*IPD*, 15).

21 On the 'non-lieu,' see Marc Augé, *Non-lieux: introduction à une anthropologie de la surmodernité* (Paris: Seuil, 1992).

22 'Développer partout, contre un humanisme universalisant et réducteur, la théorie des opacités particulières. Dans le monde de la relation, qui prend le relais du système unifiant de l'Etre, consentir à l'opacité, c'est-à-dire à la densité irréductible de l'autre, c'est accomplir, véritablement, à travers le divers, l'humain' [To develop everywhere against a universalizing and reductive humanism the theory of particular opaquenesses. In the world of relationality, which is taking over from the unifying system of Being, to consent to opaqueness, that is to say to the irreducible density of the other, is to accomplish, in truth, through diversity, the human] (*DA*, 245).

23 There is a certain distortion of Levinas's thinking in those accounts that gloss over the importance that the thinker accords to the other person (*autrui*) in contradistinction to the Other (*l'Autre*). The distinction between the two terms is illustrated by the mere fact that the other person has a face, and the face is a value central to Levinas's ethics. For this reason, certain approaches to Levinas fall into the trap of thematizing difference in the way that Levinas rejects. The page references to Levinas's works are given in the text and the works are identified by abbreviations as follows: *TI, Totalité et infini: un essai sur l'extériorité* (The Hague: Martinus Nijhoff, 1961); *HAH, Humanisme de l'autre homme* (Paris: Fata Morgana, 1972); *Autrement qu'être, ou au-delà de l'essence* (The Hague: Martinus Nijhoff, 1974) ; *NP, Noms propres* (Paris: Fata Morgana, 1976); *EI, Éthique et injini* (Paris: Fayard, 1982); *TrI, Transcendance et intelligibilité* (Paris: Labor et Fides, 1984); *HS, Hors sujet* (Paris: Fata Morgana, 1987).

24 'Depuis la fin de la guerre, le sang n'a pas cessé de couler. Racisme, impérialisme, exploitation, demeurent impitoyables. Les nations et les hommes s'exposent à la haine, au mépris, craignent misère et destruction. Mais les victimes savent au moins où porter les yeux qui s'éteignent. Leurs espaces désolés appartiennent à un monde ... Dans les discours, les écrits et les écoles, le bien a rejoint le Bien de toutes les latitudes et le mal est devenu le Mal de tous les temps' [Since the end of the war, the bloodletting has been interminable. Racism, imperialism, exploitation continue, mercilessly as before. Nations and men are exposed to hatred, contempt, and fear of poverty and destruction. But at least the victims know where to turn their dying eyes. Their devastated spaces belong to the one world ... In discourse, in writing, in schools, all agree that what is right is right

for all latitudes, just as evil is now seen as evil whatever the epoch] (*NP*, 141).

25 See Alain Finkielkraut, *La Mémoire vaine* (Paris: Gallimard, 1989).

26 Cailler, 'Totalité et infini,' 115. .

27 Simon Critchley, *Ethics, Politics, Subjectivity: Essays on Derrida, Levinas, and Contemporary French Thought* (London: Verso, 1999), 278.

28 'préférer jusque dans l'ordre humain, les identités mathématiques, identifiables du dehors, à la coïncidence de soi avec soi' [a preference even in the human domain, for mathematical identities, identifiable from outside, as against the coincidence of self with self]. Indeed, Levinas deplores the fact that 'désormais le sujet s'élimine de l'ordre des raisons' [henceforth the subject is eliminated from rational order] (*HAH*, 96).

29 *HAH*, 33, 59: 'L'ethnographie la plus récente, la plus audacieuse et la plus influente, maintient sur le même plan les cultures multiples. L'œuvre politique de la décolonisation se trouve ainsi rattachée à une ontologie – à une pensée de l'être, interprétée à partir de la signification culturelle, multiple et multivoque.' 'Une telle conception de l'universalité traduit, en somme, l'opposition radicale, si caractéristique de notre époque, à l'expansion de la culture par colonisation. Cultiver et coloniser, se sépareraient foncièrement' [The most recent, audacious, and influential ethnography situates all cultures on the same level. The political task of decolonization is thus linked to an ontology, to a notion of being seen through the perspective of multiple, diverse, cultural meanings.' 'Such a notion of universality betrays a radical opposition, so characteristic of our times, to the expansion of culture through colonization. To acculturate and to colonize are thus seen as being profoundly distinct or separate acts.]

30 'On dit: l'unité de l'être, à tout instant, consisterait simplement dans le fait que les hommes se comprennent, dans la pénétrabilité des cultures les unes aux autres; cette pénétrabilité ne saurait se faire par l'entremise d'une langue commune, traduisant, indépendamment des cultures, les articulations propres et idéales des significations et rendant, en somme, inutiles ces langues particulières ... Il existe, en effet, la possibilité pour un Français d'apprendre le chinois et de passer d'une culture dans l'autre, sans l'intermédiaire d'un esperanto qui fausserait les deux langues qu'il médiatiserait' [It is said that the unity of being consists simply in the fact that people understand each other within the context of the mutual penetrability of cultures; this penetrability cannot be achieved via a common language that could translate, independently of the cultures concerned, the specific and ideal articulations of meaning, an operation that would de facto render these specific languages useless ... It is, in fact, possible for a Frenchman to

learn Chinese and to move from one culture to the other, without the inter-
mediary of an esperanto that would distort the two languages being medi-
ated] (*HAH*, 38–9).

31 'Apercevoir à la signification une situation qui précède la culture, apercevoir le langage à partir de la révélation de l'Autre, qui est en même temps
la naissance de la morale – dans le regard de l'homme visant un homme
précisément comme homme abstrait, dégagé de toute culture, dans la
nudité de son visage – c'est revenir d'une façon nouvelle au platonisme.
C'est aussi permettre de juger des civilisations à partir de l'éthique' [To see
meaning as situated by a context that precedes culture, to see language in
terms of the revelation of the Other, that is, as the birth of morality – in the
expression of a human being facing another human being precisely as an
abstract human, free of all culture, in the nudity of his face – that means
going back in a new way to Platonism. It also means being able to judge
civilizations in relation to ethics] (*HAH*, 60).

32 Levinas does not criticize the anti-Platonic, anti-Brunschvicgian movement
(Brunschvicg having asserted that 'les progrès de la conscience occidentale
... consistent ... à épurer la pensée des alluvions des cultures et des particu-
larismes du langage' [the progress of Western consciousness consists in ...
purifying thought of the deposits associated with the cultural variability
and specificity marking language] and that the dignity and gift of the West
was to have liberated 'la vérité de ses présupposés culturels pour aller, avec
Platon, vers les significations elles-mêmes, séparées ainsi du devenir' [truth
from its cultural presuppositions so as to approach, in line with Plato,
meanings themselves, separated out from all becoming]). For Levinas recognizes all too well the danger implicit in such views ('l'émancipation des
esprits peut fournir le prétexte à l'exploitation et à la violence' [the emancipation of minds can be the pretext for exploitation and violence]), and he
agrees that philosophy (Western philosophy, he could have said) rightly
challenged this view, by studying the meaning-systems of different cultures
and also by showing that the 'hegemony' or 'excellence' of Western culture
was culturally and historically conditioned. The above citations are from
HAH, 59; in the first two, Levinas is paraphrasing Brunschvicg.

33 'L'économie seule serait véritablement orientée et signifiante. Elle, seule,
aurait le secret d'un sens propre antérieur au sens figuré. La signification
culturelle, détachée de ce sens économique – technique et scientifique –
n'aurait que la valeur d'un symptôme, le prix d'un ornement conforme aux
besoins du jeu, signification abusive et trompeuse, extérieure à la vérité'
[Economics alone is taken to be truly meaningful and orienting. It alone is
taken to hold the secret of a meaning prior to figurative meaning. Cultural

meaning, distinct from this economic, technical, or scientific meaning, is reduced to the value of a symptom, of an ornament, and its meanings are taken to be misleading, external to truth] (*HAH*, 36).

34 See Jill Robbins, *Altered Reading: Levinas and Literature* (Chicago: University of Chicago Press, 1999).

35 Gerald L. Bruns, 'The Concepts of Art and Poetry in Emmanuel Levinas's Writings,' in *The Cambridge Companion to Emmanuel Levinas*, ed. Simon Critchley and Robert Bernasconi (Cambridge: Cambridge University Press, 2002), 206–7.

36 Emmanuel Levinas, *De l'existence à l'existant* (Paris: Vrin, 1986), 211.

37 Leslie Hill, '"Distrust of Poetry": Levinas, Blanchat, Celan,' *Modern Language Notes* 120 (2005): 989. Hill is referring to Levinas's 1948 article 'La Réalité et son ombre,' *Les Temps Modernes* 38 (1948): 771–89. This article is reprinted in Emmanuel Levinas, *Les Imprévus de l'histoire* (Paris: Livre de poche, 1994).

38 Maurice Blanchot, 'Connaissance de l'inconnu' in *L'Entretien infini* (Paris: Gallimard, 1969), 76; *The Infinite Conversation*, trans. Susan Hanson (Minneapolis: University of Minnesota Press, 1993), 53. Quoted in Bruns, 'Concepts,' 207.

39 Jill Robbins, 'Aesthetic Totality and Ethical Infinity,' *L'Esprit créateur* 35.3 (1995): 66–79; reprinted in *Emmanuel Levinas: Critical Assessments of Leading Philosophers*, ed. Claire Elise Katz, vol. 5 (London: Routledge, 2005), 356–68 (version cited here), 357.

40 Robbins, *Altered Reading*, 362.

41 Bruns, 'Concepts,' 209.

42 Robbins, *Altered Reading*, 361.

43 Paul Ricoeur, *Soi-même comme un autre; Oneself as Another*, trans. Kathleen Blaney (Chicago: University of Chicago Press, 1992), 357; cited in Bruns, 'Concepts,' 233n26.

44 Bruns, 'Concepts,' 229.

45 For a discussion of Jakobson's dichotomy, see Charles Taylor, *Sources of the Self: The Making of Modern Identity* (Cambridge: Harvard University Press, 1989), 487.

46 Robbins, *Altered Reading*, 359.

47 Ibid., 358.

48 Bruns, 'Concepts,' 207.

49 Ibid., 206.

50 Levinas, *Autrement qu'être*, 70.

51 Ibid., 71.

4 French Theory[1]

JULIA KRISTEVA

Hospitality

It was with a certain degree of apprehension that I addressed the Humanities Institute of Ireland in June 2004 in what is above all, for me, the language of Joyce. If my English is far from perfect, despite years of teaching in American universities, this is – as I suggested to my Dublin audience – because of a double trauma that I suffered in my childhood and of which I had never spoken in public before. Although I was successful in my studies, I was not admitted to the British school, which was generally reserved for the children of what was known as the 'red bourgeoisie,' not my own parents' milieu. Despite their efforts to keep the cause of my non-admission secret from me, I discovered it nonetheless, and this discovery caused a feeling of bitterness which remained with me long afterwards, a bitterness at the rejection of my family by the authorities which hardened into a general rejection of anglophone culture as symbolized by the British school. Since that time, I tried to learn the language of Joyce by my own means and with the help of friends, but I suppose that the aforementioned traumatic episode has always remained a barrier to my improvement. It is for this reason that I have particularly appreciated the wonderful hospitality extended to me in English-speaking countries, and in the first place by the American universities where I have taught and which have translated my work into English. This has enabled other anglophone readers and universities to discover my work and has facilitated precious contacts between them and myself, of which my address to the Humanities Institute of Ireland was one example. The 'French Theory' which is the subject of this essay is an expression first coined in the English language, and in American universities. I must therefore begin with a brief historical sketch of my relationship to the American university. This is more than a personal story, however, for, as I hope will become clear, I believe that it is impossible today to define Europe independently of our understanding of the United States.

When I arrived in Paris, the Vietnam war was at its climax, and we often protested against the American bombing of Vietnam. It was against this background that René Girard, having attended one of my first presentations on Bakhtin in Roland Barthes's seminar, invited me to teach at the University of Baltimore. I could not see myself collaborating with the 'cops of the world,' as we used to call the Americans, in spite of the dialectical advice that I got from my professor, Lucien Goldmann – 'My dear, American imperialism has to be conquered from the inside' – for I honestly did not believe that I could not fight that fight alone. So I remained in France. This was 1966. Several years later, in 1972, I met Professor Leon Roudiez from the University of Columbia at the Cérisy conference on Artaud and Bataille. Following on this contact, I made my first trip to New York in 1973, and have been ever since a visiting professor in the Department of French of that university, which, without improving the quality of my English, has at least helped me to make many friends in American academia. From this experience, which I shall not dwell upon here, and about which I wrote in my first novel, The Samurai,[2] I would simply like to recall two symbolic images that have become a part of my psyche, and that will perhaps communicate a sense of what my attachment to the United States means.

The first one is a tiny amateur photograph, in black and white, that Leon Roudiez took of me, and which shows me with my long student hair on the ferry that took me to the skyscrapers of Manhattan. Since I do not have a picture of my arrival in Paris, this one is for me the only and the best proof of my re-naissance in the 'free world.' The second image is that of my apartment at Morningside Drive, which overlooks Harlem Park, close to where Edward Said had an apartment and to where Hannah Arendt used to live, and where I usually stay when I teach at Columbia. It is a place invaded by that unusual American light, dazzling and inviting at the same time. This is where I wrote pages that are dear to me from Tales of Love (1983)[3] and Black Sun (1987)[4] or Female Genius, a place which remains in my personal mythology a place of happy solitude.[5]

When Philippe Sollers and I decided to devote a whole issue of Tel Quel[6] to New York, many were surprised. What came across in that issue was praise of American democracy, as contrasted with French centralization, so hierarchical and jacobine. It was actually an acknowledgment of what seems to me to be the most important quality of American civilization, besides the freedom I am granted in my work there, namely, its hospitality. When I say 'American,' I mean to include Canada and the Canadian universities. By hospitality, I mean the ability that some have to offer a home to others who do not have one, or who lack one temporarily. Running away from communism to France, I did not encounter this hospitality *there*, even though France has given me my French nationality, for which I will always be grateful. Paralyzed by its administrative and cultural tradition, and at the same time trying to free itself from the latter, my adoptive country promotes innovations such as the artistic, philosophical, and theoretical avant-gardes that have seduced me, and that have contributed to its glory abroad, while, at the same time, promoting a violent rejection of, if not hatred towards, these innovations. In contrast, America seems to me to be a territory that welcomes grafts and even encourages them.

Nevertheless, I am indeed writing as a French woman, or perhaps, better said, as a gallicized European, embodying as such the very 'essence' of what *Frenchness* means. This often comes as a surprise to the French themselves, who, obviously, do not see in *me* one of *them*. Sometimes, after listening to North American intellectuals passionately discussing my work as belonging to 'French Theory,' I am even tempted to take myself to be a French intellectual. For these reasons, I have at times thought about settling in America, or more precisely, in Canada, which is more European and francophone, all the more so when I feel wounded by the xenophobia of the country which has adopted me.

In this modern world of ours, in this 'New World Order,' we seem to lack a positive definition of what it means to be human (not in the sense of the 'human species,' but rather in relation to 'the quality of being human'). We tend to operate with a purely negative and rather obscure notion of humanity when we talk about 'crimes against humanity.' My own experience, though, makes me think that the minimal definition of humanity – the degree zero of humanity, to echo an expression of Roland Barthes – is precisely hospitality. The Greeks were right when they chose the word 'ethos' to designate the concept of 'choice' – the choice between good and bad, as well as all the other possible 'choices' – a concept that gave rise to the notion of ethics. Originally, the word 'ethos' meant 'a regular resting place, or animal shelter,' finally leading to 'habitat,' 'habit,' and 'character' as characteristic of an individual and of a social group that establishes a particular type of settlement. It was just this sense of hospitality that I found in America, in many ways a country that gives us a taste of our future, a country in which everyone is a foreigner, in which society consists of foreigners dealing with other foreigners.

Nevertheless, right from when I started teaching in America, I have tried to take with me a French and, more generally, a *European* cultural memory, a mixture of German, Russian, and French traditions: Hegel and Freud, Russian formalism, French structuralism, the avant-gardes of the 'nouveau roman' and Tel Quel. I hope that Americans have been able to feel that my 'migrant personality' was less 'French' in the sense of being somewhat rigid or even arrogant and condescending, and that through the foreigner that I am, they as foreigners could have access to this French and European culture. I must admit that at times I have had difficulty recognizing the uses to which my work has been put in the United States, since it has sometimes had a kind of politically correct bias. This is not in itself a problem, since one's own work is inevitably appropriated by others in their own cultural context, as part of individual men and women's personal quests, and often in a highly original and innovative way. Nevertheless, I have not been aware of this sort of 'politically correct' reading of my work by academics in Irish or English universities, who are, I believe, closer to my own, European sensibility. It is to this particularly European sensibility which I am concerned with elaborating in my own work, that I will now turn.

A Contribution to French Theory

My personal contribution to French Theory includes four themes that I would like to sketch briefly here: intertextuality; the distinction between the semiotic and the symbolic; the concept of the abject and abjection; and finally the idea of strangeness or foreignness.

Intertextuality

The concept of intertextuality has enjoyed a certain degree of success internationally. This idea, which I developed from the starting point of Bakhtin, invites the reader to interpret a text as a crossing of texts. In formalist or structuralist approaches, this has often been perceived as a return to 'quotation' or to 'sources.' For me it is principally a way of introducing history into structuralism: the texts that Mallarmé and Proust read, and which nourish the *Coup de dès* and *À la recherche du temps perdu,* allow us to introduce history into the laboratory of writing. Mallarmé's interest in anarchism, for example, and Proust's interest in Zohar's Jewish mysticism and in the *Affaire Dreyfus* are useful material in this kind of approach. Also, by showing to what extent the internal dimension of the text is connected to the external context, such interpretations can reveal the inauthenticity of the writing subject. The writer becomes '*le sujet en procès*' – this French expression means both a 'subject in process' and a 'subject on trial' – and the speaking subject a carnival, a polyphony, forever contradictory and rebellious. The poststructuralist problematic of intertextuality also gave birth to an idea that I have been trying to work on ever since, especially in the books that I published in 1996 and 1997, namely, the connection between 'culture' and 'revolt.'

Semiotic/Symbolic

The distinction that I make between the *semiotic* and the *symbolic* has no political or feminist connotation. It is simply an attempt to think of 'meaning' not only as 'structure,' but also as 'process' or 'trial' in the sense I have already mentioned, by looking simultaneously at syntax, logic, and at what *transgresses* them, that is the *trans-verbal.* I refer to this other side of 'meaning' as trans-verbal because calling it *pre-verbal* could give rise to certain difficulties. The *semiotic* is not independent of language but rather underpins language, and under the control of language it articulates other aspects of 'meaning' which are more than mere 'significations,' such as rhythmical and melodic inflections. Bearing in mind the Freudian distinction between the *representations of things* and the *representations of words*, I try to take into consideration this double nature of the human mind, especially the constraints of biology and of instinctual drives that sustain and influence meaning and signification. This is because we could say that, although *in the beginning was the word*, before the beginning there was the unconscious with its repressed content.

I am personally convinced that the future of psychoanalysis lies in this direction, that is, between the translinguistic logic of the unconscious, and biological and neurobiological constraints. In the Institut du Vivant at the University of Paris 7, we try to bring biologists and psychoanalysts together in their work. Our basic preoccupation is the opening up of psychoanalysis to biology as well as to a more active involvement in social politics. In this connection, I fully support and have been actively involved in President Chirac's campaign for the integration of disabled citizens in French society. We hope that this approach, along with a close rereading of Freud's texts, will revitalize contemporary psychoanalysis in the long run.

This 'semiotic' trans-verbal research is connected to the archaic relation between the mother and the child, and it allows me to investigate certain aspects of the feminine and the maternal in language. That is, certain aspects of what Freud used to call 'the black continent' or Mycenaean civilization (after the name of the Greek civilization that preceded the civilization of classical Greece). This 'other logic' of the feminine and the maternal, which works against normative representation and opposes phallic representation, both masculine and feminine, is perhaps my own contribution to the effort of understanding the feminine as connected to the political via the sacred.

I am convinced that this new twenty-first century, which seems to be in such need of religion, is actually in need of the sacred, as opposed to fundamentalism. I understand the sacred as the desire of human beings to think, not in the sense of calculation, but rather in the sense of a need for fundamental questioning. It is this need that distinguishes us from other species and that, *a contrario*, brings us closer to them. As a writer, psychoanalyst, and semiotician, I believe that the human characteristic that we call *the sense of the divine and of the sacred* arises at the very point of emergence of language. 'The semiotic,' with its maternal ties, seems to be the farthest point we can reach when we try to imagine and understand the frontiers between nature, or *'phusis,'* and meaning. By understanding the 'semiotic' as 'emergence of meaning' we can overcome the dichotomies of metaphysics (soul/body, physical/psychical). My preoccupation with the sacred is, in fact, anti-metaphysical, and only becomes feminist when we come to its consequences, namely, to childbirth and the raising of children. If I am indeed passionately attached to the recognition of women in social, intellectual, and political life, this is only to the extent where we, as women, can bring a *different attitude* to the ideas of 'power' and 'meaning.' This would be an attitude that takes into consideration the need for the survival of our species, and our need for the sacred. Women are positioned at this crossroads.

The Abject

The abject and abjection are concepts that I developed out of my clinical experience dealing with the symptoms that I call 'new maladies of the soul,'[7] where the distinction between 'subject' and 'object' is not clear, and where these two pseudo-entities exhaust themselves in a dialectic of attraction and repulsion. Borderline personalities, as well as some depressive personalities, can be described in relation to this dimension of the psyche, which is also reminiscent of an archaic state, the communion of maternal holding. The mother object is the first consequence of the process of expulsion of what is disagreeable in this archaic state, in a process that I call abjection. Thus, the mother is the first 'abject' rather than object. Artists such as Picasso and de Kooning clearly understood something of this process ...

Using the concepts of 'abject' and 'abjection,' I have attempted to understand the complex universe of a writer such as Céline, master of popular fiction and of Parisian slang or *argot*, a vector of exceptional emotion. Instead of taking the cathartic road of abjection as religions do (and I believe any religion is, in fact, a way of purifying the abject), Céline insists on following imaginary abjections that he then transfers to political realities. His anti-Semitism and his despicable compromises with Nazi ideology are expressed in his pamphlets, texts that I attempted to read objectively, as an analyst, without giving in to the feelings that they inevitably arouse.

My adventures in the very dangerous territory of abjection have nevertheless been the source of many alliances. Many artists from all over the world have recognized themselves in the experience of the abject, which is close to the psychotic states that they encounter in the process of artistic creation. But my research has also given rise to sharp reaction in some academic circles and in certain journals like *The Nation*, which alleged that if I chose to analyse Céline, it was only to excuse him, as if trying to understand means necessarily trying to forgive. Founded on a misreading, that was one of the most radical rejections of my work and one which I personally perceived as a form of partisan excommunication that amounted to an attack on thinking itself. I now see it as the tragic precursor of the more recent criticism, more comic than tragic, that issued from the pen of a somewhat noisy person in New York University who thought he was exposing French 'impostors' (the name he gave to French theorists) by rejecting our 'pseudo-scientific models,' when, in fact, we have never tried to create scientific models, but rather metaphorical transfers ...

Strangeness or Foreignness

The concept of *strangeness* or *foreignness* is also something close to my heart. Writing my book *Strangers to Ourselves*[8] gave me the opportunity to outline a history of foreigners, their actual destiny, and the way in which they are perceived in the West, and also to state my own position in this debate, a position which again seems to be accepted with some difficulty. First of all, I believe that in order to fight the state of national depression that we are experiencing in France (but not only in France), as a result of globalization and of the influx of immigrants, and also in order to oppose maniacal reactions to this depression (such as that of the Front National), it is important to restore national confidence. This has to be done in the same way in which we sometimes have to restore the narcissism or the ideal 'ego' in a depressed patient, before proceeding to the actual 'analysis,' that is, to the dissolution of his system of defence and resistance. I am convinced that, in the next century, the cosmopolitan society that we have been dreaming of ever since the Stoics and throughout the Enlightenment will not be possible in the utopian shape of the 'melting pot,' as universalized and standardized by the market, the media, and the Internet. At most, this will lead to a more or less conflictual cohabitation of nations and of various 'social groups' obliged to live with and against each other. Combining a certain amount of respect for 'national identity' and support for the idea of the 'common good' (*l'intérêt général*, as Montesquieu called it), the approach that I suggest is going to have to replace the excesses of contemporary globalization. In other words, we must invent a new balance between national and general or common interests.

Two Cultures

Having situated four major threads of my own work, I would now like to consider the wider cultural and political context in which we work, and in which French Theory has been elaborated. The collapse of the Berlin Wall in 1989 brought to light the difference between two types of culture: European culture, on the one hand, and North American culture, on the other. In order to avoid any misunderstanding, I want to make it clear from the start that I am referring to two visions of freedom elaborated by democratic societies, visons that we do not, unfortunately, cherish enough. It will become clear in what I am about to suggest why I believe that Europe can be better understood in terms of her contrast with America. I am referring to two visions of freedom which both rely on the Greek, Jewish, and Christian traditions and which, in spite of episodes of shame as well as of glory, remain our most important achievement. These two visions of freedom are both, nevertheless, essential. They are sometimes, as is now the case, opposed. Fundamentally, however, they are complementary, and indeed I believe that they are both present in each of us, whichever side of the Atlantic we find ourselves on. If I continue to contrast them in what follows, the distinction is only a theoretical one.

In his *Critique of Pure Reason* (1781) and his *Critique of Practical Reason* (1789), Kant defines for the first time something that others must have experienced before him without being able to articulate it, namely, the fact that freedom is not, negatively speaking, an 'absence of constraint' but, positively speaking, the possibility of 'self-beginning,' or *Selbstanfang*. Thus, by identifying 'freedom' with the capability of spontaneously beginning, Kant opens the way to the valorization of the enterprising individual and of the initiative of the 'self,' if I may transfer his 'cosmic' thinking to a more personal level. At the same time, Kant subordinates the freedom of Reason, be it pure or practical, to a cause, divine or moral.

I will expand on this idea by observing that, in a world ever more dominated by technology, freedom becomes the capacity to adapt to a 'cause' always exterior to the 'self,' and which is less and less a moral cause, and more and more an economic one. In an ideal situation, the two operate at the same time. In this line of thought, which is favoured by Protestantism (I am referring here especially to Max Weber's work on the connection between capitalism and Protestantism), freedom becomes freedom to adapt to the logic of cause and effect, or, as Hannah Arendt would say, 'to the calculus of consequences,' the logic of production, of science, and of the economy. To be free would be, then, to be able to benefit from adapting to this logic of causes and effects, and to the economic market. This kind of freedom culminates in the logic of globalization and of the unrestrained free-market; the Supreme Cause (God) and the Technical Cause (the Dollar) are its two co-existing variants, which guarantee the functioning of our freedom within this logic of 'instrumentalization.' I am not denying here the benefits of this kind of freedom; it has the advantage, notably, of being able to adapt to the logic of 'causes and effects' that culminates in the specific way of thinking that we might term 'thinking-as-calculus' and scientific thinking. I believe this vision to be crucial for our access to technology and automation. American society seems to be better adapted to this kind of freedom, which is not, however, the only kind.

There is another vision of freedom which emerges within the Greek world at the very heart of its philosophy, with the pre-Socratics, and which develops in the Socratic dialogue. This fundamental variety of freedom is not subordinate to a cause, which means that it is prior to the concatenation of Aristotelian 'categories,' which are already a premise for scientific and technical thinking. This vision of freedom relies on *Being* and, moreover, on *the Being* of *Language Which is Delivered (l/'Etre de la Parole Qui se Livre)*, a Being which delivers (itself) to itself and to the Other, and thus liberates itself, 'sets itself free,' liberates the Self/Other. The liberation of the Being of Language that occurs in the encounter between the Self and the Other is emphasized in Heidegger's discussion of Kant.[9] This approach inscribes freedom into the very essence of philosophy, as eternal questioning, before allowing it to become fixed, but also after initial fixation, in the succession of causes and effects and the ability to master it. *Poiesis* as questioning is a privileged space of French Theory, and it is inseparable from style, narration, fiction. In other words, it is inseparable from poetics in the broad sense of this term, embracing narrative, style, fiction (Jakobson), and the disclosure of language (Heidegger). Rather than venturing much further into the debate, which I have already oversimplified, surrounding notions of freedom in Kant and Heidegger, what I am interested in pursuing here is this second concept of freedom in the context of the modern world. This second kind of freedom is very different from the kind of calculating logic that leads to unbridled consumerism; it is a notion evidenced in the Being of Speech via the Presencing of the Self to the Other. It is important to understand its psychological and social connotations since they constitute the essential themes of French Theory. The *poet* is its main custodian, together with the *libertine* who defies the conventions of social causes and effects in order to formulate a desire for dissidence. Not to mention the *psychoanalyst* via the experience of transference and counter-transference, or the revolutionary who places the liberties of the individual above any other convention. It provides the foundation of Human Rights, and the slogan of the French Revolution, Liberty-Equality-Fraternity, which at the time reinforced the ideas of the English *Habeas Corpus*, and in paying attention to these figures we distance ourselves from the abstract universalism that handicaps the legacy of the Enlightenment.

But I would like to return at this point to contemporary reality. We Europeans are in the process of building a European Community in spite of all the associated difficulties that we cannot ignore. In this often chaotic European assembly, the voice of France, which sometimes finds it hard to make itself heard, still finds allies in other governments and in the public opinion of various countries, all of them deeply attached to their cultural tradition and all implicitly or explicitly sharing our notion of freedom. We French are trying to promote a 'type of society' which is not exclusively that of laissez-faire capitalism, often identified as 'the American model.' Our imperative of 'cultural difference' – usually referred to as the 'exception française' – derives not only from the fact that we belong to a tradition and possess a memory which may be older, 'more refined,' and 'more sophisticated,' and so on, because it originates in the 'Old World,' but also from the fact that we have a different vision of freedom, namely, one that privileges the uniqueness of the individual over economic and scientific factors. When the French government, whether it be of the Left, or of the Gaullist Right, insists on our 'solidarity' in opposition to 'liberalism' in the classic sense of unregulated economic and social competition, we have to understand this as expressing recognition of varying notions of freedom. We French are fully aware of the risks that may accompany such an attitude: ignorance of contemporary economic reality, excessive union demands, an inability to take part in international competition, idleness, backwardness. This is why we need to be alert to the new constraints of our technological world and to the imperatives of the domain of 'causes and effects.' But, at the same time, we are aware of the advantages of this other type of freedom, to which certain other European nations aspire also. It is an aspiration rather than a fixed project, driven by real concern for the uniqueness and fragility of each and every human life, and, not least, the poor, the disabled, the retired, and those who rely on social benefits. It requires special attention to sexual and ethnic differences, to men and women considered in their unique intimacy rather than as simple groups of consumers.

From this perspective, the main characteristic of European culture could well be its emphasis on the intimate, the particular, the art of living, taste, leisure, 'idle' pleasures, grace, pure chance, playfulness, wastefulness, our 'darker side,' or, to put it in a nutshell, freedom as the essence of 'Being-in-the-World' prior to any 'Cause.' (I recently attempted to describe this aspect of human uniqueness in my 'Feminine Genius' trilogy on the life and work of Arendt, Klein, and Colette. For the notion of individual feminine genius can take us beyond mass feminism, a movement in which the uniqueness of each woman risks being submerged, although obviously the notion of genius can be applied to both sexes.) Can we preserve this understanding of freedom as a general human value? This still remains to be seen, since we are overwhelmed by the maelstrom of our calculus thinking and consumerism. The only counterpoint to this seems to be the rebirth of religious sects for whom the sacred is no longer 'a permanent quest,' as the very concept of human dignity would require, but rather a subordination to absolute causes and effects – in this case, the authority of sects and fundamentalist groups. This means that today's religious alternative, to the extent that it degenerates into a clash between fundamentalisms, is not only an unreliable counterpoint to technological mastery, but even reinforces its logic of competition and conflict. It is therefore rather unlikely that the alternative vision of freedom that I am attempting to rehabilitate here can become more than an aspiration, but the die is cast, and this is the bet we have placed.

Of course, Europe is far from being homogeneous and united. In the context of the crisis in Iraq and faced with the terrorist threat, some have claimed that a rift has opened up between the countries of (to use their terminology) 'Old Europe' and those of the 'New Europe.' Without going too deeply into this complex set of problems, I would like to express two, highly personal, opinions on this issue. Firstly, I believe that it is important that 'Old Europe,' and France, in particular, take very seriously the economic difficulties encountered by the 'New Europe,' difficulties that have the consequence of making these countries dependent to some degree on the United States. But we (Old Europeans) must also recognize the cultural and, in particular, the religious differences that separate us from these countries, and we must respect these differences. Our famous 'French arrogance' does not equip us very well for this task, and the Orthodox Christian countries, in particular, feel this very keenly. My second point is this: the knowledge that we in Europe have of the Arab world, after so many years of colonialism, has made us very sensitive to Islamic culture and able to soften, if not to entirely avoid, the 'clash of civilizations' to which I have referred; but, at the same time, the insidious anti-Semitism of our countries should make us vigilant towards the rise of anti-Semitism today, whether it emanates from the Right or from the Left.

To return now, however, to the domain of the university and, in particular, to the question of French Theory. I have been speaking briefly about the political implications of a certain European vision of freedom, a vision which is deeply ingrained in our social experience as well as in our *way of thinking*. This dimension of our freedom often takes the form of political opposition, but it is fundamentally more than that: it is a way of being that reveals itself in the act of revolt. In fact, politics, *stricto sensu*, can also be seen as the betrayal of this freedom of thinking. This is why, in my last two books on the culture of revolt (published in a single volume in English under the title *Intimate Revolt*),[10] I discuss the idea that 'political revolution' (the French Terror of 1793 and the Russian Revolution of 1917) can be seen as the stifling of revolt in the sense of free questioning and permanent restlessness. Nevertheless, and paradoxically, the horror of totalitarianism, which took over the idea of revolt only to become a deadly dogma, has not managed to compromise entirely the possibility of thinking-as-revolt, which is also a part of our political experience, and not only of our spiritual life.

The deformation imposed by 'political correctness' has hardened, however, the political implications of the philosophy at the heart of the works of French theoreticians as an implicit dimension of our way of thinking. Some of our readers in American universities have simplified these implications; others have forgotten them. What is neglected by this (mis)reading is *the working through of thought*, just as Freud used to speak of the *working through of dreams*. That is, '*unconcealed*' thinking in the sense of Heidegger, or what Hannah Arendt calls the 'disclosure' of thinking, a kind of thinking that opposes calculus thinking. In this way, thinking finds its source in fiction and also in the sensitive human body, thus revealing the 'third type of cognition' described by Spinoza, but also in free association and transference in psychoanalytical experience.

I would like to think that this drive for freedom is continuing to grow in France. I believe that there is neither decline nor stagnation of intellectual life in contemporary France. This is visible in the ever-increasing emphasis on '*the speaking subject*' in the humanities. This does not mean, however, that objective facts are ignored, but, quite on the contrary, that, by taking them into consideration, the researcher is much more subjectively involved in their interpretation. France will soon initiate a national debate on the role of human sciences around this general theme of 'fact and interpretation.' It goes without saying that the part played by psychoanalysis in this is crucial.

Moreover – and this is undoubtedly the result of the psychoanalytical perspective – the imagination is more and more perceived as an essential component of the human psyche. This is indeed the space wherein emerges that 'alternative' version of freedom that I am trying to rehabilitate today. We humans are alive precisely because we have a psychic life. This is the intimate dimension of our existence (what we call in French our *for intérieur*) which allows us to shelter from internal and external attacks on our being, that is, psychological and biological traumas, as well as social and political external aggression. The imagination transforms them all, sublimates them, works for us and keeps us alive. Which part of our imagination? Well, for example, precisely the fantasies that psychoanalysis works with. Literature, for its part, offers a refuge for our loves and insomnia, our states of grace and crisis, while religion opposes laissez-aller capitalism and its logic of causes and effects by adding that supplement of the 'human soul.' In the modern state of human sciences, thinking is now ripe for a fruitful and critical (and not exclusively condemnatory) encounter with the religious imagination. For religion also becomes analysable. Here, too, I believe, French Theory can make an important contribution. I recently created, along with colleagues in Paris, the Institute for Contemporary Thought, the core of which is the Roland Barthes Interdisciplinary Center, dealing with questions situated at the interface between literature, philosophy, psychoanalysis, and ethics, questions centred on those characteristics that I believe to be essential to the French Theory under discussion here.

I have placed a great deal of emphasis in this essay on the European origins of the type of freedom which, in my opinion, underpins what we call 'French Theory.' Still, nobody has the monopoly over this vision, neither the Catholics, nor the Protestants, on either side of the Atlantic. They both have an equal potential for dealing with these problems. Also, I believe that the idea of 'being chosen' in Judaism, although different from the Greek idea of freedom that I have tried to outline here, makes a person coming from the Jewish tradition particularly capable of restoring what we lack so much, namely, the interaction of both versions of freedom – both economic neo-liberalism and fraternal and poetic freedom, both causal and 'disclosing' versions of freedom.

Earlier, when criticizing the resurgence of French nationalism, I pointed out that this intimate and fraternal type of freedom is indeed a difficult, if not an impossible, choice. Still, this is the challenge that France is ready to face, and, in the long run, the challenge that Europe as a whole must be willing to take. Personally, I feel highly committed to this vision. In this context, America – the America that I love, an America which has, however, silenced all its opponents – risks becoming a fourth Rome, after Byzantium and Moscow. In the new economic order, and in the context of the terrorist crisis following September 11, America has imposed a financial, economic, and cultural oligarchy that excludes or puts at risk an important dimension of human freedom. Other civilizations, and our European civilization among these, have different visions of human freedom. They also need to be heard in this globalized world and to be allowed to bring their own correction, through diversity, to this new global vision of human destiny. The diversity of cultural models is the only guarantee for the humanity that I referred to in the beginning of my lecture, a humanity that we could describe as 'hospitality' for lack of a better definition. But hospitality is not only the simple juxtaposition of differences with one model dominating all the others, and pretending to respect these others while being indifferent to them. On the contrary, hospitality is a real attempt to understand other kinds of freedom in order to make every 'way of being' more multiple, more complex. The definition of humanity that I was looking for is perhaps precisely this process of 'complexification.'

In this sense, understanding (or lack of understanding) on the part of the Americans for a European alternative could turn out to be a decisive step. The creed of French moralists is well known: if God did not exist, we would have to invent Him. I would paraphrase this by saying: if Europe did not exist, the world would have to invent her. This is in the interest of our plural world, and in the interest of America. Whatever the economic and diplomatic competition between the Old and the New Worlds, our 'old' Europe needs to make herself heard in the 'new' America, and European intellectuals have a particular responsibility here. The most urgent and the noblest mission of 'French Theory' (and of European thought more generally) is, after all, that of drawing attention to human diversity in its experience of freedom. French Theory is just another term for the experience of freedom.

NOTES

1 This is the text of a talk written and delivered in English at the Humanities Institute of Ireland at University College Dublin in June 2004. It has been slightly amended for publication, and versions of the same material were presented at lectures given in certain American universities and in Julia Kristeva's acceptance speech at the Prix Holburg reception ceremony.

2 Julia Kristeva, *Les Samouraï* (Paris: Fayard, 1990); *The Samurai*, trans. Barbara Bray (New York: Columbia University Press, 1992).

3 *Histoires d'amour* (Paris: Denoël, 1983); *Tales of Love*, trans. Leon. S. Roudiez (New York: Columbia University Press, 1987).

4 *Soleil noir: dépression et mélancolie* (Paris: Gallimard, 1987); *Black Sun: Depression and Melancholia*, trans. Leon S. Roudiez (New York: Columbia University Press, 1989).

5 Julia Kristeva, *Le Génie féminin I, Hannah Arendt* (1999); *II, La Folie: Mélanie Klein* (2000); *III, Colette* (2002).
6 *Tel Quel* 71/73 (Autumn, 1977).
7 *Les Nouvelles Maladies de l'âme* (Paris: Fayard, 1993); *New Maladies of the Soul*, trans. R. Guberman (New York: Columbia University Press, 1995).
8 *Étrangers à nous-mêmes* (Paris: Fayard, 1989); *Strangers to Ourselves*, trans. Leon S. Roudiez (New York: Columbia University Press, 1995).
9 In a 1930 seminar, 'The Essence of Human Freedom,' published in 1982.
10 Julia Kristeva, *La Révolte intime: discours direct* (Paris: Fayard, 1997); *Intimate Revolt: The Powers and Limits of Psychoanalysis*, trans. Jeanine Herman (New York: Columbia University Press, 2002).

5 Redrawing the Hexagon: The Space of Culture in Malraux and Blanchot

DOUGLAS SMITH

The schematic representation of metropolitan France as a hexagon has a long history. Its symbolization of a homogeneous national territory governed by abstract principles is particularly associated, however, with the republican ideology developed from the Third Republic onwards, and culminating in the Gaullist technocracy of the late 1950s and 1960s.[1] From 1870 to 1962, the characterization of France as a hexagon holds important, and ambiguous, implications for the country's national identity as defined through territorial integrity. On the one hand, to describe France as a hexagon in the late nineteenth and early twentieth century is to insist on its rightful claim to the provinces of Alsace and Lorraine annexed by Germany in the aftermath of the Franco-Prussian War, since the approximate resemblance of French territory to a hexagon depends on the inclusion of these eastern provinces. On the other hand, to reduce France to a hexagon is to define it solely in terms of its metropolitan territory and thus to ignore the Empire so conscientiously developed by the Third Republic, partly as compensation for the loss of Alsace and Lorraine. By the 1950s, the term had taken on a strongly polemical connotation in the context of bitter debate over the colonial war waged in Algeria. To refer to France as a hexagon was implicitly to endorse withdrawal from North Africa, and white Algerian settlers often described the (in their view) unreliable metropolitan French as 'les hexagonaux.' It is in this context that the hexagon becomes identified with the Gaullist project of the modernized metropolitan state, shorn of the rough edges of its colonial past, able to engage in neatly interlocking sets of relations with Europe and the wider world. The image of the hexagon, then, is bound up with the geopolitical repositioning of France within the post-war and post-colonial world. A spatial problematic (that of the place of France in a world increasingly defined by the Cold War superpowers and by the new non-aligned nations emerging after decolonization) invites a spatial solution (the geometric figure of the hexagon emphasizing the abstract values of the republic – freedom, equality, and fraternity – and their universal application). The purpose of this essay is to investigate alternative spatial reponses to the post-war predicament of France, responses developed primarily within the context of aesthetic debates, but which nonetheless have clear political and ethical implications. Two of the more significant figures in this regard are André Malraux and Maurice Blanchot.

The association of Malraux and Blanchot in the context of a discussion of globalization and aesthetics might seem a little unlikely. In the first place, the conjunction of Malraux and Blanchot may well appear incongruous in itself. What could the rhetorical public interventions of the high-profile Gaullist minister of culture have in common with the rare and discreet pronouncements of the reclusive defender of an ontology of literature? But the terms of such a question neglect the complex intineraries of both figures and the ambiguous nature of the cultural politics of 1950s France. Leslie Hill has remarked how the political trajectories of both writers intersect in the 1950s, as Blanchot moves from Right to Left and Malraux moves from Left to Right, forming a chiasmic relationship.[2] Philippe Lacoue-Labarthe has further noted how both writers rework what he sees as one of the founding myths of Western literature, the descent to (and return from) the Underworld, as enshrined in the work of Homer, Virgil, and Dante.[3] The following argument seeks to articulate these two readings, the political and the literary, through an examination of the question of aesthetic space. In my view, the models of aesthetic or cultural space proposed by Malraux and Blanchot, the theories of the imaginary museum and the space of literature respectively, are not only defined by common motifs but by their shared global context involving post-war decolonization and the Cold War. Both writers invoke spatial models for the understanding of culture at a moment when the territorial boundaries of the French state and empire are being redrawn and the global position of France as a world power among a community of traditionally imperial nations is being challenged by the new bipolar supremacy of the United States and the Soviet Union. Both Malraux's and Blanchot's conceptions of cultural space involve a reorganization of the traditional canon of artistic achievement, a reorganization that involves crossing the boundaries of the isolated nation-state, hexagonal or otherwise. Thus Blanchot's space of literature is defined by a wide range of non-French texts, while Malraux's imaginary museum expands to embrace a global rather than a national heritage. Both projects are concerned more with the ontology than the history of culture and represent a formidable process of deterritorialization, removing culture from the narrow framework of the history of the nation-state defined by its territorial integrity to place it within a global and philosophical context.[4] Ultimately, however, this deterritorialization is ethically and politically ambiguous. On the one hand, it is the culture of late imperial nations such as France that is deterritorialized as the logic of culture itself is shown to dissent from any essentialist or identitarian politics (such is Blanchot's position). On the other hand, the deterritorialization extends also to former colonized nations, uprooting their indigenous cultures and so allowing their appropriation (and re-territorialization) by a still pre-eminent European civilization that 'discovers' and rehabilitates the arts of the non-Western world (as in Malraux's imaginary museum). In other words, both new models of aesthetic space reflect the ambiguities of French decolonization and also the compensatory geopolitical repositioning of France within a Cold War world, precisely the context that determines the image of France as hexagon. In what follows, I propose to trace this dual development through a comparative and contrastive reading of the work of Malraux and Blanchot, examining in turn their respective treatments of the themes of death and survival, cultural space, the political and the ethical. This comparative approach will turn in many respects on the central ontological and ethical questions posed respectively by death (of both self and other) and its appropriation (by both self and other).

Surviving Death in Malraux and Blanchot: Life, Writing, and Theory

Death and survival are central themes in the work of Malraux and Blanchot and are subtly linked in their work to art or writing. This section proposes to examine the treatment of the two themes in the overlapping modes of autobiography, theory, and myth. In late works, both writers relate their experience of surviving execution by firing squad during the German Occupation. In his *Antimémoires*, Malraux describes how he was subjected to a mock execution after being wounded and taken prisoner by German troops at Gramat in the south of France.[5] In *L'Instant de ma mort*, Blanchot recounts a similar experience of escaping from execution by firing squad during the latter days of the German Occupation, filtering his account through a third-person protagonist.[6] Malraux emphasizes his perception of the unreality of the situation and his refusal to believe in the apparently imminent danger (*AM*, 176). Elsewhere he underlines the importance of the experience only to qualify its significance by attributing his preoccupation with mortality to a sense of history that predates his wartime experience: 'Etre l'objet d'un simulacre d'exécution n'apporte pas une expérience négligeable. Mais je dois *d'abord* ce sentiment à l'action singulière, parfois physique, qu'exerce sur moi l'envoûtante conscience des siècles' [The experience of being subjected to a mock execution is not a negligible one. But *in the first instance* I owe this feeling to the singular, sometimes physical, effect that the spellbinding awareness of past centuries has on me] (*AM*, 15). Blanchot, in contrast, stresses the feeling of lightness that overcomes the imminent victim, and seems to insist on the foundational nature of the experience: 'Désormais, il fut lié à la mort, par une amitié subreptice' [From that moment on, he was tied to death by a surreptitious friendship] (*IM*, 11). The nature of this relationship with death is such as to place the non-executed beyond life and death, already dead but also immortal: 'comme si la mort hors de lui ne pouvait désormais que se heurter à la mort en lui' [as if the death outside him could from now on only collide with the death within him] (*IM*, 15). But like Malraux, Blanchot also relates the experience to a sense of history, represented by the references to Hegel's sighting of Napoleon at Jena in 1807 (*IM*, 13–14). The reference to Hegel occurs in relation to an attempted explanation of why the Germans did not burn the château in which the almost-executed protagonist was found; Blanchot speculates that perhaps their commanding officer recognized that the building was built in the historic year of 1807 and was cultivated enough to spare it for that reason. Blanchot further alludes to Hegel's celebrated idea that Napoleon's victory over Prussia at Jena marked the end of history, just as the contemporary completion of his *Phenomenology of Mind* marked the end of philosophy. To recall the Hegelian theory of the end of history as embodied in a historical battle against the backdrop of a later historical conflict demonstrates how history has outlived its end, just as Blanchot's protagonist has outlived his death. The ambiguous historicity thus established is heightened by Blanchot's dating of the battle of Jena to 1807 rather than to 1806, the actual year of the historical event. The date of the end of history necessarily remains uncertain.[7]

Beyond the near-death experience itself and its relation to a certain sense of history, the accounts of Malraux and Blanchot are linked by a third common element: the loss of a manuscript, as noted by Blanchot in the final (unpaginated) section of *L'Instant de ma mort* (*IM*, 17). The text of Malraux's novel *La Lutte avec l'ange*, the second part of *Les Noyers d'Altenburg*, was, as Malraux recounts, destroyed by the Gestapo during the Occupation (*AM*, 17). Blanchot alludes to this loss but (mis)identifies the text as a theoretical reflection on art (*IM*, 17). Similarly, in his own narrative, Blanchot describes how a hefty manuscript, perhaps mistaken for war plans, was removed from the château where his protagonist had been living. This motif of the lost manuscript constitutes a further implicit allusion to Hegel, whose *Phenomenology* manuscript was almost lost in the post during the Napoleonic campaign that culminated at Jena. More importantly, the loss of a manuscript in the context of a near-death experience suggests that the loss of the book stands in for the loss of life, that the (lost) text is substituted for the (preserved) life. This exchange implicates writing (and, by extension, cultural activity in general) in the complex relationship between life and death explored in the work of Malraux and Blanchot. If the lost text redeems the life of Malraux and in some sense permits his 'resurrection,' Blanchot's missing manuscript accords the literary work the same suspended status as his survivor protagonist, existing virtually beyond death and destruction.

The narration of these episodes in autobiographical texts suggests that the experience of near execution operates as a foundational moment within the life and work of Malraux and Blanchot. But we have already seen how Malraux tends to downplay the significance of a potentially highly dramatic episode, while Blanchot chooses to relate his experience through third-person narration. In fact, in different ways, both writers break the pact or contract identified by the critic Philippe Lejeune as the basis of autobiography (the understanding that an autobiographer undertakes to tell the truth about himself or herself in his or her own voice).[8] Malraux frankly characterizes his autobiographical writings as anti-memoirs, refusing the coherence of chronology and even of a stable self – the last section of his autobiography attempts to capture in writing what he calls a 'je-sans-moi' [I-without-me], a first-person pronoun without a clearly defined personal identity.[9] As for Blanchot's narrative, it switches from first person (the title *L'Instant de ma mort*) to third person (the body of the narration) back to first person (the last line of the text): 'Seul demeure le sentiment de légèreté qui est la mort même ou, pour le dire plus précisément, l'instant de *ma* mort désormais toujours en instance' [All that remains is the feeling of lightness that is death itself or, to be more accurate, the moment of *my* death that from now on is always pending] (*IM*, 18; my emphasis). The switch from first to third person and back again refuses to posit the experience in question as that of the author, while also blurring the boundaries between the death of the self and the death of the other. Further, this final line of *L'Instant de ma mort* is part of an unpaginated coda that follows the conclusion of the main body of the text and so finds itself situated ambiguously both after and before the end of the text.

Far from grounding the themes of death and survival securely in personal experience, then, these autobiographical texts question the experiential status of the episodes related and stress instead the textual nature of their concerns, going so far as to substitute the loss of a manuscript for the loss of life. In fact, these autobiographical versions of death and survival represent on the part of both writers a late variation on persistent themes treated in different modes in earlier texts. In the immediate post-war period, both writers addressed the question of death and survival in two related ways: in overtly theoretical or philosophical terms and through the medium of myths or archetypes drawn from the Western cultural inheritance.

Death and the Poetics of Culture

Both Malraux's theory of art and Blanchot's theory of literature are centred on the question of death and survival. The problem that Malraux's account of culture seeks to solve is that posed by the survival of works of art beyond the death of the cultures that created them: 'le problème qui se pose, c'est précisément de savoir ce qui assure la transcendence partielle des cultures mortes' [the problem posed is precisely that of knowing what it is that ensures the partial transcendence of dead cultures].[10] Malraux's answer to this question is the theory of the *musée imaginaire* or imaginary museum.[11] The imaginary museum is the exhaustive photographic archive of world art embodied in the illustrated art book and made possible through the conjunction of three historical factors: the colonial encounter with non-Western cultures; the rehabilitation of non-Western art undertaken by Western modernism; and the invention of sophisticated techniques of reproduction. The juxtaposition of the totality of available art in the imaginary museum reveals the characteristic signature of an individual artist through an examination of his or her complete works, the characteristic style of a civilization or period through an exhaustive inventory of its artefacts, and ultimately the underlying shared purpose of art as a whole through a cumulative aggregation of forms drawn from all over the world throughout history. For Malraux, the common denominator of all art is its defiance of mortality through the creation of forms that outlive their creators. Art, according to Malraux, is the vehicle for an existentialist humanism, which defines humanity in terms of its confrontation with death and its refusal to submit meekly to the biological imperative of mortality. Works of art survive the artists who create them and the civilizations that give them their initial meaning. They are then subject to cycles of forgetting and (re)discovery that Malraux describes alternately as 'métamorphose' or 'résurrection.' Thus, the imaginary museum is responsible for the metamorphosis that transforms African fetishes into works of art in a Western sense and for the resurrection that raises from the dead neglected European styles such as Romanesque sculpture and architecture. This theoretical emphasis on resurrection is expressed in mythical or archetypal form in Malraux's invocation of the New Testament story of Lazarus, miraculously raised from the dead by Christ. For Malraux, the story of Lazarus is the subtext of a global cultural history, as well as the archetypal framework for understanding his own near-death experiences (CS, 419–541).

At roughly the same time as Malraux was proposing his theory of the imaginary museum, Blanchot was developing the bases of his theory of literature, whose most programmatic expression is to be found in the essay 'La Littérature et le droit à la mort.'[12] First published in two parts in Critique in 1947 and 1948 , the essay operates within a dual context. First, it represents a sustained exploration of the literary implications of the reading of Hegel proposed by Alexandre Kojève.[13] Second, it offers an implicit response to Sartre's theory of literature as expounded in Qu'est-ce que la littérature?[14]

Kojève's interpretation of Hegel is based essentially on a reading of the Phenomenology of Mind. For Kojève, the key to Hegel's work as a whole is the master-slave dialectic, a struggle for recognition between rival consciousnesses whose outcome confronts the loser with the invidious choice between death or ignominious surrender and enslavement (ILH, 9–34). According to Kojève, this primal conflict marks the foundation of recognizably human society, with its hierarchical structure dominated by masters and its productive capacity underwritten by forced labour. In these terms, the violence of the master-slave dialectic is 'anthropogenic'– it produces the human. This, for Kojève, is the beginning of human history, which continues as a process of violent negation of the given conditions of nature through human labour. According to Kojève, then, the motor of human history is negation, expressed through labour and the struggle for recognition, but embodied ultimately in human mortality itself.

Sartre's post-war theory of literature takes the form of a phenomenological account of culture as the product of interacting consciousnesses, the sum of the free intentionalities of artist and audience together generating the work of art as an aesthetic object. For Sartre, the work of art is both the product of the free choices of artist and audience and an incitement to the exercise of freedom in other domains: 'l'œuvre d'art est une valeur parce qu'elle est appel' [the work of art is a value because it is a calling forth] (QL, 62). Sartre's own version of that incitement to freedom is to call explicitly for a committed literature, fully engaged in the social and political life of its time: 'l'écrivain "engagé" sait que la parole est action' [the 'committed' writer knows that the word is action] (QL, 30). For, in spite of his general phenomenological model, according to which all art is an expression of and an incitement to freedom, Sartre distinguishes between forms of literature on the ethical and political grounds of greater or lesser potential for commitment to social causes. Thus, prose is identified as a transparent and transitive medium that seeks to change the society that surrounds it, while poetry is dismissed as an opaque and intransitive medium bound up with its own rules and conventions (QL, 17–18).

Blanchot's essay 'La Littérature et le droit à la mort' might be described as a Kojèvian reply to Sartre. Blanchot refuses Sartre's distinction between engaged transitive literature (prose) and an autonomous intransitive literature (poetry). Instead, Blanchot stresses the role of all language and literature as work and negation in the Hegelian sense. Literature is as engaged as any other human activity because it transforms the world in the same way, through a negation of given circumstances. As for Kojève, for Blanchot this negation is a form of death, and throughout the essay, he frequently paraphrases a celebrated Hegelian formula, quoted by Kojève, that insists on the centrality of death to the movement of human life: 'Or la vie de l'Esprit n'est pas la vie qui s'effarouche (scheut) devant la mort et se préserve (rein bewahrt) du ravage (Verwüstung), mais celle qui supporte la mort et se conserve (erhält) en elle' [Now the life of the Mind is not the life that bridles before death and preserves itself from devastation but the life

that tolerates death and conserves itself in it] (*ILH*, 540–1). In a significant displacement, Blanchot remodels the sentence by substituting 'language' for 'life of the Mind': 'le langage est *la vie qui porte la mort et se
maintient en elle*' [language is *life that carries death and maintains itself in it*]
(*LDM*, 324). In Blanchot's adaptation of Kojève's Hegel to a theory of
literature, it is language that becomes the domain of negation and
death. This is possible not simply because all human activity is a form
of negation but also because language possesses specific qualities as a
means of negation. For Blanchot, following Mallarmé, language evokes
an absent object by naming it, but thereby denies its actual physical
presence. So language, and by extension literature, operates through
negation, but a negation that is ambiguously related to the evocation of
a physical presence that it both affirms and denies. In this sense, language and littérature embody death, the negation that both gives life its
meaning and ultimately deprives it of meaning.

As this might suggest, death for Blanchot is ambiguous and elusive.
Death both defines life as negation and negates that negation. The significance of death depends on its ability to define life and embody negation, in such a way that to undergo death and thus pass beyond life and
negation is paradoxically to deny its importance. Upon dying, the state
of death defined by negation no longer exists, and so to die in the sense
understood in advance of death, that is, to leave definitively a world
defined by negation, is impossible. In other words, to die is to leave the
realm of the human, defined by mortality, and thus become in a sense
immortal, incapable of death. For Blanchot, in sum, death is impossible,
because with death the negation that makes death what it is passes
away also (*LDM*, 325). According to Blanchot, organized religions
attempt to deal with this paradox by humanizing it, and the impossibility of death is reinterpreted as proof of the existence of an immortal soul
destined for either resurrection or reincarnation. Blanchot himself
favours confronting the paradox and recognizing its implications for a
kind of post-human existence, opened up by the possibility of 'surviving' death in a state suspended between life and death. The mythical
archetype that Blanchot uses to express this account of death and survival is the story of Orpheus and Eurydice, the story of the poet who
fails in his attempt to bring his wife back from the dead but thereby
enters into a new suspended relationship with death.[15]

Malraux and Blanchot thus approach the relation of death to culture
in significantly different ways. For Malraux, culture represents the defiance of mortality through creation and through the foundation of an

existential humanism. For Blanchot, literature is the paradoxical embodiment of the essence of life that is death, simultaneously affirming and negating, both dead letter and living spirit, suspended beyond life and death in what might be described as a post-human or ahuman condition. The relation between these two definitions of culture represents a kind of asymptote, a convergence without intersection.[16] For there are moments when Malraux's theory of metamorphosis seems to approach Blanchot's view of the impossibility of death. For Malraux, the affirmation of cultural continuity is ultimately premised upon the breaks and ruptures in history that threaten the complete destruction of civilizations. Without death and destruction, survival would have no meaning and no pathos. In this sense, cultural artefacts carry the mark of death (in the form of the decline of cultures) as much as that of a creative life force.

Cultural Space in Malraux and Blanchot: The Imaginary Museum and the Space of Literature

The question of death and survival defines the central cultural preoccupations of Malraux and Blanchot and leads to their reconfiguration of cultural space. For Malraux, the imaginary museum is the space of the death and resurrection, or metamorphosis, of cultures. But this ontological space of metamorphosis is the product of the intersection of three other spaces: the global space of cultural contact opened up by colonialism, the flat surface of modernist painting that helped to rehabilitate non-perspectival, non-Western arts, and the virtual space of photographic reproduction. Embodied provisionally in the illustrated art book, the imaginary museum exists everywhere and nowhere, a universal repertoire of forms reduced to two dimensions.

The new space opened up by the imaginary museum is problematic. It appears abstract and universal, but its premises are concrete and culture-specific. Notwithstanding its openness to other cultures, it remains a Western invention, the result of a fusion of imperial access to other civilizations, modern art and technology, and European philosophy. For Malraux's aesthetics is informed by an existential humanism that identifies the human with the refusal of biological destiny as embodied in death. This is a very specifically modern Western worldview, albeit one that draws on a wide variety of other cultures to illustrate its convictions. In the 1970s, Malraux drew attention to the fact that the publication of the first edition of Le Musée imaginaire in 1947 coincided with the independence of India and the beginning of the era of decolonization: 'le Musée imaginaire naît avec l'indépendance du Tiers Monde, et le procédé photographique sans lequel il serait né beaucoup plus tard, la détrame, est curieusement contemporain de la libération de l'Inde' [the Imaginary Museum is born with the independence of the Third World, and the photographic technique without which it would have been born much later, desampling, is curiously contemporary with the liberation of India].[17] Indeed, the imaginary museum does recognize the value of other cultures, but only on the basis of their illustrative relationship to the preoccupations of Western European civilization: 'Mais en notre temps où la reproduction donne peu à peu à chacun la possession d'un musée imaginaire qui embrasse le monde tout entier, les perspectives de ce musée imaginaire continuent à être imposées par l'Europe occidentale et, nommément, par la France' [But in our time when reproduction puts the possession of an imaginary museum that embraces the whole world within almost anyone's grasp, the perspectives of this imaginary museum continue to be imposed by western Europe, and specifically France].[18] It is not so much the era of decolonization and national independence that the imaginary museum anticipates as the age of post-colonial relationships of patronage, where culture functions as a means of exercising soft hegemony.

Decolonization is not the only geopolitical context for Malraux's theory; the imaginary museum is also a stake in the Cold War. Essentially, Malraux presented his aesthetic as a European alternative to market-driven American popular culture and party-line Soviet propaganda. He saw the democratization of a high culture intimately engaged with issues of life and death as an effective means of combatting the simplistic but persuasive appeals of advertising and ideology. Malraux greatly admired Russian literature and was on occasion disparaging about American civilization, but his cultural third way was ultimately more sympathetic to the United States than to the Soviet Union. Indeed, Malraux envisaged the development of a 'culture atlantique,' where European high culture would be underwritten by American productive capacity and military power, as each continent compensated for the other's weakness in a cultural version of NATO (MND, 171).

So the imaginary museum represents a dual strategy to reposition European (and French) culture globally in relation to both a post-colonial and a bipolar world, to formerly colonized nations and to the Cold War superpowers. In a time of decolonization and Cold War, it envisages a cultural space that is at once global and Atlantic, and that secures the pre-eminence of European values and ideals. The imaginary museum might appear an exploded or decentred space in relation to the versions of cultural tradition that it supersedes, but its virtual global space is actually firmly centred on Europe. The expanded canon of the imaginary museum is a vehicle for an atemporal humanism that manifests itself through the stubborn persistence of cultural objects beyond their initial context. This atemporal humanism is in turn a means of reasserting the cultural pre-eminence of Europe in a period of intense geopolitical transformation.

Blanchot's vision of cultural space is very different. For Blanchot the space of literature is the space opened up by the notion of impossible death central to his theoretical work and exemplified by his reading of the Orpheus myth (EL, 224–32). The space of literature is the non-place between the Underworld and the surface where Orpheus loses Eurydice for the second time, where the repetitive conflict between the positive impulse of the literary work (œuvre) and the negativity or death of unworking (désœuvrement) is enacted. It is for this reason that Blanchot identifies his interpretation of Orpheus as the unlocatable, ever-shifting centre of the book in which it appears (EL, 9). For Blanchot there is no resurrection after death, only a paradoxical survival in a time that is a non-time and a place that is a non-place.

While Blanchot's critical work extends the canon well beyond the confines of traditional French literature, it does not move beyond the West, limiting itself to European and North American authors for the most part (the Argentinian Borges is a limit case, although his cultural background, it might be argued, is essentially European).[19] At first glance, this may appear a narrow cultural ethnocentrism on Blanchot's part, particularly in comparison with the global range of reference deployed by Malraux. But while Malraux expands the canon to include non-Western art, he does so in order to secure the primacy of Western art; in other words, he reterritorializes what he appears to deterritorialize. Blanchot, on the other hand, restricts himself for the most part to the deterritorialization of the Western canon, dismissing national boundaries as irrelevant in the elaboration of a kind of negative ontology of literature. Literature for Blanchot is a negative process of unworking that denies origins and grounding and decentres cultural space. It cannot be recuperated for ideological or national ends, short of gross misreading. While Malraux's ontology of art appears politically motivated, an aesthetic appropriation of non-Western art in the services of a post-colonial strategy, Blanchot's version removes literature from the arena of conventional politics altogether, denying its capacity to ground or justify political action and stressing instead its tendency to question in ontological and ethical terms the assumptions of identity and essence that usually underpin such action. So, whereas Malraux's expanded canon is ethnocentric, Blanchot's Western canon is deterritorialized, no longer based on any territorial integrity or national identity. The aesthetics of both Malraux and Blanchot, then, have clear political and ethical implications, which an examination of their respective attitudes to Gaullism helps to clarify.

Politics, Death, and the Nation: For and against Gaullism

General de Gaulle returned dramatically to the forefront of French political life in May 1958 after a twelve-year absence. Following four years of war in Algeria between French forces and the the armed independence movement, the Front de Libération Nationale, extreme elements of the French settler population, acting with military support, challenged the authority of the metropolitan government led by Pierre Pflimlin by forming a Committee for Public Safety in Algiers. Pflimlin resigned as Prime Minister, and President René Coty, faced with a constitutional crisis, invited de Gaulle to form an interim government charged with constitutional reform. De Gaulle promptly initiated the process that was to lead to the foundation of the Fifth Republic and tentatively moved towards the resolution of the Algerian question. In so doing, he laid the groundwork that was to establish Gaullism as the dominant force in French politics throughout the 1960s.

Schematically, Gaullism might be defined as the project of restoring to France the status of major international power (*la grandeur*) premised on national unity. The instrument of this project was a strong state apparatus, with supreme executive powers vested in the office of the President. Its immediate aims were the institutional and economic modernization of France and the reorganization of the traditional French Empire to take into account the growing demand for greater autonomy and independence on the part of overseas territories. The main outlines of this program were in place from the mid-1940s, but de Gaulle was unable to implement them in the immediate post-war period, when the inter-party discussions of the new constitution for the Fourth Republic moved decisively in the direction of a parliamentary rather than a presidential model, prompting his resignation as head of the provisional government in 1946. It was only after his return to

power in 1958 that de Gaulle found himself in a position to pursue the
program he had conceived some fifteen years before. Two key texts of
the 1940s outline the main elements of the Gaullist project: the speech
given at Bayeux on 16 June 1946, where de Gaulle presented his view of
the kind of constitution required for post-war France, and the speech
delivered at Brazzaville on 30 January 1944, where he recognized the
need to rework the relationships between metropolitan France and its
colonized territories.[20]

In his Bayeux speech, de Gaulle identifies internal division and inter-
party strife as a constant of French political life that often threatens to
obscure and even obstruct the national interest (*BX*, 7). For de Gaulle,
the national interest can only be adequately promoted and defended by
a strong State with a strict separation of powers, defining the party-
dominated national assembly as an essentially legislative body and
vesting executive powers in the office of President (*BX*, 9). It is the task
of the President to ensure the primacy of the national interest over the
narrow interests of the parties and to guarantee the continuity of institutions in times of social and international conflict (*BX*, 10). In many
respects, the Bayeux speech outlines the main principles behind the
drafting of the constitution of the Fifth Republic in 1958.

If the 1946 Bayeux speech anticipates de Gaulle's later domestic
reforms, the address delivered two years earlier in Brazzaville indicates
the direction of his thought on the subject of France's imperial status.
The speech reaffirms the 'vocation civilisatrice' or 'civilizing vocation'
of France (*BE*, 371) and so participates in the traditional ideological justification of colonization as 'white man's burden,' but it also envisages
a radical reorganization of the Empire in terms of greater autonomy for
dependent territories 'capables de participer chez eux à la gestion de
leurs propres affaires' [capable of participating at home in the management of their own affairs] (*BE*, 373). De Gaulle's view of Empire at this
time does not explicitly include full-fledged independence for colonized territories, but it does recognize the existence of a growing desire
for autonomy and the need for structural reform of the relations
between metropolitan France and its overseas territories. Just over a
year later, in August 1945, de Gaulle remarked to President Truman of
the United States: 'Le XXe siècle sera celui de l'indépendance des peuples colonisés' [The twentieth century will be the century of the independence of colonized peoples].[21] Further, in his subsequent memoirs,
de Gaulle not only claims to have recognized that the age of Empire
was over but also that the interests of France lay in the development of

post-colonial relations with the newly independent nations: 'Il était clair que c'en était fait des lointaines dominations qui avaient fondé les empires. Mais peut-être serait-il possible de transformer les anciennes relations de dépendance en liens préférentiels de coopération politique, économique et culturelle?' [It was clear that the time of the long-distance domination that had founded the empires was over. But perhaps it would be possible to transform the old relations of dependence into preferential links of political, economic, and cultural cooperation?].[22]

The dual commitment to national regeneration and decolonization may appear contradictory, since renunciation of overseas territories could be construed as damaging rather than enhancing the international prestige and global influence of France. Paul Marie de la Gorce and Rosalind Krauss see in Gaullist foreign policy and Malraux's aesthetics respectively a tension between nationalism and internationalism.[23] But Gaullism's political and aesthetic commitments on a national and international level are in fact underwritten by the single conviction that the nation-state rather than empire represents the dominant political form of the twentieth century. It is through bilateral and multilateral arrangements between independent states rather than imperial hegemony that the future world order is to be constructed. If such a policy abandons the traditional type of international prestige associated with empire, it compensates by cultivating the support and goodwill of newly independent nations.

There is no doubting Malraux's commitment to Gaullism in both its national and international guises.[24] He has even been credited with inventing the term, although he denied that this was so (CS, 204, 251). But Malraux's version of Gaullism adds a different dimension to the practical politics outlined above. This is not to say that he was indifferent to policy. On a number of occasions, he succinctly identifies the main elements of the Gaullist program: the creation of a strong State, economic modernization, and decolonization (AM, 118; CS, 249). He is quick, however, to deny that Gaullism represents a system (CS, 268). Far from being an ideology, he asserts, Gaullism is a kind of incarnation (CS, 252). De Gaulle as President is not just the constitutional guarantor of the national interest but the incarnation of the national destiny; through him, the essential presence of France manifests itself (CS, 252). Beyond the constitution of the Fifth Republic, the 'contract' that binds de Gaulle to the French people is not the standard legalistic pact of conventional political theory; its real basis lies, not in electoral legitimacy, but in the act of refusal of 18 June 1940, the day on which de Gaulle launched his appeal for the continuance of the struggle against Germany after military defeat in metropolitan France (*CS*, 137).

For Malraux, the key idea of Gaullism is not any particular policy but its ambition of 'rassemblement,' the uniting of diverse social groups beyond sectional interests in the service of the nation. This 'rassemblement' has its origins in the communion of the Resistance struggle (*CS*, 513) and in the subsequent collective exaltation of the Liberation of France (*CS*, 262). National unity is ultimately grounded in fraternity in the face of death (*CS*, 513, 530). Malraux's Gaullism is then founded on a mystical idea of the nation-state, construed as an essence that persists through time and undergoes many transformations in a series of mythical incarnations, the latest of which is de Gaulle. Like the work of art, the nation is subject to metamorphosis, or a series of deaths and resurrections that constitute its History beyond the factional struggles of politics (*CS*, 255). De Gaulle's special status rests in his ability to defy the destiny of defeat and to transform it into the anti-destiny of victory. Through him and the communion of *rassemblement*, the nation-state becomes immanent.

Blanchot's view of Gaullism and de Gaulle is diametrically opposed to Malraux's in terms of sympathy, even if some of the terms of analysis overlap. Blanchot's attitude to Gaullism is most clearly expressed in two texts of 1958.[25] In 'Le Refus,' first published in October 1958, Blanchot calls for a refusal, not of the attempted putsch of 13 May 1958, the formation of a Comité de salut public in Algiers with the support of the army in defiance of the metropolitan government, but of the apparent solution offered by the subsequent intervention of de Gaulle. For Blanchot, political refusal is not so much a question of refusing what should clearly be refused (the German Occupation in 1940 or the revolt of the Algerian settlers and army in 1958) as of refusing the apparently providential solution that ensues (Pétain's Vichy in 1940 or de Gaulle's constitutional reform in 1958). For Blanchot, the proposed solution is in both cases compromised, a part of the problem it appears to address, and must be resisted firmly on that basis.

Blanchot's second text on the events of May 1958, 'La Perversion essentielle,' looks back on the crisis from a year later, providing a more analytic, if no less vehement, appraisal of de Gaulle's role. Blanchot begins by noting how in conventional political terms the return of de Gaulle can be discussed ad infinitum in terms of its advantages and disadvantages, but that to most people his intervention came as a welcome relief from the threat of outright military dictatorship by an Algeria-based junta. For Blanchot, however, such an attitude implies an opportunistic concept of politics that fails to address the more fundamental problems raised by the crisis (*PE*, 14–15).

The key issue for Blanchot is the transformation in the nature of political power wrought by the events of May 1958. De Gaulle is not an active dictator who seizes power, but a passive incarnation of sovereignty that acquires power without seeking it (*PE*, 16). For Blanchot, he embodies a providential force, a religious power of salvation, rather than conventional political authority (*PE*, 17). The paradox of this ultimate sovereignty is that it is both omnipotent and impotent; its unimpeachable authority rests on inaction, a refusal to immerse itself in the messy debates and decisions of day-to-day politics.

According to Blanchot, de Gaulle's sovereignty invokes the national destiny of France, and his capacity to incarnate it is premised upon his role in resisting the German Occupation and Vichy collaboration during the Second World War. At a moment of complete political collapse, de Gaulle's refusal to capitulate on 18 June 1940 represented the values of national permanence and certainty within an otherwise disastrous vacuum (*PE*, 19). De Gaulle effectively became the visible presence of an absent nation; a refugee in London, the exemplary value and authority of de Gaulle's refusal derived from his lack of real power and status. He passively preserved an authority without content in cooperation with the Allied forces that actively sought to affirm a set of anti-fascist values. This wartime experience made de Gaulle aware of his ability to symbolize an exceptional sovereignty, coinciding at dramatic periods of political crisis with the essential presence of the national destiny.

But Blanchot insists that history does not repeat itself, and that May 1958 is not June 1940 (*PE*, 21). For if, in the 1940s, the Allied powers left de Gaulle more or less free to develop his own notion of national sovereignty, in 1958 the political groups that returned him to power remain present and in a position to use his passive sovereignty as a cover for the pursuit of their own interests. If the precise nature of the links between de Gaulle and the political forces that enabled his return are unclear, the forces themselves are easily identifiable: an upsurge in nationalist feeling coinciding with a reaffirmation of the colonial presence in Algeria; technocratic pressure for economic modernization; the political ambitions of the army (*PE*, 21–2). The return of de Gaulle might seem an appropriate response to the despair and frustration manifested by nationalist and pro-colonial elements, but the passive sovereignty embodied in the general cannot satisfy their expectations and he is obliged to delegate such a task to the active political forces that have brought him to power (*PE*, 23). On the one hand, the nationalist and military factions use Gaullist sovereignty to pursue their defence of colonialism, while the economic forces of neo-capitalism use centralized authority to secure the technocratic planning of development that they require (*PE*, 24). The Gaullist regime is not what it appears; its apparent absolute sovereignty is a mere cover for the activities of irredentist nationalism and modern technocratic capitalism; its apparent authority masks an indecision that hands the initiative to its unscrupulous supporters; its apparent unity hides the tensions between these competing groups; its apparent disinterestedness and sense of responsibility cover the irresponsible pursuit of sectional interests. Under these circumstances, de Gaulle ceases to be a providential war leader or saviour of the nation and becomes instead a symbolic Managing Director figure, the mere function of forces beyond his control (*PE*, 24). If he is not himself a dictator, his transformation of political sovereignty, his perversion of its sacred function into the vehicle for militant nationalism and technocratic capitalism, paves the way for dictatorship, which necessarily follows the corruption of political power into an instrument of salvation (*PE*, 25).

Thus, while Malraux insists on the Gaullist commitment to decolonization, Blanchot in 1958 condemns de Gaulle for his complicity with an ultra-colonialist military caste and settler population in Algeria. Ultimately these different views of de Gaulle point to radically different notions of politics and ethics, and of the way the two domains are linked through the themes of community and death.

Ethics and Politics: The Self, the Other, and the Social

In many respects, the terms for the discussion of the constitution of social groups or communities in post-war France were set by the sociology and ethnology of the early twentieth century, and, in particular, by the work of Émile Durkheim and Marcel Mauss. In *Les Formes élémentaires de la vie religieuse* (1912), Durkheim defined religion as the indirect worship of the power of the social group itself through the detour of totemic symbols.[26] For Durkheim, periods of collective celebration produced a shared sense of 'effervescence' or euphoric social turbulence that generated the idea of religion: 'c'est donc dans ces milieux sociaux effervescents et de cette effervescence même que paraît être née l'idée religieuse' [it is thus in these effervescent social milieux and from this very effervescence that the religious idea appears to be born] (*FE*, 385). In a sense, effervescence is the origin not just of religion but of the social itself; it is the binding agent that ensures the cohesion of the social group. But it is also a collective celebration that has the capacity to destabilize the order of the social group, and it is this paradox, that effervescence both founds and threatens the social order, that recurs in Malraux's and Blanchot's discussion of Gaullism. De Gaulle himself identified the dissension of French political life as a form of effervescence and considered that it required strong institutional controls to keep it in check: 'il est nécessaire que nos institutions démocratiques nouvelles compensent, par elles-mêmes, les effets de notre perpétuelle effervescence politique' [it is necessary for our new democratic institutions to compensate by themselves for the effects of our perpetual political effervescence] (*BX*, 8). Similarly, ventriloquizing the general, Malraux describes how true *rassemblement* or unity has its origins in collective exaltation (*CS*, 262), and in his own voice outlines how the 'illusion lyrique' or 'lyrical illusion' of collective struggle must be converted into the practical construction of a State.[27] Blanchot's comments on the role of effervescence in politics are more ambivalent, as a comparison of his reactions to the events of May 1958 and May 1968 reveals. In his critique of the return to power of de Gaulle in 1958, Blanchot identifies the reactionary forces behind the Algerian settler revolt of 13 May as 'des mouvements d'effervescence qu'on peut appeler tantôt racistes, tantôt fascistes' [movements of effervescence that might be called alternately racist or fascist] (*PE*, 22). Effervescence figures here as a negative force contesting the due authority of the constitutional state. Over twenty years later, however, in a retrospective appraisal of the student revolt of May 1968, Blanchot describes the events as an example of utopian communication and community 'où l'intelligence calculatrice s'exprimait moins que l'effervescence presque pure' [which did not so much express calculating intelligence as effervescence in an almost pure state].[28] Effervescence here is beyond not just reason but the reason of State itself.

For all the authors cited here, effervescence constitutes the loss of the self in a collective gathering, even if the value attributed to that loss differs considerably. For de Gaulle, it represents a loss of cohesion that must be secured by the countervailing discipline of institutions. For Malraux, it represents the foundational moment of a State in collective emotion, but one that must be transcended for the practical creation of a State to become possible. For Blanchot, effervescence represents rather a challenge to the organized State, either negative and reactionary as in 1958 or positive and revolutionary as in 1968. As discussed in these texts, the loss of the self in effervescence can lead to two consequences: the reabsorption of the self into a larger entity modelled on the self (the nation-state of de Gaulle and Malraux; the irredentist empire envisaged by the Algerian coup of 1958); or the creation of a paradoxical collective constituted by the assembly of fragmented selves open to communication with the fragmented others that surround them. The first alternative is that of a politics based on the conception of community as communion, a merging of self through identification with a greater self, as in Malraux's Gaullism; the second alternative is that of a critique of conventional politics based on a theory of an unavowable or inoperative community, as developed by Blanchot and Jean-Luc Nancy.

Blanchot's ideas on community as elaborated in *La Communauté inavouable* (1983) represent a response to an article by Jean-Luc Nancy subsequently collected in *La Communauté désœuvrée* (1986).[29] Both Blanchot and Nancy propose a critique of the nation-state founded on the myth of immanence (the fantasy that a national community – conceived in the implicitly Christian terms of communion and incarnation – is immanent to itself and to its political forms). In contrast, Blanchot and Nancy suggest an alternative model of community developed from the ideas of Georges Bataille. This alternative community, labelled variously by Bataille as 'impossible' (*communauté impossible*), by Nancy as 'inoperative' (*communauté désœuvrée*), and by Blanchot as 'unavowable' (*communauté inavouable*), is a paradoxical community of fragmented selves whose communicative openness to one another is premised on their individual lack of coherence. This community is based, not on immanence, the experience of being within and embodying the self, but on ecstasy (*extase*), the experience of being outside oneself. Ultimately, this experience of exteriority to the self is founded in a relation to death.

For both Gaullist nationalism and also for its critique, the relation between the self and the social is based on death. The common background here is the place of the theme of death in the philosophy of Heidegger. In *Being and Time* (1926), Heidegger famously described the mode of being that characterizes human life (*Dasein*) as 'Being-towards-death' (*Sein zum Tode*), defined essentially by the finite horizon of mortality.[30] According to Heidegger, death is the inalienable property of the human being (*BT*, 240). In broad terms, this theme has been interpreted in two ways in French thought. On the one hand, existentialism founds the authenticity of the self in its recognition and acceptance of finitude, in a conscious appropriation of the death of the self. Deconstruction, on the other hand, contests the idea that death can be appropriated, insisting that death is instead the ultimate instance of expropriation – how can death be anyone's property since death does away with ownership (the dead, after all, own nothing)? Malraux is often portrayed as an existentialist writer, and Sartre described him as demonstrating a Heideggerian attitude towards death.[31] Malraux responded many years later by insisting that his work was not concerned with 'Being-towards-death' but rather with 'Being-against-death' ('être contre la mort').[32] For Malraux, culture is conceived as a defiant refusal of an inevitable mortality. His existentialist premises (that the meaning of human life is to be found in its relation to death) lead to essentialist conclusions (that culture embodies a universal human spirit of defiance). In the process, the negative force of death is appropriated and recuperated as a transitional moment in an affirmative process of human self-expression.

Blanchot, too, has often been described as a Heideggerian thinker, but his deviation from his German predecessor is both more radical and more faithful. He accepts the centrality of death to human experience but insists on its expropriating force rather than its status as human property. As Emmanuel Levinas has pointed out, Blanchot's work represents a deracination or ungrounding of Heidegger's thought.[33] Death is not the founding property of humanity but the movement of expropriation or eviction that inhabits the very notion of property. This is one reason why death is impossible for Blanchot: to appropriate death one must die, but if one is dead, one cannot appropriate anything. Culture embodies this paradox, as art is both an affirmative project and the negation that inhabits it, both work and unworking. For Blanchot, in contrast to Malraux, then, culture does not defy death but rather incarnates its force of negation.

So both Malraux and Blanchot modify Heidegger in different ways: Malraux's theory of culture contradicts the existential acceptance of death, while Blanchot radicalizes Heidegger's emphasis on finitude to arrive at his own account of the impossibility of death. This difference can be seen clearly in their respective treatments of the theme of death of the other. The Lazarus myth as deployed by Malraux represents an appropriation of the death of the self as the basis for an affirmative view of culture, while the Orpheus myth as retold by Blanchot presents the death of the other as an expropriation of the self, a break that confronts the witness with the impossibility of his or her own death.

The recurring motif of Malraux's work as identified by himself near the beginning of the *Antimémoires* is that of a 'return to earth,' a vertiginous confrontation with death followed by a safe landing: 'le sentiment de devenir étranger à la terre, ou de revenir sur la terre, que l'on trouve ici à plusieurs reprises, semble né, le plus souvent, d'un dialogue avec la mort' [the feeling of becoming a stranger to the earth, or of returning to earth, that is to be found here on several occasions, seems most often to be born from a dialogue with death] (*AM*, 15). The hesitation here between 'becoming a stranger to the earth' and 'returning to earth' is significant, and indicates something of the ambiguity of Malraux's attitude to death and survival; survival is figured as both alienation or defamiliarization on the one hand, and simple return, on the other. It is both an experience of dispossession and restoration. Critics have chosen to read this ambiguity in one of two ways. Both André Chastel and Fredric Jameson describe Malraux as a modern practitioner of the sublime.[34] In terms of both content and style, the vertiginous brushes with death that mark Malraux's fictional and autobiographical writings are matched by the accelerating and disorienting torrent of references in his art criticism. Both confrontations with the infinite lead to a redemptive or restorative glimpse of an absolute that transcends and unifies the disparate elements of physical reality. So for Chastel and Jameson, the excesses of the sublime ultimately underwrite the unity of the self. In contrast, Michel Beaujour and Jean-François Lyotard choose to emphasize the discontinuity introduced into self and world as a result of the confrontation with death.[35] For Lyotard, the rupturing of human identity finds its analogue in the historical breaks that mark the decline and disappearance of cultures, and the work of art becomes a way of resisting the inevitability of death by imposing a signature on organic materials otherwise doomed to decay. So Malraux's treatment of death has been read in two ways: either death leads to resurrection, or death disrupts life definitively and initiates a compensatory creation of form.

Malraux's appropriation of his own death is not, then, exclusively self-centred. Indeed, it serves as the prelude to the identificatory appropriation of the death of others, both culturally and literally. Such is the tenor for example of his funeral orations, a genre that he practised regularly while Minister for Culture. The best-known example is probably the address that accompanied the transfer of the remains of the Resistance hero Jean Moulin to the Pantheon: 'Puissent les commémorations des deux guerres s'achever par la résurrection du peuple d'ombres que cet homme anima, qu'il symbolise' [May the commemorations of the two wars conclude with the resurrection of the people of shadows to whom this man gave life and whom he symbolizes].[36] For Malraux, the death of the other in the context of the Resistance struggle represents a sacrifice that unites the national community. As he states elsewhere in his memoirs, armed struggle forges a fraternal communion: 'la fraternité du combat est, rigoureusement, communion' [the fraternity of combat is, rigorously understood, communion] (CS, 530). It is this fraternal communion that is capable of defying death: 'la communion est quelquefois aussi forte que la mort' [communion is sometimes as strong as death] (CS, 529). In Malraux's work, the death of the other is effectively appropriated by the larger self of the national community.

For Blanchot, however, the death of the other cannot be appropriated in terms of selfhood because it expropriates not only itself (the dead cannot own their own death) but also the self of the witness (the witnessing of death confronts the self with the impossibility of its own death, the realization that it is both already dead and can never die). So the dominant motif of Blanchot's work is not the resurrection of Malraux but arguably that of the double death: either witnessing the death of the other, who dies twice, as in L'Arrêt de mort (1948), or the conjoined death of the other and the self, as with the floating first-person/third-person narrative of L'Instant de ma mort. This repetition of death makes dying infinite: it ceases to be an appropriable instant and ·becomes instead a repeatable moment within a suspended state of impossibility, an impossible experience and possession that hollows out the integrity of the self.

So Blanchot does not seek to appropriate the death of the other to shore up an individual or collective self, but his work poses problems of an opposite nature: when faced with an account of the self that insists upon its integrity, his interpretation tends to expropriate that self. This may be seen as a therapeutic move in approaching the work of someone like Malraux, whose self-centred ontology of art is the basis of a questionable nationalist politics, but it becomes highly problematic in the case of a writer such as Robert Antelme, whose concentration camp memoir L'Espèce humaine (1947) insists on the inability of the camp regime to expunge the essential humanity of the inmates.[37] Colin Davis has argued that Blanchot enlists Antelme in a critique of humanism that expropriates the self in the interests of a privileged relation to the other and in the process fails to respect the essentially humanist argument of Antelme's work.[38] For Antelme, murder represents the final futile attempt of the executioners to destroy the humanity of the victims, futile because death removes the victim from the realm of the human altogether and so from the possibility of further dehumanization through humiliation and torture: 'Le mort is plus fort que le SS. Le SS ne peut poursuivre le copain dans la mort ... Le mort n'offre plus prise. S'ils s'acharnaient sur sa figure, s'ils coupaient son corps en morceaux, l'impassibilité même du mort, son inertie parfaite leur renverraient tous les coups qu'ils lui donnent' [The dead man is stronger than the SS. The SS cannot pursue the dead friend beyond death ... The dead man offers no further purchase. If they were to brutalize his face, cut his body to pieces, the very impassiveness of the dead man, his perfect inertia would return all the blows that they gave him] (*EH*, 104). According to Blanchot, Antelme's work illustrates the paradox that the human being is both indestructible and extremely vulnerable (*MEH*, 77). For Blanchot, the experience of the camps reduces the self to its paradoxical core, its internal otherness that manifests itself through an impersonal or collective need and desire. Davis reads this interpretation as a distortion of Antelme's project, a transformation of a humanist defence of the identity of the self into a critique of traditional humanism that privileges the other over the self. But this is to reduce Antelme's work to a traditional humanism and Blanchot's to a simplistic critique of that humanism, when both are in different ways exploring the relationship between self and other in an extreme situation. So in some ways Antelme's humanism is paradoxically grounded in what might be called animal, rather than specifically human, acts or bodily functions (such as excretion) that to a certain extent escape the total control of the camp regime and so allow a margin of autonomy (the freedom from surveillance offered by the latrine). Conversely, Blanchot's critique of self-centred humanism proposes an alternative humanism that may be oriented towards the other but remains nonetheless a humanism whose other-centredness in potential at least protects and respects the self as the other's other. It is nevertheless true that at points Blanchot's model of alterity runs the risk of absorbing the self into the collective other of the impossible community.

Conclusion

The multiple modes through which Malraux and Blanchot address the question of death and survival (autobiography, theory, myth) are underpinned by two opposed definitions of culture: for Malraux, culture represents the defiance of death that constitutes humanity; for Blanchot, culture is the embodiment of an ambiguous impossible death that defines the paradox of human existence. Each of these views of culture implies a different kind of cultural space. If both Malraux and Blanchot expand the traditional canon of French art and literature, they do so in different ways; while Malraux opens up Western art to the outside, absorbing the art of the entire world into the aesthetic tradition first developed in the West, Blanchot hollows out Western literature from the inside, through an examination of its paradoxical model of art. Malraux envisages culture as a total space, Blanchot as an empty space. The two spaces are different versions of deterritorialization: Malraux removes the monopoly of Western art on aesthetic value only to reinstate it by subordinating the arts of other cultures to the preoccupations of its existential humanism (deterritorialization is followed by reterritorialization); Blanchot, on the other hand, deterritorializes his home culture from the inside and so avoids the trap of subordinating non-Western cultures to his own preoccupations. These reconfigurations of space are related to the new post-war geopolitics of decolonization and the Cold War and represent different attempts to reposition French culture in relation to that of other nations and of the two superpowers. So Malraux's imaginary museum insists both on the pre-eminence of French and European culture among the non-Western cultures it has 'discovered' and promoted, and on the superiority of traditional European high culture to both American popular culture and Soviet propaganda. Blanchot's space of literature has no explicit political agenda and actually does away with the notion of national literatures, but it still presents an implicitly European canon of works whose shared ontology arguably remains very European in its rejection of any essentialist identity.

In both cases, the cultural spaces envisaged are bound up with the question of death and its appropriation. The openness of Malraux's canon is underpinned by the Western appropriation of other cultures, by the self's assimilation of the other (including the inalienable property of death). But Malraux's Gaullism, for all its post-colonial manoeuvres, contains nonetheless the utopian possibility of shared global culture. In contrast, the relative narrowness of Blanchot's Western canon avoids the appropriation of other cultures, opting instead to expropriate Western literature as the expression of a propertyless regime of death and unworking. The Western work of art is only itself (the affirmation of work) insofar as it is other than itself (the negation of unworking), and so posits an open relation to external others (including other cultures). Nevertheless, Blanchot's work poses a further problem as it runs the risk of appropriating the self of the other as other rather than as self, as his reading of Robert Antelme suggests.

In conjunction, then, the work of Malraux and Blanchot delineates the complex problem of the encounter with other cultures at a time of rejection of the (collective) other in ideological confrontation (Cold War) and of assertion of the (collective) self in newly emergent nations (decolonization). In such a context, where self-assertion and openness to the other carry ambiguous connotations, neither rejection of the self (Blanchot) nor assimilation of the other (Malraux) offers an entirely adequate response to the ethical and political problem of relations between cultures. But in spite of all their paradoxes and ambiguities, it is the merit of the imaginary museum and the space of literature to have begun the ongoing reconfiguration of French cultural space in the post-war era, rejecting the neat lines of the hexagon for a variable geometry closer to the complex geopolitics and cultural ethics of the late twentieth century.

NOTES

1 See Nathaniel B. Smith, 'The Idea of the French Hexagon,' *French Historical Studies* 6.2 (1969): 139–55; and Eugen Weber, 'L'Hexagone,' in *Les Lieux de mémoire*, ed. Pierre Nora, 3 vols (Paris: Gallimard/Quarto, 1997), 1: 1171–90.

2 See Leslie Hill, *Bataille, Klossowski, Blanchot: Writing at the Limit* (Oxford: Oxford University Press, 2001), 189–91.

3 See Philippe Lacoue-Labarthe, 'Fidélités,' in *L'Animal autobiographique: autour de Jacques Derrida*, ed. Marie-Louise Mallet (Paris: Galilée, 1999), 215–30.

4 On the logic of deterritorialization and its counterpart, reterritorialization, see Gilles Deleuze and Félix Guattari, *Capitalisme et schizophrénie I: l'anti-Œdipe* (Paris: Minuit, 1972), 306–7. In the context of a fusion of Marxism and psychoanalysis, Deleuze and Guattari are concerned with the ways in which the schizophrenic logic of capitalism disrupts and reconstitutes identities through its overdetermination of human desire. I am using the terms in a looser sense to designate the subversion and reconsolidation of notions of national identity vested in territorial integrity.

5 See André Malraux, *Le Miroir des limbes I: antimémoires* (Paris: Gallimard/Folio, 1972), 175–6. Subsequent references are given in the text using the abbreviation *AM*.

6 See Maurice Blanchot, *L'Instant de ma mort* (1994; Paris: Gallimard, 2002). Subsequent references are given in the text using the abbreviation *IM*.

7 On Blanchot's manipulation of dates and the ambiguous historicity of his narratives, see Leslie Hill, *Blanchot: Extreme Contemporary* (London: Routledge, 1997), 148–50.

8 See Philippe Lejeune, *Le Pacte autobiographique* (Paris: Seuil, 1975), 13–46.

9 See André Malraux, *Le Miroir des limbes II: la corde et la souris* (Paris: Gallimard/Folio, 1976), 487. Subsequent references are given in the text using the abbreviation *CS*.

10 See André Malraux, 'Appel aux intellectuels' (1948), in *La Politique, la culture: discours, articles, entretiens (1925–1975)*, ed. Janine Mossuz-Lavau (Paris: Gallimard, 1996), 178–99 (187).

11 See André Malraux, *Essais de psychologie de l'art I: le musée imaginaire* (Geneva: Skira, 1947). Subsequent references are to the revised edition, *Le Musée imaginaire* (Paris: Gallimard, 1965), and are given in the text using the abbreviation *MI*.

12 See Maurice Blanchot, 'La Littérature et le droit à la mort' (1947/48), in *La Part du feu* (Paris: Gallimard, 1949), 291–331. Susequent references are given in the text using the abbreviation *LDM*.

13 See Alexandre Kojève, *Introduction à la lecture de Hegel*, ed. Raymond Queneau (1947; Paris: Gallimard, 1968). Subsequent references are given in the text using the abbreviation *ILH*.

14 See Jean-Paul Sartre, *Qu'est-ce que la littérature?* (Paris: Gallimard, 1948). Subsequent references are given in the text using the abbreviation *QL*.

15 See Maurice Blanchot, 'Le Regard d'Orphée,' in *L'Espace littéraire* (Paris: Gallimard, 1955), 224–32. Subsequent references are given in the text using the abbreviation *EL*.

16 For the convergence between Malraux and Blanchot, see Blanchot's sympathetic review articles, 'Le Musée, l'art et le temps' (1950/51) and 'Le Mal du musée' (1957), in *L'Amitié* (Paris: Gallimard, 1971), 21–51 and 52–61 respectively.

17 André Malraux, *La Tête d'obsidienne* (Paris: Gallimard. 1974), 234.

18 See André Malraux, 'Malraux nous dit: entretien avec Albert Olivier' (1946), in *La Politique, la culture*, 162–73 (171). Subsequent references are given in the text using the abbreviation *MND*.

19 On Blanchot's reconstruction of the canon, see Fredric Jameson, *A Singular Modernity: Essay on the Ontology of the Present* (London: Verso, 2002), 185–6.

20 See Charles de Gaulle, 'Discours prononcé à Bayeux' (1946) and 'Allocution prononcée à l'occasion de l'ouverture de la conférence de Brazzaville' (1944), in *Discours et messages*, 5 vols (Paris: Plon, 1970), 2:5–11 and 1:370–3

respectively. Subsequent references are given in the text using the abbreviations *BX* and *BE* respectively.

21 See 'Note établie par Henri Bonnet, au sujet de l'entretien du général de Gaulle et du Président Truman, le 24 août 1945,' in Charles de Gaulle, *Mémoires de guerre*, 3 vols (Paris: Plon, 1959), 3:553–5 (554).

22 Charles de Gaulle, *Mémoires d'espoir: le renouveau (1958–62), l'effort (1962...), allocutions et messages (1946–1969)* (Paris: Plon, 1994), 19.

23 See Paul Marie de la Gorce, 'De Gaulle et la décolonisation,' in *De Gaulle en son siècle 6: liberté et dignité des peuples* (Paris: Institut Charles de Gaulle / La Documentation française / Plon, 1992), 11–34 (14–15); and Rosalind Krauss, 'The Ministry of Fate,' in *A New History of French Literature*, ed. Denis Hollier (Cambridge, MA: Harvard University Press, 1989), 1000–6 (1005).

24 On Malraux's Gaullism, see Janine Mossuz-Lavau, *André Malraux et le gaullisme* (1970; Paris: Presses de la Fondation Nationale des Sciences Politiques, 1982); and François Gerber, *Malraux–De Gaulle: la nation retrouvée* (Paris: L'Harmattan, 1996).

25 See Maurice Blanchot, 'Le Refus' and 'La Perversion essentielle,' in *Écrits politiques: guerre d'Algérie, mai 68 etc. (1958–1993)* (Paris: Lignes et manifestes / Léo Scheer, 2003), 11–12 and 13–25 respectively. Subsequent references are given in the text using the abbreviations *R* and *PE* respectively.

26 See Émile Durkheim, *Les Formes élémentaires de la vie religieuse: le système totémique en Australie* (1912; Paris: Livre de poche, 1991), 52–3. Subsequent references are given in the text using the abbreviation *FE*.

27 'Deuxième entretien d'André Malraux avec *L'Express*' (1955), in *La Politique, la culture*, 226–46 (236–7).

28 Maurice Blanchot, *La Communauté inavouable* (Paris: Minuit, 1983), 53. Subsequent references are given in the text using the abbreviation *CI*.

29 See Jean-Luc Nancy, 'La Communauté désoeuvrée,' in *Alea* 4 (February 1983): 11–49; reprinted in extended form in *La Communauté désœuvrée* (1986; Paris: Christian Bourgois, 1990), 9–105. Subsequent references are to the latter version and are given in the text using the abbreviation *CD*.

30 Martin Heidegger, *Being and Time*, trans. John Macquarrie and Edward Robinson (1962; Oxford: Basil Blackwell, 1988), 259. Subsequent references are given in the text using the abbreviation *BT*.

31 See Jean-Paul Sartre, *L'Etre et le néant: essai d'ontologie phénoménologique* (Paris: Gallimard, 1943), 615–16 and 630–1.

32 Gaëtan Picon, *Malraux par lui-même* (Paris: Seuil, 1974), 74–5.

33 See Emmanuel Levinas, 'Le Regard du poète' (1955), in *Sur Maurice Blanchot* (Paris: Fata Morgana, 1975), 7–26 (25).

34 See André Chastel, 'André Malraux: métamorphose de l'art,' *Critique* 478 (1987): 185–202 (188–9); and Fredric Jameson, 'Transformations of the Image in Postmodernity,' in *The Cultural Turn: Selected Writings on the Postmodern 1983–1998* (London: Verso, 1998), 93–135 (122–3).

35 See Michel Beaujour, 'L'Invention comme antimémoire,' in *Miroirs d'encre: rhétorique de l'autoportrait* (Paris: Seuil, 1980), 294–303; and Jean-François Lyotard, 'Le Monstre a occupé mes décombres (D'une biographie de Malraux),' *Critique* 591–2 (1996): 628–45, *Signé Malraux* (Paris: Grasset & Fasquelle, 1996), and *Chambre sourde: l'antiesthétique de Malraux* (Paris: Galilée, 1998).

36 See André Malraux, 'Transfert des cendres de Jean Moulin au Panthéon' (1964), in *La Politique, la culture*, 295–305 (295).

37 Robert Antelme, *L'Espèce humaine* (1947; Paris: Gallimard, 1957). Subsequent references are given in the text using the abbreviation *EH*. For Blanchot's reading, see 'L'Espèce humaine,' in *L'Entretien infini* (Paris: Gallimard, 1969), 191–200; reprinted in Robert Antelme, *Textes inédits, Sur L'Espèce humaine, Essais et témoignages*, ed. Daniel Dobbels (Paris: Gallimard, 1996), 77–87. Subsequent references are to the latter edition and are given in the text using the abbreviation *MEH*.

38 See Colin Davis, 'Ethical Indifference: Duras,' in *Ethical Issues in Twentieth-Century Fiction: Killing the Other* (Basingstoke: Macmillan, 2000), 131–51 (140).

6 Not Your Uncle: Text, Sex, and the Globalized Moroccan Author

RICHARD SERRANO

Sexual mores and practices are particularly susceptible to the pressures of globalization, since the exported American aesthetic is so much about selling sex, or about selling via sex, while the Western touristic impulse is so much about buying sex or at least about buying into the eroticization of other places. Yet, somehow homosexual practices and mores are also especially resistant to the sorts of standardization demanded by globalization. In this essay, I explore the construction of meaning and dissolution of significance surrounding what most Euro-Americans would consider homosexuality in the works of two Moroccan writers, Driss Chraïbi, who first published in the early 1950s, and Rachid O, who first published in the mid-1990s. I do not read these texts sociologically; in other words, I do not believe that they merely represent the practice of homosexuality in Morocco nor the place of the homosexual in Moroccan society, since all of these terms are far too monolithic and unnuanced to be helpful. Instead, I propose to examine how the texts acknowlege the intersection of homosexuality as praxis and the transformation of Morocco as it becomes increasingly implicated in the global economy, indeed in global economies of language, exchange, and sexuality.

The publication of Driss Chraïbi's first novel, *Le Passé simple*, in 1954 provoked a scandal both in France and Morocco because of what was perceived as its harsh portrayal of a traditional Muslim family in Casablanca while Morocco was struggling to free itself from French rule after the Second World War.[1] Some Moroccan nationalists criticized the novel for giving metropolitan French readers further excuse for supporting France's so-called *mission civilisatrice* while Morocco was struggling for independence. Indeed, the novel was banned in Morocco until

1977, and, although Chraïbi himself renounced the work, he continued to live in exile in France until 1985. I would like to suggest here, however, that Chraïbi's unsavoury depiction of this particular family attacks, not the traditional Muslim family itself, but this particular family as evidence of the corruption of traditional Moroccan culture by French colonialism.[2] Whereas critics of Chraïbi view the traditional family as a potential site of resistance to colonialism, Chraïbi depicts a family that has already been co-opted by French colonialism and American economic imperialism. In his novel, the site of resistance to colonialism is found, not in the traditional family, which is always already corrupted, but instead in the specifically Arabo-Mediterranean construction of what Europeans and Americans would call homosexuality.

Jacqueline Kaye and Abdelhamid Zoubir, two of Chraïbi's most vociferous critics, claim in their book *The Ambiguous Compromise* that he subverts 'the Arabo-Islamic basis of Moroccan culture by suggesting that Islam is no more an expression of authentic culture than French.'[3] The incongruity of contrasting a religion (Islam) with a language (French) is somewhat mitigated when placed in the overall context of their book, which argues against the benefits of written language in Morocco and Algeria (whether French or Modern Standard Arabic), especially since most Algerians and Moroccans are ethnically 'Berber.' However, the contrast does remain startling. Kaye and Zoubir see the French language as the most important part of an ideological system – French national secularism translated into Empire – that distorts any attempt at representing Maghrebi reality. They accuse Chraïbi of further misrepresenting Morocco in what they regard as his attempt to make Islam seem as inauthentic a part of Moroccan existence as the alienating French language, a tactic presumably designed to make his use of the French language as a vehicle of literary expression seem less alienating. However, I want to argue that under colonial rule the practice of Islam and the imposition of French should not be seen as antithetical but rather, as in this case, as potentially complementary.

While it is certainly true that Islam as practised by Moroccans under French colonialism in the 1940s appears hopelessly corrupt in *Le Passé simple*, Chraïbi's novel seems more a criticism of the hypocrisy of its practitioners than of Islam itself. Moreover, all the characters in the novel other than the narrator, whether Muslim or not, are either hypocritical or craven or both. In other words, Chraïbi does not represent any European characters as less hypocritical than the Moroccans. Joseph Kessel, for example, the French professor who evaluates the narrator's *bac* exam, praises him for being an exceptional indigenous student lifted into civilization by the French. When the narrator proves less than grateful for this praise, the professor says, 'J'aurais dû vous mettre un beau zéro' [I should have given you a big fat zero] and threatens to fail him at the oral exam (213). Or again, when the narrator is thrown out of the house by his father, his closest European friend, Albert-Raymond Roche, refuses to take him in because he no longer takes the passive role in sex (200). As these examples show, Chraïbi does not provide a moral European alternative to the corrupt practice of Islam surrounding him. Contrary to Kaye's criticism, Chraïbi does not mean to suggest that Islam is no more an expression of authentic culture than the French language and the ideology it has transported to Morocco, but instead that the practice of Islam has been distorted by the exigencies and accommodations of colonialism.

The critic Houaria Kadra-Hadjadji is much more sympathetic to Chraïbi, but in her encyclopedic *Contestation et révolte dans l'œuvre de Driss Chraïbi*, she provides us with numerous examples of Chraïbi's misunderstandings, whether wilful or naïve, both of the Qur'an and of traditional Muslim practices in Morocco. According to Kadra-Hadjadji's meticulously researched book, Chraïbi invents and conflates *hadith*, orally transmitted anecdotes recounting the sayings and doings of the Prophet, and even renders some of them obscene. The most shocking instance is the narrator's supposed citation of Abu Bakr, one of the companions of the Prophet and the first caliph after the latter's death: 'Vous croyez avoir pété. Mais réfléchissez, peuple de Dieu. Votre anus a-t-il éjecté une once de fèces? Non? Alors, tranquillisez-vous: vous n'avez pas pété' [You think you've farted? But think, people of God, has your anus ejected an ounce of feces? No? Then don't worry, you haven't farted] (169). I am not convinced, however, that Driss Chraïbi, the author, is to be condemned for this adolescent mocking of Islam; perhaps the blame should be placed instead on the adolescent narrator, Driss Ferdi. Most critics neglect to distinguish between the author and his pseudo-autobiographical narrator. Although both are named Driss, thus implying that we are intended to understand them as intimately related, I would suggest, nonetheless, that we should read the novel as something of a palinode. Chraïbi's narrator, after all, is not terribly sympathetic to any reader who has managed to mature beyond his James Dean or *Catcher in the Rye* phase. In creating this irascible and erratic narrator, Chraïbi is surely criticizing the young man he once was, as well as the family and system that created such a Moroccan youth.

If the narrator misunderstands the Qur'an and Muslim practices, it is because his Western education has erased all memory of his Qur'anic education, except for the corporal punishment and furtive groping inflicted on him by his teacher. For we should not forget that this narrator is constantly misidentified as European. Even his uncle does not recognize him when he returns to Fez after several years absence: 'Sombre chrétien, vous désirez? J'ai payé mes impôts, je n'ai ni poux ni puces à déclarer, je ne fais pas de politique et tous ceux qui gîtent dans cette maison ont été maintes fois vaccinés contre toutes les maladies de la création' [Sombre Christian, what do you want? I paid my taxes, I have neither lice nor fleas to declare, I'm not interested in politics and everyone who lives in this house has been vaccinated many times against all the maladies of creation] (79). Indeed, the narrator has been so thoroughly transformed by his French education that even his family finds it difficult to recognize him as Arab. At one point an American soldier looking for authentic local colour addresses Driss in broken French:

– Toi Français? me demanda-t-il.
– Non, répondis-je. Arabe habillé en Français.
– Then ... où sont Arabes habillés en Arabes, parlant arabe et ...
J'étendis la main en direction du vieux cimetière musulman.
– Par là. (208)

[–You French? he asked me.
– No, I responded, Arab dressed as French.
– Then ... where are Arabs dressed as Arabs, speaking Arabic and ...?
I pointed in the direction of the old Muslim cemetery.
–Over there.]

There are many Arabs dressed as Arabs and speaking Arabic in *Le Passé simple*, but here the narrator sarcastically suggests that even they lack the authenticity the tourist seeks. Real Arabs are dead and buried; the narrator who passes for French is as authentic an Arab as the American can hope to find.

Yet the narrator remains an extreme case, to the extent that, late one night when he is trying to find a place to stay after an argument with his tyrannical father, a dog that has been trained by its owner to distinguish between Arabs and Europeans whimpers at its inability to determine to which of the two groups he belongs. We are meant to understand that Chraïbi is criticizing here, not the uncle, not the American soldier, not the dog – none of whom recognize Driss as an Arab – and not even the narrator himself, but rather his father. This criticism, however, is not directed at the father *qua* traditional Moroccan patriarch. Rather, the father is at fault for having transformed his son into an Arab in French garb, by selecting him as the single member of the family to be Westernized in order that he might learn how to protect the family's economic interests, interests that are not at all traditional in nature or scope. The father casts the narrator into the jaws of the wolf, to borrow a phrase from the Algerian writer Kateb Yacine, not to protect the faith, nor to encourage Moroccan nationalism, but in order to create a new being at home in both worlds who could then help him beat the French at their own colonial game.[4]

Le Passé simple has also been criticized for misrepresenting the traditional Muslim family in that the patriarch of the narrator's family seems to style himself after God, which would be the ultimate blasphemy in Islam. Kaye and Zoubir, while conceding that 'the use of French makes possible a kind of guerilla assault on French itself,' insist that its use 'can also encode an implicit assault on Arabo-Islamic values, thus mimicking the double alienation of the writer' (34). The *Seigneur*, as the narrator's father insists his family call him, is consistently depicted in terms of God the Father, which Kaye correctly points out is a Christian and not a Muslim image of the deity. Kaye seems to suggest that, because he writes in French, Chraïbi cannot help but distort his representation of the Moroccan family (although, in this case, she values this distortion as an 'assault'). Again, however, I would insist that since the entire novel is filtered through the consciousness of the narrator, this misrepresentation of the father functions as part of the characterization of the narrator as son. We can thus read the son's misrepresentation of his Muslim father in Christian terms as a function of the son's Western education and not simply as evidence of the author's inability to faithfully represent contemporary Morocco using French words. In this way, the narrator's use of *Seigneur* in referring to his father can be seen as part of Chraïbi's representation of the institution of Islamic patriarchy as being already corrupted by French colonial influence. This father, although he does not speak French and is a Hajji twice over, should not, then, be considered representative of traditional Moroccan culture. It was, after all, by manipulating the economic system imposed by the French that this man went from destitution to wealth and power. One of the most important, but most consistently overlooked, elements of the novel is the patriarch's establishment of a monopoly in the trading of tea and, especially, the way in which he turns a potentially disastrous over-supply of tea into a lucrative short-age thanks to his dealings with French officials and American traders. Far from being a representative of the traditional Moroccan aristocracy, the father is an *arriviste*, one of the *nouveaux riches* that made their for-tunes by cooperating with the French. As we further discover, he also drinks, fornicates, and lies, retaining only the trappings of the pious Muslim. Whereas his son is an *Arabe habillé en Français*, I would charac-terize the father as a *Français habillé en Arabe*. I do not mean to imply that alcoholism, fornication, and dishonesty are particular to French culture, but rather that the father had adopted customs proscribed by Islam but encouraged by Western capitalism even before he made a pseudo-Westerner of his son. Again, I would argue that Chraïbi is criticizing here neither the Moroccan family nor the Moroccan patriarch per se, but rather a clan and a father corrupted by contact with the West. In fact, the greatly exaggerated elements of Chraïbi's portrayal of the fam-ily – the illiterate, weepy, craven, suicidal mother, the illiterate, obese, crude friend of the family who sells prayers, the silent, terrified chil-dren, the omnipotent self-righteous father – indicate a desperate desire on the father's part to compensate for the illegitimate and Western-tainted source of the family's wealth and power. Chraïbi is thus criticiz-ing this particular Moroccan family and this Moroccan father as well as the compromised and distorted traditional values that they ostensibly represent, but that do not characterize all Moroccan families or all Moroccan fathers.

I have used the word 'traditional' repeatedly without defining pre-cisely what I mean. Traditions, of course, are invented and not fixed or eternal. Nonetheless, I would argue that one site of resistance to Euro-American ideology can be found in the narrator's adherence to a tradi-tional and non-Euro-American economy of sexuality. Indeed, the narra-tor's progression through different stages of what North Europeans and Americans would call homosexuality until he arrives at heterosex-uality is perhaps the only thing about the narrator that marks him as Moroccan and therefore Arab and distinguishes him from the French.[5] Western discourse on same-sex erotic contacts among men in Arab cul-tures may be divided into three different categories. First is the 'but he didn't even kiss me' accounts of dissatisfied European and American sexual tourists. Second is the orientalist outrage or swooning, depend-ing on the scholar's perspective, over allusions to pederasty in classical Arabic texts. Finally, there has recently been more serious and careful scholarship into the multiplicity of (homo)sexual experiences and identities specific to particular eras, places, and cultures within the context of Arab and other Islamic histories and cultures. Examples of this new scholarship can be found in two recent anthologies, *Sexuality and Eroticism among Males in Moslem Societies* and *Islamic Homosexualities: Culture, History, and Literature*, as well as in a collection of essays concerned entirely with classical Arabic literature, *Homoeroticism in Classical Arabic Writing*.

Rather than exhaustively summarize the oft-contradictory conclusions of this research, I would like to distill it to a few points for the purposes of my argument. On the whole, the researchers agree that with the exception of small, Westernized circles, sexual contact among Arab men is not constructed as homosexuality is in Northern Europe and America. In the Arab world, they say, men are not divided into heterosexuals and homosexuals; instead, partners tend to be differentiated on the basis of age, role, or class status. In other words, interest in sexual relations exclusively with men does not make a man 'gay.' Instead, younger, poorer, or more 'feminine' men take on the receptive role otherwise reserved to women, while older, wealthier, or more 'masculine' men take on the active role strictly reserved to men. Nor is one's sexual role fixed for life; as a boy matures into a man, he moves from one role to another. In fact, a man who continues to be the receptive partner after he has passed his adolescence, or who never takes up his role as husband and father is considered ill, defective, or worse.[6]

Driss the narrator becomes a man – what Northern Europeans and Americans would call a heterosexual man – over the course of *Le Passé simple*. He goes from being, according to his own terminology, passive to the European Roche's active at the beginning of the novel, to taking the active role with boys, and thence 'progresses' to taking the man's role with women. He describes himself and Roche as *adultères* and himself as a *péderaste passif* (16). Much later in the novel, however, when he needs Roche to protect him from his father, Roche refuses, replying, 'Si tu étais encore passif ... mais tu ne veux être qu'actif' [If you were still passive ... but you only want to be active] (200). I think we are meant to contrast the unchanging sexuality of European Roche with the shifting roles of Driss, although we know too little about Roche to develop an argument around this contrast beyond pointing it out. When the single most repulsive character of the novel, Si Kettani, ogles him, Driss himself declares himself *actif* (95). Si Kettani, however, does not mind, implying that he would be willing to take the passive role. We are meant to see, I believe, that this supposed man of God is so corrupt that he would not mind giving up the role reserved for the older, wealthier man. In a very odd way, then, at this moment Driss the narrator is taking a traditional position in conflict with the man who is supposed to be a pillar of Muslim tradition.[7]

Driss does not fully become a man until after he performs exceedingly well in a brothel. Becoming a man by visiting a prostitute is a cliché of francophone Maghrebi literature, but while such scenes are funny or sordid in the novels of Albert Memmi and Rachid Boudjedra, Chraïbi takes Driss's introduction to heterosexuality to Hollywood-esque extremes, for it is implied that he runs through the house's bevy of girls during his night-long stay. After this rite of passage, Driss's father begins to deal with him as an equal, just as Driss begins to take on some of the characteristics of his father, treating his younger brothers with contempt and cruelty. It is also telling that his mother commits suicide on the very night that Driss spends with prostitutes. She knows nothing of his nocturnal activities and he knows nothing of her death until he returns to face his father, so that the connection between the two events must be buried at some other level of significance in the novel. Perhaps it is necessary for the mother to be eliminated once Driss has reached the point in his evolution where he can, if not supplant his father, then at least become like his father; that is, take on the sexual role reserved for a father.

How does the narrator's adherence to a specifically Arabo-Mediterranean sexual evolution serve, then, as a site of resistance to Euro-American ideology? The novel ends with Driss the narrator leaving Morocco to pursue his studies in Paris. He has already achieved a certain level of maturity, since he has successfully completed the traditional sexual evolution. According to contemporary researchers of Middle Eastern and Maghrebi sexuality, many young men resist taking the passive role even once, because it is believed to be addictive. A boy can come to like it so much that he will have difficulty giving it up as he matures into a man. Driss, however, twice refuses to take the passive role in the novel. He refuses the entreaties of Si Kettani and the corrupted Islam that the latter represents, and he refuses to continue his passive pederasty with Roche, the novel's representative of European intellectual life. By permitting himself to be sodomized by either a corrupt Muslim or a corrupting European, Driss could gain the protection he needs, but instead, he refuses the sexual analogue of domination by either European ideology or the corrupt Morocco that the latter has wrought. While his father maintains some hold over him as provider of financial support for his studies in France, it is clear that the narrator's fealty is contingent and transitory and will last only so long as he needs this financial support. As a student and worker in France, he in time will replace his father as patriarch and as such make his own way through the world. One of the disappointments of this novel is that the narrator, despite his rebellion against both the West and the corrupt Morocco it has wrought, does as so many other protagonists of francophone novels in the 1950s do – he leaves his native land for Paris. Whatever resistance has been enabled by his following an Arabo-Mediterranean process of sexual maturation is subsumed by the trope of departure. Resistance was temporary: its site is abandoned and its moment erased as the narrator leaves for France, where his sexual practices may be read as simply heterosexual and not as the end of a different process of sexual maturation.

A little more than forty years after Driss-narrator's fictional departure for Paris and exactly forty years after the publication of Chraïbi's novel, the gay – and this time the adjective seems appropriate beyond dispute – Moroccan writer Rachid O appeared on the literary scene with the publication of L'Enfant ébloui (The Astonished Child) with Gallimard in 1995. This book of interrelated narratives was followed by the similarly structured Plusieurs vies (Several Lives) in 1996, the novel Chocolate chaud (Hot Chocolate) in 1998, and the novel Ce qui reste (That Which Remains) in 2002. Although, like Chraïbi, Rachid O is never graphic about sex in his writings – indeed, he usually sees fit to tell us that nothing happened, meaning nothing sexual happened – he is more forthcoming about the complexities and vagaries of how the homosexual lives in Morocco. While Chraïbi's account of Driss's sexuality is wholly believable (more so than some of the other details of the novel, which sometimes strain credulity), it seems that it was always intended as a vehicle for polemic. Rachid O, on the other hand, does not engage in polemic, nor does he strain credulity. Indeed, Rachid O never strains to do anything. The narrative voice that he creates is that of a matter-of-fact, normal, unambitious post-adolescent. However, although his narratives seem overtly autobiographical and largely artless, it would be as great a mistake to identify Rachid O with Rachid-narrator as it would be to insist on a simple correspondance between Driss Chraïbi and Driss-narrator.

The Morocco of Rachid is not the Morocco of Driss, but they do overlap, they do imply co-existence, they do implicate one another. Those

1950s Moroccan readers of *Le Passé simple* who wanted Chraïbi to have written a different book, apparently a Manichaean one in which the French were evil and Moroccans virtuous, refused to see that in the world Driss inhabited, a world marked by accelerating globalization represented as French colonialism and Moroccan reaction, such distinctions were no longer possible or valuable, but instead merely obscured the rapacious collaboration of the native bourgeoisie. Even the process of sexual maturation that I described above as Arabo-Mediterranean, perhaps the only element of his character not fully or immediately assimilated into European culture, results in Driss's becoming a man who can then fly to Paris and inhabit Chraïbi's next novel, *Les Boucs* (1955), in which no reference is made to homosexuality. What could be understood in *Le Passé simple* as a sign of Driss's difference, can later be read, therefore, as a sign of his having always been heterosexual according to the Euro–North American model. In Rachid O's first two books, we get the sense that Rachid may be working his way through the receptive stage of the same process of sexual maturation that Driss experienced, but by the time we reach the two works identified as novels, it is clear that he is not going to evolve beyond receptive homosexuality. The narrator's feelings about this state of affairs are not wholly unambiguous, although he never seems to suffer from a complex about his sexual orientation. Nor do we have any evidence that his family is particularly concerned that he give up men and marry a woman.

In a development sure to make an American, especially an American teacher, squirm, Rachid's first love affair is with his Arabic teacher, who first beds the boy when the latter is thirteen. This would seem to be both acceptable and unacceptable in Morocco. The teacher's family is aware but pretends not to know, while the other students in the class encourage Rachid to become the teacher's lover in order to facilitate their own sexual conquest of the boy:

> Ils voulaient juste coucher avec moi comme ça se passe au Maroc quand il y a un plutôt joli garçon dans une classe, on lui répète qu'il est mignon jusqu'à ce qu'il craque et accepte de se faire enculer, et là ils pensaient que ce serait encore plus facile puisque j'étais déjà le petit ami du professeur.

> [They just wanted to sleep with me as happens in Morocco when there is a pretty boy in the class. They keep telling him that he's cute until he gives in and lets them sodomize him, and they thought that it would be easier in

this case, since I would already be the teacher's boyfriend.] (*L'Enfant ébloui*, 66)

Nowhere in this account is there any sign that Rachid's classmates disapprove; instead, they are eager for the affair to begin. Rachid also insists on the normality of his experience, suggesting that this is what typically happens in Morocco. The erotic dimension of the teacher-student relationship has been a component of Mediterranean culture since at least the height of classical Athenian culture, but it would be a mistake for us to consider it merely a shard of the past that has survived in present-day Morocco, since the ensuing 2,500 years and the great distance separating the Aegean from the Atlas have remade the context of these practices many times over. Rachid O's stories demonstrate how complicated the reality of teacher-student love in contemporary Morocco has become. Stereotypically such a relationship would end once the junior partner reaches manhood. In other words, the junior partner's termination of the relationship would mark the latter's entry into adulthood.

However, Rachid and his teacher do not end their relationship because Rachid turns to women as he matures (à la Driss). During a moment when Rachid expresses tenderness by kissing his teacher all over his back, the latter upbraids him:

> Tu ne devrais plus faire ça. Un garçon doit s'intéresser aux filles pour devenir un homme. On ne devrait plus se voir.

> [You shouldn't do that anymore. A boy should take interest in girls in order to become a man. We shouldn't see each other anymore.] (*L'Enfant ébloui*, 69)

Although this does not mark the end of their affair, the teacher shows a keen interest in Rachid's maturation. For example, the first time Rachid ejaculates during their love-making, the teacher takes him out to dinner to celebrate (*L'Enfant ébloui*, 73). And as it transpires, their relationship comes to an end when the teacher, and not Rachid, falls in love with a woman. Rachid, who earlier had been proud that he was the only boy the teacher had been with or whom the teacher had even looked at, falls short of recognizing just who has evolved: 'Mais j'ai vu que maintenant c'était finie sa période pédé, c'était un hétéro, il ne pouvait plus m'aimer moi personnellement, le seul et dernier garçon qu'il ait connu'

[But I now saw that his pederastic period was over, he was a hetero, he could no longer love me personally, the only and last boy he'd known] (*L'Enfant ébloui*, 79). There is a contradiction at the centre of Rachid's understanding of his teacher. He describes the teacher as heterosexual, but in the same sentence also recognizes that the pederastic chapter of the latter's life was coming to an end. This was the sort of evolution the teacher expected of Rachid, having seen evidence of maturation into heterosexuality in Rachid's first ejaculation, but instead it is Rachid who witnesses the teacher's maturation into exclusive heterosexuality.

Rachid's understanding of this shift is further confused by the terminology he employs. 'Pédé' can refer specifically to a pederast as well as to homosexuals more generally, and since Rachid places 'pédé' in opposition to 'hétéro,' it is obvious that here he means 'pédé' as 'gay.' In another story, 'Rue de la gare,' when Rachid is among a group of Swiss gay men, he uses the term's ambiguity to provocative effect:

Vincent détestait les pédérastes et trouvait que le mot 'pédé' que moi je prononçais était vulgaire et ne s'appliquait qu'aux pédérastes et qu'il se sentait plus gay que pédé, tous étaient d'accord là-dessus.

[Vincent hated pederasts and thought the word 'pédé' that I pronounced was vulgar and applied only to pederasts and that he considered himself more gay than 'pédé,' everyone was in agreement on that.] (*Plusieurs vies*, 75)

As far as we can tell (and we do not have much access into his interior world), the teacher does not and would not consider himself gay. As Rachid notes, he looks at women and is heterosexual, but he has a pederastic interlude when he wants an underage boy, or at least wants this one. The boundaries between different kinds of sexual behaviour are thus blurred and elastic, while the vocabulary used to describe them is inadequate and contradictory, due in part to importing French terminology to describe Moroccan experience. That 'pédé' means one thing in Morocco and another thing among Europeans, and that Rachid-narrator knows this and can provoke gay Europeans by pretending *not* to know this perhaps means that Jacqueline Kaye is naïve when she believes that Moroccans unconsciously mimic their double alienation when using French. Or perhaps it means instead that Rachid O lives in a world in which a Moroccan can be more adept at manipulating situational French than a group of Swiss also speaking French as a second language. Unlike in the Morocco of *Le Passé simple*, there is no authoritarian French teacher threatening Rachid with a big fat zero if he uses a French word in a way not intended by most French speakers. Since Rachid visits Zurich, unlike Driss, who moves to Paris, authoritative use of the French language is decentred. Driss the narrator's father wants him to learn French to become French enough to outsmart the French, whereas Rachid the narrator learns French to master the word 'pédé' to the point where he can make his Swiss hosts feel stupid.

Nonetheless, 'pédé' is not a word we can imagine Rachid saying to his teacher. Whatever its ambiguities and contingencies, it can only be applied to him fleetingly, even wistfully. Rachid must romanticize (and thereby mystifiy) his teacher's attachment to him, insisting repeatedly that he was the only boy the teacher ever 'knew.' We do not know enough about the teacher's life before he met Rachid to determine if he participated in the earliest stages of traditional Arabo-Mediterranean sexual maturation. Was he once a receptive pre-adolescent boy? We also do not know if it is true that he was never involved with another boy. We must take Rachid's word for it. The teacher engages in the sort of behaviour that Rachid's Swiss gay friends would label as 'pédé' and therefore disdain and distance themselves from. There would seem to them to be something irreducibly Other about the teacher's sexual behaviour and maturation, his passing attraction to a pre-pubescent boy putting him into a category in which they do not want to find themselves.

Nor can Rachid put himself into the same category as his teacher. On the rare occasion when Rachid, in his later books, shows an interest in pretty boys his own age or younger, we are always assured that nothing happens between them. As we progress through the stories and novels, we also discover that Rachid grows too old to attract the sort of man who wants a boy. It would seem, then, that he is caught between two different economies of same-sex relations. It would be a mistake to argue that in Rachid's world there is a European system and an Arabo-Mediterranean system, since they overlap and inform one another, but Rachid's involvements with older European men, which sometimes take on all the trappings of full-blown domesticity, either affect the choices he makes or, at the very least, allow him to make choices about sexual partners and understand these choices in a way that does not make him feel guilty or defective. Thus, his teacher's turn to exclusive heterosexuality does not cause him to reflect on his own inability to do so. Rather, he accepts himself for who he is, that is, at the very centre of globalized Oprah Winfrey pop psychology discourses of personal happiness (which might make us wonder if Oprah has read Gide's *L'Immoraliste* or *Corydon* at least). Morocco, speaking through the teacher, wants him to take up his proper role as a husband and, eventually, father, while the globalized world wants him to self-affirm and adapt his language to the situation rather than adapt his behaviour to the norms of one system or another.

This is not to suggest that normative sexuality is less coercive in Europe. In 'Luc,' another story in *Plusieurs vies*, the title character is an older 'pédé,' but this time meaning pederast rather than simply gay. Rachid notes that Luc, a tourist from Paris, was

> frappé par la présence de vieux pédés euoropéens dans cette ville. Il me disait: 'Je ne vois jamais ce genre de vieilles folles à Paris,' que ça ne pouvait pas exister dans le métro parisien, dans des lieux publics, mais qu'il trouvait que c'était totalement accepté au Maroc.

> [struck by the presence of old European pederasts in this city. He told me, 'I never see these sort of old queens in Paris,' that this wouldn't happen in the métro or in other public places in Paris, whereas it seemed to him to be completely accepted in Morocco.] (*Plusieurs vies*, 45)

Rachid does not offer any commentary on Luc's observations, but it would seem to be the case that what is considered normal in Morocco – or at least not discounted as aberrant – is considered so abnormal in France that, if it exists at all, is hidden from view. When a Moroccan boy who mistakes Luc and Rachid for lovers asks if they need a guide to visit the tomb of Jean Genet, Luc asks him

> s'il couchait beaucoup avec les touristes. 'Oui, ça m'arrive.' On lui a demandé s'il aimait les hommes. 'Au départ, pas vraiment, mais maintenant j'ai pris l'habitude avec mon ami et j'aime ça. De toute façon, je suis le plus beau de la ville.' Il était très beau, vraiment.

> [if he often slept with the tourists. 'Yes, sometimes.' We asked him if he liked men. 'At first, not really, but now I've gotten used to it with my boyfriend and I like it. In any case, I'm the most beautiful boy in the city.' He was truly beautiful.] (*Plusieurs vies*, 42)

Other than noting his beauty, Rachid does not offer any commentary on this boy's statement. If we take the latter at his word, he has learned to enjoy sex with men (his boyfriend is French). But far more important, since it most clearly explains why he has sex with men, is that he is the most beautiful boy in the city. Although it would seem to be the case that he learns to enjoy sex with men because of his encounters with foreign tourists, which would indicate that he is not inherently homosexual, he is inherently beautiful, which means that, like Rachid at thirteen, men want him and expect him to take the receptive role with men older than himself. In other words, he is homosexual because of tourists, but not, apparently, homosexual *like* the tourists.

Rachid's experience of sexuality within his family is also perplexing. His grandfather's way of kissing and hugging him makes others uncomfortable. One of his classmates is shocked: 'Pour lui, son grand-père ne ferait jamais ça de serrer son petit-fils dans les bras de cette manière frappante qui était pour lui à la limite presque sexuelle' [For him, his grandfather would never do that, holding tight his grandson in his arms in this astonishing way that was for him approaching the very limit of being sexual] (*Plusieurs vies*, 53). We might dismiss this commentary as unusually prudish, but Rachid's father is also uncomfortable with the grandfather's behaviour: 'Mon père détestait mon grand-père ... quand il venait dormir à la maison il voulait absolument que je dorme avec lui' [My father despised my grandfather ... when he came to sleep at our house he absolutely insisted that I sleep with him] (53). As usual, Rachid does not offer his own interpretation, but his juxtaposition of the father's dislike of the grandfather with the latter's desire to sleep with Rachid suggests that he understands (or thinks he does) the grandfather's apparent lechery as the source of his father's enmity.

The erotics of this family are complex in other ways, as well. In one of the best-wrought stories of *Plusieurs vies*, 'Mon oncle,' Rachid's account of his crush on his uncle is at first endearing, but as he matures and as the attraction grows more urgent, it would be difficult for an American reader not to feel some discomfort at the incestuous undertones. At the end of the short story, this discomfort is displaced, but in such a way as to raise yet more questions about erotic practice in Rachid's family. The story begins with a description that intertwines Rachid's love for his uncle with his father's love for his uncle:

Peu importe le nombre de fois où je pense à lui, une fois, dix fois ou trois cents fois par jour, mais il est là. Je l'aimais, et mon père aussi. Son apparition était perpétuellement comme une fête. Toujours surprenant, si grand, si délicat, et, par-dessus tout, tellement beau. Sa beauté ressemblait à tout ce qui venait de lui et à tout ce qu'il pouvait dire. Sa vie était si élégante, mon père trouvait ça.

[It doesn't matter how many times I think of him, once, ten times, or three hundred times a day, but he is here. I loved him, and so did my father. Whenever he showed up it was like a party. Always surprising, so tall, so delicate, and above all, so handsome. His beauty was like everything that came from him and everything that he could say. His life was so elegant, that's what my father thought.] (*Plusieurs vies*, 7)

We do not immediately understand why it matters, but Rachid's admiration and feelings for his uncle are filtered through his father's own similar feelings. Similarly, his appreciation for his uncle's beauty is filtered through the desire for him expressed by women in the family. The narrator likes the way women talk about his uncle. It is only much later that he comes to understand that he himself was 'très attiré par lui' [very attracted to him] (9). There is a constant alternation between what the narrator knows because others know it, and what he does not know because he has not been told. It is not clear whether he assigns his feelings to others in order to mask their erotic dimension, or if we should read desire back into the feelings of others. The ambiguity of his father's feelings towards this uncle becomes central to our (mis)apprehension of how Rachid's homosexuality fits into his family.

It soon becomes obvious that the uncle has a taste for rough trade. While still a boy, Rachid inadvertently interrupts a 'type' [guy] brandishing a knife who demands money from the uncle (*Plusieurs vies*, 15). Also, when the uncle takes Rachid on a trip with him, they stay at a house that seems to be of ill repute. Rachid notices his uncle take a boy with him into his room and suddenly realizes that his uncle's relationship with the knife-brandishing guy years earlier must have been of the same sort. Because Rachid comes to know all these things about his uncle while still less than ten years old, that is, before his love affair with his teacher, there is no attempt to explain, or even indicate, how the uncle fits into the various paradigms of homosexual behaviour structuring Rachid O's other stories. The narrator's desire to see his uncle completely naked – a desire he satisfies by hiding when his father wants to take him to the public *hammam* before a wedding celebration so that he ends up staying behind and showering with his uncle instead – is not given a name, although this is virtually the only erotic moment described with any detail in any of Rachid O's four books. In this case, the narrator does not tell us that 'nothing' happened, since it is quite clear that *something* happens: he washes his uncle's beautiful, naked body. In other words, Rachid has his first erotic experience, an experience that he not only initiates and demands, but that he brought about by deceiving his father. Regardless of whether or not he knows what to call this desire for his uncle, he knows that satisfying it requires subterfuge. It is not quite the same desire for the uncle that the women he knows as a child experience and express laughingly, nor is it the same kind of love, apparently, that his father feels, but some sort of longing that includes both.

Perhaps sensing that Rachid has reached an age when he must begin to sort through all these different sorts of feelings and desires, the uncle has taken him on this journey in order to explain that he is not really his uncle:

'Je ne suis pas ton oncle,' me dit-il. Sur le coup, je ne comprenais pas du tout ce qu'il voulait dire, il n'arrivait plus à continuer ce qu'il voulait dire, il articulait très mal ses mots, c'en était émouvant de le voir trembler. Il prend sa tête entre ses deux mains pour se maudire, regretter ce qu'il allait me dire, ce qu'il venait de me dire. Mais il a continué quand même à me faire du mal, qu'il n'a jamais été mon oncle, qu'il était simplement le meilleur ami de mon père et qu'il était presque comme l'un de mes frères puisqu'il avait grandi auprès de mon père, que depuis le jour où j'ai commencé à le surnommer 'mon oncle' ça avait été un ordre de mon père de me laisser l'appeler comme ça et que tout le monde m'a laissé me tromper ...

['I am not your uncle,' he says. All at once, I did not understand anything he wanted to say, he was unable to continue to say what he wanted to, he could hardly articulate his words, it was moving to see him tremble. He held his head in his hands to curse himself, regretting what he was about to tell me, what he had just told me. But he still continued to hurt me, saying that he had never been my uncle, that he was simply my father's best friend, that he was almost like one of my brothers, since he'd grown up with my father, that since the day I'd begun calling him 'my uncle' my father had ordered everyone to let me call him that and that everyone let me make this mistake ...] (*Plusieurs vies*, 28)

Since the uncle retreats into incoherence, we never discover why he felt compelled to tell Rachid the truth about their relationship and about his relationship to Rachid's father. It would seem to be that the word 'uncle' obscures some dimension of their relationship. What is most interesting is that it was Rachid himself who labels this man and thereby makes him part of the family in name. Just as he does with 'pédé' in Switzerland, Rachid has the power to make words mean what he wants, but in this case there is a price to be paid for the distortion of the word 'uncle.' While the hitherto incestual tension between the not-uncle's role and Rachid's desire is artificial and contingent upon the latter's having forgotten his own earlier act of naming validated by his father, the stripping away of the label 'uncle' does not lead to the realization of that desire. This is truly the love that cannot be named.

After he returns to Rabat, Rachid refers to his 'uncle' by his name, which shocks his father. Once Rachid explains what had passed between them, his father tells him, 'C'est juste qu'il est dans un moment difficile de sa vie' [He's just going through a difficult period of his life] (*Plusieurs vies*, 32). Rachid would seem to have inherited from his father his penchant for keeping things ambiguous. We never discover what the uncle's difficulty was or why it would cause him to disavow the label that Rachid had assigned to him many years earlier. The father knows things that the son does not, and Rachid seems disinclined to question him further.

The short story ends abruptly:

La mort de mon oncle a été la chose la plus horrible, je crois, que mon père a connue. Il s'est tué en voiture. C'était un peu moins de deux ans plus tard. Il voyageait de nuit. Je n'ai jamais connu une réaction pareille, le jour en apprenant la nouvelle mon père s'est endormi plus de vingt-quatre heures tellement il aimait son ami.

[The death of my uncle was the most horrible thing, I think, that my father ever experienced. He was killed in a car accident. It was a little less than two years later. He was travelling at night. I've never seen such a reaction: the day he heard the news, by father slept for more than twenty-four hours, he so loved his friend.] (*Plusieurs vies*, 33)

The text closes on the word 'ami,' shifting the focus of the short story away from the relationship between the man and Rachid, to that between the man and the father. The father's terrible grief is evidence of the profound ties that linked him to the 'uncle.' It is as if this grief returns the latter to the father. The 'uncle' had attempted to explain to

Rachid that he wasn't his uncle and not his father's brother, but rather his father's best friend. Whatever the terminology, it does not seem to fully account for either Rachid's erotic attraction nor the father's sorrow. At the emotional centre of Rachid O's work is something unnameable, perhaps even unknowable.

In Chraïbi's *Le Passé simple*, the Arabo-Mediterranean process of sexual maturation that sees receptive homosexuality as the first step on the path that ultimately leads to exclusive heterosexuality is, as we have seen, presented schematically at best and represents a place of temporary and limited resistance to French colonialism as an example of the sort of globalization practised in the 1950s. Rachid O's books, on the other hand, are nearly wholly devoid of politics. They do not indicate a place where resistance can be practised, in part because Rachid O does not seem to recognize the necessity of resistance. The practice of homosexuality in contemporary Morocco as seen by Rachid O is not a potential means of even brief and ineffectual resistance to the latest forms of globalization, but is instead a sign of the latter's apparent inevitability. Various types of homosexual practice that we might label either 'European' or 'Arabo-Mediterranean' co-exist in Morocco, although neither Rachid O nor his narrator label them as such, nor do his characters show much understanding of, or curiosity about, whence their sexual practices might come. Nonetheless, by reconstructing his earliest erotic memories in 'Mon oncle,' Rachid O's narrator seems to reach a core of experience that does not match any of his models nor submit to any particular labels. His childhood entry into the manipulation of language ('oncle') obscures the meaning of that core of experience, which somehow exists beyond either traditional Arabo-Mediterranean understanding of erotic love or the newly adapted modes of homosexuality practised by and with Euro-American tourists.

What disappears between the 1950s and 1990s is any sense of France either as the source of a civilization or a set of values towards which the Moroccan may aspire, or as the source of an oppression against which he may revolt. Rachid does express a vague yearning to visit Paris, but mostly because his European lover, who had been living in Morocco, returns to the French capital leaving him behind. Indeed, Rachid's eventual journey to Europe is boring and disappointing. Europeans in Morocco are delighted to cast off value judgments, while Europeans in Europe are judgmental.

It may seem odd that I have avoided using the word 'ethics' in an essay for a volume concerned as much with ethics as with poetics, but in Rachid O's Morocco there is no ethics of sexuality. Indeed, his Morocco is no longer the site of any sort of sexual ethics at all. Whereas the narrator of *Le Passé simple* could rely on his completion of an histor-ically and culturally contingent Arabo-Mediterranean process of sexual maturation in order to conceive of himself as positioned in ethical opposition to both his father and to France, however temporary and illusory that opposition might be, the narrator of Rachid O's fiction has no such option. In other words, in Morocco at the early stages of global-ization, *passif* and *actif* as words denoting sexual positionality have a fixed meaning to which a certain, culturally variable, ethical signifi-cance is assigned. The passage from one to the next is also culturally and ethically meaningful, especially in the narrator's self-construction. He cannot defeat his father and go to France until he has completed this rite of passage. His ethical superiority is rooted in a transition into exclusive heterosexuality that henceforth mimics the predominant par-adigm of ethical sexual behaviour in France, or at least in the France that matters to the decolonizing Moroccan.

In the globalized Morocco of Rachid O, on the other hand, the mean-ing (including the ethical meaning) of key words is subject to interpre-tation, revision, and dispute. Because we cannot know precisely what 'pédé' means, we cannot be certain what ethical value it has at any given moment. Indeed, when a group of Europeans assign it a negative value, they succeed only in demonstrating the greater intellectual agil-ity of the Moroccan among them, who is able to revalue the word, although since they occupy a position of power as First-Worlders to his Third, he is not able to revalue the word for *them*. Even a word whose meaning we might assume to be fixed, 'oncle,' turns out to function instead as an uneasy sign of a boy's desires and his father's feelings, but these desires and these feelings remain ill-defined. Indeed, we cannot be certain that the boy's desires and the father's feelings are not some-how the same and do not have the same meaning and ethical value. The very reticence of Rachid O's texts on this point emphasizes the fact that resistance – surely the central value, the very ethos, of *Le Passé simple* – is no longer possible, just as fixed meaning and value are impossible, indeed no longer exist, because everything of importance already means at least two contradictory things at once.

In *Le Passé simple*, Driss the narrator's achievement is to have com-pleted an Arabo-Mediterranean process of sexual maturation in order to take up in France a life that need not acknowledge the unassimilable elements of what he no longer is but still remembers. This achievement is commonplace in Rachid O's Morocco, however, and becomes instead an 'achievement' of uncertain value. No one in this writer's works – certainly not Rachid the narrator nor, then, we might suppose, Rachid O the author – criticizes the power imbalance demonstrated by the sorts of sexual relations practised between European and Moroccan men in Rachid O's novels, although the exploitation of at times very young boys is implied at virtually every mention of inter-cultural sex. The gay men in Switzerland do not object to pederasty itself, but rather to the word; they can practise pederasty in Morocco and reject the idea in Zurich.

Rachid O would seem to have faith in that curious idea common to both postcolonial and postmodern theory that discourse is all. However, his ability to manipulate language, to practise a polysemic poetics, does not prevent his French lover from gradually abandoning him for younger and younger Moroccan boys, or from leaving him behind when he returns to France. Nor does Rachid's ability to live out an ambiguous, ambivalent, complex, sexual life, his ability to live simultaneously in two different (mis?)representations of sexual practise, prevent the Moroccan police from interrogating him nor skinheads in Zurich from terrifying him. Rachid O can practise a polysemic poetics, but globalization places the practice of a *poethics* beyond his grasp. For Rachid O, the ethical dimension implied by the *h* embedded in the neologism *poethics* is absent from the poetics of his text. If in the globalized world meaning is always contingent and situational, that does not necessarily mean that the globalized world can account for the meaning of all contingencies and situations. When Rachid's father hears of the 'uncle's' untimely death, he reacts by going to sleep for twenty-four hours. Rachid laconically interprets this as a sign of grief, but we might see it instead as a pretext for silence, as a means of 'disappearing' the father from the text, from meaning, from discourse, and from ethical value. Perhaps the poetics of equivocal positions and shifting meanings, and its prolongation into a poetics of silence, is now the only possible act of resistance in globalized Morocco, since anything you say can and will be used against you if your only source of power is discursive.

NOTES

1 Chraïbi was not the first Moroccan writer of French Expression, but the notoriety of *Le Passé simple* was in part due to his being the initiator of a

modern Moroccan literature in French that did not conform to the newly triumphant Moroccan nationalism. In Morocco's neighbour Algeria, Kateb Yacine's *Nedjma* (Paris: Seuil, 1956) was similarly the initiating text of modern Algerian literature in French, but was much more easily – perhaps too easily – assimilated into Algerian nationalist ideology, at least until the acceleration of the Arabization of Algerian public life in the 1980s.

2 In his 1972 novel, *La Civilisation, ma mère!* Chraïbi represents a similar family (we are to understand that both are based at least distantly on Chraïbi's own family) quite differently. French ideology and especially French things bring liberation to a household depicted as far less corrupt than that of *Le Passé simple*.

3 Jacqueline Kaye and Abdelhamid Zoubir, *The Ambiguous Compromise: Language, Literature and National Identity in Algeria and Morocco* (London and New York: Routledge, 1990), 58.

4 See Jacqueline Arnaud, *Recherches sur la littérature maghrébine de langue française: le cas de Kateb Yacine* (Lille: Atelier National Reproduction des Thèses, 1982), 504.

5 The text insists on distinguishing between Arab and French (rather than between Moroccan and French or between Arab and Western), since according to the Moroccan nationalist ideology of the 1950s, which has only recently been nuanced to account for the majority 'Berbers' (yet another fraught category), all Moroccans were Arab, while the French were the most salient representatives of the West, since they were the colonizers. This essay further blurs this distinction by insisting that the sexual economy in which Driss participates is not restricted to Morocco or the Arab world, but is instead 'Arabo-Mediterranean,' since similar practices are to be found throughout the Mediterranean world, although they are less and less common in the member states of the European Union. In other words, the Mediterranean paradigm of same-sex sexual practices is likely to disappear first from the rest of the Mediterranean world, while it lingers in the Arab world in attenuated form.

6 This Arabo-Mediterranean process of sexual maturation is in sharp distinction to the predominant sexual paradigm of homosexuality in the twentieth-century West, in general, and France, in particular. The French paradigm focuses on self-discovery followed by self-liberation. In other words, once you know who you really are in terms of your sexual orientation, it is then your right or even responsibility to assure yourself the ability to live out the self you have discovered yourself to be. André Gide is one of the foremost architects of this discourse of liberation. As Lawrence Schehr points out, however, this 'discourse of liberation [is] predicated on the ine-

quality of subjects ... the freedom to be homosexual comes at the expense of someone else's lack of freedom to be homo- or heterosexual' (Lawrence Schehr, *Alcibiades at the Door* [Stanford: Stanford University Press, 1995], 116). Since Gide's literary and actual self-liberation depend on erotic contact with North African adolescent boys, I would further nuance Schehr's argument by insisting that Gide's freedom to be homosexual – in a specific, defined, and liminal space – depends on someone else's living in an erotic economy that does not define sexuality as a question of *liberté* or *égalité* or even *fraternité*. Gide's attraction to North African little boys is not just a question of pedophilia, but is also a reflection of his penetration into a sexual economy in which little boys would be the only sexual objects readily available to him, since sexual relations with men of his own age would have been considered grossly perverse and with women of any age dangerously transgressive.

7 The issue of what sort of sexual activity is permitted by Islam is fraught with complication. The simple answer is to insist that homosexuality is prohibited by Islam, although there is no such prohibition in the Qur'an itself. Numerous *hadith*, however, proscribe sex between men (though whether this includes sex between men and boys is subject to debate), although one of the rewards of Islamic paradise is the attention of cupbearers, pretty boys who serve the righteous. A classical Arabic term for what Euro-Americans would call homosexuality, although the categories are not perfectly congruous in this case, is *liwat*, which is taken from the proper name Lut or Lot, the biblical and qur'anic character who fled Sodom with his family. *Lata*, however, also derived from Lut/liwat, refers to the insertive partner only. Other, various and generally far more derogatory terms were used for the passive partner. The Arabo-Mediterranean homoerotics I describe in this essay are more deeply influenced by the sexual ideology (pre-existing Islam) that Arabs largely adopted once they conquered the major urban centres of other, much more ancient empires. I would argue that the contemporary ideology of heterosexuality in Arab countries is based primarily on pre-Islamic tribal traditions about ownership of women, which are also complicated by contact with the ideologies of conquered empires. For a thorough, if dated, discussion of *liwat*, see the *Encyclopaedia of Islam* article (2nd edition; Leiden: Brill, 1986),vol. 5, 669–776.

7 Rationality, Realism, and the Poet(h)ic Problem of Otherness: J.M. Coetzee's *Elizabeth Costello*

If by 'globalization' we mean a newly extensive and intensive connect-edness between formerly remote or disconnected peoples, then cer-tainly notions of such things as a 'global economy,' 'world culture,' and 'human interaction' have to be newly assessed. Our customary tools for comprehending and representing human behaviour, both in the social sciences and the humanities, no longer have the luxury of focusing only on discrete and separate objects, phenomena, and behaviour, since these are now mingling with and cross-referencing each other in unprece-dented and sometimes discrepant manners. Ironically, it would seem, then, that knowledge of others has become even more of a problem in an age when the distance between others is continually shrinking.

Yet for some, especially those social scientists predisposed towards rational choice theory, the matter seems uncomplicated: 'The combined assumptions of maximizing behaviour, market equilibrium, and stable preferences, used relentlessly and unflinchingly, form the heart of the economic approach ... I have come to the position that the economic approach is a comprehensive one that is applicable to all human behav-iour, be it behaviour involving money prices or imputed shadow prices, repeated or infrequent decisions, large or minor decisions, emo-tional or mechanical ends, rich or poor persons, men or women, adults or children, brilliant or stupid persons, patients or therapists, business-men or politicians, teachers or students.'[1] In short, the 'economic approach' would seem to overcome the unruliness of difference, subor-dinating it to a universally applicable analytic.

Indeed, while nearly all disciplines claim they hold the key to unlock one or another of life's mysteries, few have made such wholesale claims of universal applicability across disciplines and across all areas of human behaviour, both individual and collective. In short, with regard to describing human behaviour, no more powerfully 'elegant' model exists in the social sciences than rational choice theory. While Becker's claim may not seem excessive to some, I have come to the position that the 'economic approach' to understanding how humans behave extends well beyond the confines of the academy and the boardroom. Assumptions that all people maximize utility and have stable preferences – in other words, the basic tenets of economic rationality – have come to be embedded in everyday speech and in common sense, naturalized in sentences like 'Everyone knows X will do Y if they want Z,' and applied broadly to diverse populations in distant and near places.

Here I intend to suggest that the 'economic approach to human behaviour' can go only so far in helping us understand how people come to make choices, especially choices regarding their behaviour towards others. What does the saliency of this approach tell us about how we have come to relate to others, and about how we understand them to be part of the world we live in? How does this unabashedly universal formalistic model accommodate (or not) the heterogeneity of subjects living in the world today? And, perhaps most important of all, if we accept this parsimonious and elegant (again, to use the vocabulary of rational choice theory) model, so committed to the description of individual, self-interested choice, can it help us to understand how our choices might have anything to do with others? That is, what can it tell us about ethics in an age of unprecedented globalization?

It used to be that art, and particularly imaginative literature, was seen as the antidote to too much rationality: it was through art that the sphere of the irrational, the emotional, the intuitive, could help us understand human being in a more complex and rich sense. Human relations, in this perspective, were better understood in thicker ways, especially when dealing with distant others, whose notions of rationality and choice – if they had such notions at all – would often stand outside of the normative definitions of the modern West. It was (and is) argued that it was precisely the things that were written out of rational choice (as 'exogenous') that, on the contrary, form the core of what makes people both different and similar in profound ways. And it was art, so we once believed, that captured this complexity and subtlety.

In this essay, I ask how literature challenges the assumptions about, and descriptions of, human behaviour that appear in rational economic accounts. Can literature still afford us insights into diverse populations and cultures, or have 'we' human beings indeed become so similar as to be able to be read through a single formula? Does rationality as seen in this model of human behaviour and choice offer a uniform and useful benchmark with which to measure and evaluate the actions and choices of others? And these questions lead to a final query. Outside of mere economic and species survival, why and how do we know that others matter to us? In short, if 'globalization' includes the assumption that the world is now suddenly more intensively and extensively pulled together by common financial, economic, political, and ecological interests and concerns, and that the Other is now more immediately integrated into various spheres which used to seem to include predominantly or even solely an 'us,' particularly understood, then how are we supposed to address our new neighbours? How are our new neighbours presented to us, channelled into our consciousnesses, how is their behaviour (returning to Becker) made legible?

This essay focuses on how a literary text can indeed destabilize and denaturalize certain assumptions that undergird rational choice theory, and point the way towards a different sort of ethics, and on how it can bring forth different ways of construing and acting towards others. But in so doing, it refers to a text that destabilizes not only our notions of rationality and choice, but also the imaginative possibilities of literature. This text points the way out of the easy dichotomies of emotion versus rationality, economics versus art, and towards a more complex and vexed picture of human behaviour. It rescinds, I believe, the ideal vision of literature as antidote to reason and shows not only the interpenetration of these seemingly opposite arenas, but also an abiding problematic that is the legacy of this deconstructive operation. J.M. Coetzee's *Elizabeth Costello* precisely dramatizes the terrible logic of isolation that is produced when reason and art both come up short, and when they spill out over their respective domains.

Peter Abell presents a useful sketch of rational choice theory in relation to sociology.[2] As he describes it, rational choice theory strives 'to understand individual actors (which in specified circumstances may be collectivities of one sort or another) as acting, or more likely interacting, in a manner such that they can be deemed to be doing the best they can for themselves, given their objectives, resources, and circumstances, as they see them' (252). One of the most prevalent criticisms of rational choice theory, however, is that it does not handle well the issue of interaction and motivation, that it discounts ambiguous interactions and irrational motivations. Both these issues are, of course, intimately attached to the issue of regarding others and their choices, and, again, it is to art and literature that we have customarily looked for a way to imagine others.

In *Nuts and Bolts for the Social Sciences*, Jon Elster's discussions of storytelling and literature provide an interesting set of observations regarding the goals of rational choice theory, as well as its limitations.[3] Elster points to both the benefits and dangers of literature (and the kind of thinking it engages) within the rational choice enterprise. Thus, he gives credit to storytelling for its ability to present the individual with a set of choice options and a particular imaginative space for weighing those choices (and the example he gives is itself enormously revealing): 'Storytelling can suggest new, parsimonious explanations. Suppose that someone asserts that self-sacrificing or helping behaviour is conclusive proof that not all action is rational ... Could it not be in one's self-interest to help others? Could it not be rational to be swayed by one's emotions? The first step toward finding a positive answer is telling a *plausible story* to show how these possibilities could be realized' (7–8). But in the same passage, Elster cautions: 'storytelling can be harmful if it is mistaken for the real thing.' Furthermore, 'With some ingenuity – and many scholars have a great deal – one can *always* tell a story in which things are turned upside down' (8). In sum, storytelling allows us to increase the body of information upon which we form our beliefs, but fiction also may be deployed to instantiate false or irrational beliefs. It contributes to a body of emotions that Elster calls 'counterfactual emotions,' which arise 'out of what could have happened but didn't' (63). In other words, the benefit that storytelling might offer rational choice-making in terms of its speculative and hypothetical power is offset by its illusory quality, its tendency to be confused for fact, for turning things 'upside down.' In this case, the key issue will become, as it does in *Elizabeth Costello*, that of literary realism – a mode of constraining the full range of fiction into plausible accounts of what can be significant for certain characters. And this involves not only rational choices but emotionally charged ones, as well. Elster describes, for example, 'other-oriented emotions,' that is, emotions predicated on the belief that 'it could have been me' (64). We can see in these last two instances a connection that points directly at fiction and affect: storytelling allows the individual to speculate on a range of possible scenarios; 'other-oriented emotions' predicate stories in which the individual might feel the effect of actions upon a hypothetical stand-in for him- or herself. These two issues – realism and otherness – are announced early on in Coetzee's novel and remain key elements of its thesis.

At the very beginning of the novel, we are presented with a statement on literary realism that brings together the topics of narrative art, rationality, choice-making, and otherness. Here, Coetzee borrows precisely the discourse of problem-solving and choice-making: 'There is first of all the problem of the opening, namely, how to get us from where we are, which is, as yet, nowhere, to the far bank. It is a simple bridging problem, a problem of knocking together a bridge. People solve such problems every day. They solve them, and having solved them push on.'[4] We find here two key elements that tie together the issue of rationality and otherness. First, of course, is the idea of choice – in the poetics of realism one identifies one's preferences, one's utility, and then works out the ways to remove obstacles and maximize efficiencies towards that end. But, secondly, the poetics of realism is also a poet(h)ics, for that bridge is built not only between discrete choices and actions but also between people and other creatures of the earth. In fact, the latter connection is implicated in the former. The connection between *those* two relies on and puts tremendous pressure on the imagination, so much so that it may strain against the constraints of reason. It is no accident that Coetzee's fictional protagonist, the speaker of these lines, presents him with this key problem of otherness and imagination: how to bridge the distance between his biological and biographical self and the sixty-six-year-old Australian female author who is his chief character and organizing point of view. How will he solve the engineering problem he sets forth for all realist literature? [5]

Costello confidently asserts that for realism the task is to 'supply the particulars [and] allow the significations to emerge of themselves' (4). However, the problem set forth in the novel is an historical one: it relies on a reader who is able to see the bridge and to connect the particulars into a meaningful unit. Moreover, the novel will proceed to outline a problematic in which it is precisely the difficulty of envisioning a broader, global set of readers, each bringing her or his set of interests and values to the text, that makes signifying a fraught and unsure venture. Time and again in this text, we find that the significations do not easily or unambiguously 'emerge of themselves.' Coetzee suggests that the audience for realist literature may be deaf to those connections and significations, and this is in no small way attached to a different and problematic condition of understanding why and how different people who now exist within our sphere of life (as opposed to existing as distant and distinct) act.

Again, the beginning of the novel sets up the conditions of its success and failure. On the one hand, Costello opines: 'Realism is driven to invent situations ... in which characters give voice to contending ideas and thereby in a certain sense embody them. The notion of *embodying* turns out to be pivotal. In such debates ideas do not and indeed cannot float free: they are tied to the speakers by whom they are enounced, and generated from the matrix of individual interests out of which their speakers act in the world' (9). On the other hand, as we will see, the characters so invented by Coetzee embody chaotic and inconsistent ideas, and the entire notion of an identifiable individual is shown to be questionable, just as the line between Self and Other is seen to be blurred. As such, characters are intensely problematic anchors for any realist position, and as a consequence of this, the 'matrix of interests' thus turns out to be anything but coherent; rather, we are confronted by a matrix composed of conflictual gestures and aspirations. It is critical here to insist that the problematic of the novel itself is not (simply) an arbitrarily invented series of paradoxes; the problematic is indeed produced by the twin failures of artistic realism and rationality.

Both the failure of 'bridging' and the incoherence of interests stem from the same source: the essential inability to imagine an other. This ability has been a cornerstone in Western philosophical aesthetics since Kant, and has an intimate connection with ethics. It shows up especially in Kant's notion of the *sensus communis*, a term which is difficult to translate fully, but which might be called a common sense (*not* 'common sense'): 'For the principle [of *sensus communis*] while it is only subjective, being yet assumed as a subjective universal (a necessary idea for every one), could, in what concerns the consensus of differing judging Subjects, demand universal assent like an objective principle, provided we were assured of our subsumption under it being correct. This indeterminate norm of a common sense is as a matter of fact, presupposed by us' (85). As Antoon Van Den Braembussche argues: 'Kant tries to construct sensus communis as an operation of reflection which enables us to free ourselves from our own prejudices by comparing "our own judgment with human reason in general" ... We compare our judgments not with the actual but rather with the merely possible ones of others in order to put ourselves in the position of everyone else.'[6] It is, in short, a particular form of empathy that tries to intuit the universally shared affect of a work of art: 'we introduce this fundamental feeling not as a private feeling, but as a public sense.' One's disinterested free play of the imagination is thus an image of the morally good; the *sensus communis* is connected to acting in such a way that one's actions can be the basis for a universal order. In short, the private is connected to the intersubjective and the public.[7] And within the first dozen pages of the novel we find that the imagining of others is articulated as a core element of Costello's dicta: 'It is otherness that is the challenge. Making up someone other than yourself. Making up a world for him to move in' (12).

What becomes clear as the novel progresses is that the true difficulty of this challenge is to create a *plausible* world for the fictional character, a 'realistic' one which, according to what we have learned thus far, must be able to present a matrix of interests and behaviours associated with that person as a unified subject. The reader's imaginative construction of that 'bridge' between discrete acts and events forms the crux of the realist project, but it must be supported at base by a faith in the consistent behaviour of an individual character, and *Elizabeth Costello* not only blurs the line between human beings, but also between humans and animals. Costello ups the ante in her next articulation of realism. She presents a lecture entitled 'What Is Realism?' and alludes to a parable by Kafka in which an ape (or so it appears) stands before an audience and delivers a speech. Costello uses this as a challenge to her own audience: can they reside in that space in which the human and the ape can cohabit a form of the imagination? What is our capacity to imagine otherness in a trans-species fashion? What do our senses of the real and the rational rely upon as foundational, and how does that foundation act as a barrier to other modes of reasoning or imagining? Turning precisely then to the act of writing fiction, she questions the bounds of rhetoric, the tropes and figures that stand outside its signifying protocols:[8] 'For all we know, the speaker may not "really" be an ape, may simply be a human being like ourselves deluded into thinking himself an ape, or a human being presenting himself, with heavy irony, for rhetorical purposes, as an ape' (18).

This is not a trans-historical question regarding the elasticity of the imagination and poetic language. As I argued above, Coetzee locates the problem of poetics, realism, and imagination at a specific moment in time when we witness a particular strain placed upon the logic and reason of realism, a crisis predicated by the expanding field of otherness: 'There used to be a time when we knew. We used to believe that when the text said, "on the table stood a glass of water," there was indeed a table, and a glass of water on it, and we had only to look at the word-mirror of the text to see them. But all that has ended. The word-mirror is broken, irreparably, it seems. About what is really going on in the lecture hall your guess is as good as mine: men and men, men and apes, apes and men, apes and apes ... There used to be a time, we believe, when we could say who we were. Now we are just performers speaking our parts. The bottom has dropped out' (19). There is no way to avoid the radical quality of the last statement, especially, for if 'we' as human subjects are simply performers playing parts set forth by history, then with the blurring of boundaries, the evaporation of the containers of the real, with the flooding-in of otherness, comes too the dissolution of subjectivity. And yet this dissolution is regarded in *Elizabeth Costello* as not necessarily a bad thing. There is a wonderful and at the same time terrible price to pay for meeting the challenge of inventing something truly other than oneself.

Crucially, to fully embrace the potential of this terrible success, one must first abandon reason as absolute: 'Both reason and seven decades of life experience tell me that reason is neither the being of the universe nor the being of God. On the contrary, reason looks to me suspiciously like the being of human thought; worse than that, like the being of one tendency in human thought. Reason is the being of a certain spectrum of human thinking' (67). And to maintain the belief that reason is universal rather than particular is to maintain the boundaries of the imagination and the limits of the Self: 'Might it not be that the phenomenon we are examining here is, rather than the flowering of a faculty that allows access to the secrets of the universe, the specialism of a rather narrow self-regenerating intellectual tradition whose forte is reasoning, in the same way that the forte of chess players is playing chess, which for its own motives it tries to install at the centre of the universe? Yet, although I see that the best way to win acceptance from this learned gathering would be for me to join myself, like a tributary stream running into a great river, to the great Western discourse of man versus beast, of reason versus unreason, something in me resists, foreseeing in that step the concession of the entire battle' (69).

Costello resists this concession because it would not only acknowledge the assumptions that undergird that dichotomy, but also because it would also leave intact the illusion that the question of reason and its separation from unreason is a neutral, unmotivated one. Instead, she sees behind the very posing of such questions a continuing program of subordination, of dominance that allows precisely for the maintenance of the boundary between Self and Other. She uses psychologist Wolfgang Köhler's treatise of 1917, 'The Mentality of Apes,' as a prime example. Köhler tries an experiment on an ape he names 'Sultan,' withholding food from the him until the ape is forced to use his intelligence in a way that confirms Köhler's assumptions of what an animal *should* think. 'As long as Sultan continues to think the wrong thoughts, he is starved. He is starved until the pangs of hunger are so intense, so over-riding, that he is forced to think the right thought, namely, how to go about getting the bananas ... From the purity of speculation (Why do men behave like this?) he is relentlessly propelled towards lower, prac-tical, instrumental reason (How does one use this to get that?)' (73).

Thus, as Costello says, 'A carefully plotted psychological regimen conducts him *away* from ethics and metaphysics towards the humbler reaches of practical reason' (74). Indeed, to put it more bluntly, as long as the ape thinks in any other fashion than pragmatically, his behaviour confirms his status as animal (and not human), and the creature is pun-ished. This critique has, of course, a broader application: as long as *any* animal or sentient creature defies its placement in the schematization of reason, it will be forcefully disciplined. What does this tell us about our stance towards other human beings? Conversely, and this is Costello's next topic, much as we seek to maintain a careful watch over the bor-ders between human and animal life, policing the line with reason as our yardstick, we can also relegate other human beings to the other side when our motives require. This is only possible, Costello claims, when we deny ourselves the faculty of sympathy. And this brings her discus-sion fully back into the realm of her declared topic, realism and litera-ture. At this point in Costello's disquisition, the demand for rationality placed on others is replaced by a demand placed upon ourselves to be able to feel sympathy.

We recall that the key challenge presented to the author is to create fictional others, and worlds in which they would act. And yet this chal-lenge seems insurmountable precisely because it puts us face to face with a number of imperatives: for example, how to displace (or at least 'bracket') oneself enough to allow for the imagining of an other that endows that other with her or his (or its) own sphere of action and choice, without mandating that the other has to act as we do? And yet, how can we make a bridge between their discrete acts and our realm of understanding reasonable, that is, 'realistic,' if we do not retain (as if we could truly give it up) our own particular sense of the real, the rational, the reasonable? This line of questioning thus links the ethical aspect of writing to that of being human in general. Costello is moved to make the bold assertion: 'If I can think my way into the existence of a being who has never existed, then I can think my way into the existence of a bat or a chimpanzee or an oyster, any being with whom I share the substrate of life' (80). And yet we are forced to wonder if mere 'sharing' is all we (can) do in life, for both practical and moral reasons. The move into the realm of the real and historical exerts tremendous critical pressure on Costello's idealism (though from what we have learned about her, that word does not exactly fit), not to mention on her politics.

Using the Holocaust as her historical example, Costello argues, 'The question to ask should not be: Do we have something in common – reason, self-consciousness, a soul – with other animals? ... The horror is that the killers refused to think themselves into the place of their victims, as did everyone else ... In other words, they closed their hearts. The heart is the seat of a faculty, *sympathy*, that allows us to share at times the being of another' (79). Taken alone, this argument seems noncontroversial. It is when Costello makes more explicit what she means by 'other animals' that her audience rises up in protest: how can she compare the slaughter of humans with the 'culling' of livestock? Is she not desecrating the human in order to elevate the animal and to create a world in which we 'share' the planet? The issue thus recedes from being a purely ethical one and emerges full force as an historical and eminently political one.

Along with this forced entry into the realm of the political, we note, as well, a logical problem. An audience member thus questions Costello: '[T]he very fact that you can be arguing against this reasoning, exposing its falsity, means that you put a certain faith in the power of reason, of true reason as opposed to false reason' (100). Behind every critique of reason there is another sort of rationality that founds that critique. It is at this point in the novel that, as if this line of reasoning were exhausted, the scene abruptly shifts to a new locale: Africa.

Costello there meets her sister Blanche, now Sister Bridget, and finds herself defending precisely reason, beauty, and choice. We find that Costello's beliefs respond to this new environment and to her tenuous relationship with her sister. Costello finds herself unwittingly recruited to be the defender of not only humanism, but the faculty of reason. And reason is no better borne out than in choice. Emblematic in this section is the episode of Joseph the woodcarver, a person revered by the religious community for his absolute dedication to God, which he manifests every minute by his laborious carving, over and over again, of crucifixes. In response to her sister's comment that Joseph can take gratification in Jesus' joy over this 'choice,' Costello replies sardonically, 'I would think Jesus would be gladder still ... if he knew that

Joseph had some choice. That Joseph had not been dragooned into piety' (138). In the same way that Sultan the ape is 'dragooned' away from ethical questions and into the sheer practicality of remaining alive, Costello claims that Joseph has been lured away from choosing a broad range of aesthetic life (which she relates to the ideal aesthetic of the ancient Greeks) and into the mere repetition of a single figure, depicted in exactly the same pose and posture, over and over again. To her, this makes no sense. Yet to Blanche it not only makes perfect sense to adhere to this constraint, which is a source of joy, not suffering, but it is also senseless to abandon it in order to gain something so pointless in her sister's aesthetic: 'I do not need to consult novels ... to know what pettiness, what baseness, what cruelty human beings are capable of' (128). That is to say, even in sheer economic terms, the cost is hardly worth it; in fact, it is to trade down one life choice for another. Frustrated by the failure to win her argument with her sister, Costello undergoes another transformation.

First performing the role of aesthete against the hegemony of cold reason, and then the role of liberal secular humanist armed with reason against the hegemony of cold, choiceless religious passion, Elizabeth next takes on the role of a moralist who will constrain the very realm of artistic choice that she has just championed against religious constraint. She is invited to give a talk in Amsterdam on 'Witness, Silence, Censorship,' and during that period becomes deeply disturbed by Paul West's novel *The Very Rich Hours of Count von Stauffenberg*, in which the author offers a horrifyingly graphic account of the final, tortured existence of the conspirators against Hitler.[9] If previously she championed literary art for its aesthetic humanistic value, and for its ethically critical ability to put us in touch with others of all species, now Costello draws back and blocks off certain 'realities' from our scope of empathy, for our own sake: 'She is not longer sure that people are always improved by what they read. Furthermore, she is not sure that writers who venture into the darker territories of the soul always return unscathed. She has begun to wonder whether writing what one desires, any more than reading what one desires, is in itself a good thing' (160). We have come some distance, then, from the imperative to be able to choose one's poetic investments, as seen in the episode of the crucifix-maker, to the delimiting of aesthetic choice found in this passage. Indeed, choice is taken out of the realm of aesthetics and placed squarely into the realm of ethics: 'she no longer believes that storytelling is good in itself ... If she ... had to choose between telling a story and doing good, she would rather, she thinks, do good' (167). Nevertheless, this transition is not founded in anything logical or rational. With neither aesthetic nor rational criteria to guide her, Costello is cast into the realm of sheer faith, or belief. And this is indeed the subject of the penultimate sequence of the novel.

Costello finds herself in a Kafkaesque situation, in a remote Italian village, petitioning before an anonymous tribunal to cross over to 'the other side,' and we seem to have come full circle back to the novel's initial statement cited at the start of this essay regarding the first problem of realism: 'There is first of all the problem of the opening, namely, how to get us from where we are, which is, as yet, nowhere, to the far bank. It is a simple bridging problem, a problem of knocking together a bridge. People solve such problems every day. They solve them, and having solved them push on.' We have come, in other words, to the final 'bridge' to be crossed, the final solution to be arrived at, and it is a problem precisely of crossing over, between events, locales, and subjectivities, between life and death. In this state of limbo, Coetzee plumbs the depths of language and articulation, of intersubjectivity, of Costello's adamant individual will and the social nature of writing and of speaking to and with an other.

The judges have one and only one question: what does Costello believe in? As should be clear by this point in my essay, the novel is about nothing if not the inventory of possible modes of belief: in reason, in art, in religion, in other human beings, in our capacity to imagine lives other than our own, and in the reasonableness of choices we ourselves would perhaps not have made (poetic and otherwise). Here, near the very end of the novel, we find Costello unable, or unwilling, to admit to believing in anything, even if it means release: a highly irrational choice, if her intent is to reach the other side. Naming her belief will mean release precisely because, according to the belief of the tribunal, it will attest to nothing less than her humanity: 'Without beliefs we are not human' (200). But Costello rejects this statement, interpreting it as requiring that beliefs be rational: 'Beliefs are not the only ethical supports we have. We can rely on our hearts as well. That is all. I have nothing more to say' (203). Yet, crucially, the retreat is not from rationality to sentimentality, and the reliance on 'our hearts' leads rather to an evacuation of self and a merging with the other. Costello's refusal to state her beliefs is paradoxically founded on a belief in an indistinct and fluctuating self. She defiantly asks the tribunal: 'But who am I, who is this *I*, this *you*? We change from day to day, and we also stay the same. No *I*, no *you* is more fundamental than any other. You might as well ask which is the true Elizabeth Costello: the one who made the first statement or the one who made the second. My answer is, both are true. Both. And neither. *I am an other'* (221).

At this point in the novel, the 'bridge' to be made between individuals and the significance of their choices and actions collapses, and this also marks the implosion of the enclosure of the Self. However, this is a riposte that has been with us since the beginning of Costello's lecture on realism. We can thus read *Elizabeth Costello* as following the vacillating, inconsistent trajectory of reason, emotion, belief, art, and religion, all ultimately tied to the problematic of otherness: how do we 'know' or understand others; what constitutes our emotional response to their lives; how can reason, art, religion form the foundations upon which we meet the other; and, crucially, are we capable of conceptualizing ourselves either as apart from, or as indistinct from, the other? And what are the costs of both conceptualizations? While the novel spends the bulk of its time challenging us to imagine otherwise, the end of the novel presents the vertiginous descent into a maelstrom not only of oneness but also of paralysis.

This conclusion is dramatically articulated in the text that introduces the postscript to the novel, Hugo von Hofmannstahl's 'Letter to Lord Chandos from Lord Bacon': 'It is as if everything, everything that exists, everything I can recall, everything my confused thinking touches on, means something' (226). This statement achieves its full significance only in the light of, again, Costello's opening comments on realism: for realism the task is to 'supply the particulars [and] allow the significations to emerge of themselves' (4). The problem now before us is precisely that there is an overabundance of particulars, so much so that everything 'means something,' and that the discriminations and hierarchies secured by reason are under attack: with the proliferation of diversity, reason turns to confusion.

The co-extensivity of language and being, of rational discrimination and ontological indistinction, is paralleled in the companion piece to Lord Chandos's agony over the influx of irrationality. I am referring to Lady Chandos's agony over the influx of otherness, as found in the 'Letter of Elizabeth, Lady Chandos, to Francis Bacon': 'All is allegory, says my Philip. Each creature is key to all other creatures. A dog sitting in a patch of sun licking itself, says he, is at one moment a dog and at the next a vessel of revelation. But I ask you can I live with rats and dogs and beetles crawling through me day and night, drowning and gasping, scratching me, tugging me, urging me deeper and deeper into revelation – how? *We are not made for revelation'* (229). This seems to be a final rebuttal of Costello's project of writing, a rebuttal of the challenge of projecting oneself outside oneself and of 'sharing' the planet with all other life forms. Whether through art or religion, this project or challenge, and the attendant revelation, are to be rejected, for they will ultimately strip one of reason and selfhood at once. And yet even as language itself is dragged along unremittingly by a flood of otherness, as each creature allegorizes another, and each word then bleeds into another ('It is like a contagion, saying one thing always for another'), the final appeal is made precisely through language, and more precisely through writing, to a man who is known to the writer of the letter as one who 'selects' his words and 'sets them in place' and 'builds his judgments' with discretion and discernment. And here, in this linguistic free fall, we can see the trace of Levinas's call to radically reconceive our ontological presumptions and see the emergence of self as always preceded by an irreducible Other. Levinas himself uses language as a key corollary for this: 'Everything depends on the possibility of vibrating with a meaning that is not synchronized with the speech that captures it and cannot be fitted into its order; everything depends on the possibility of a signification that would signify in an irreducible disturbance.'[10] In this passage from *Elizabeth Costello,* I would assert, we find such a disturbance perpetrated by the constant slippage of signifiers, unmoored from 'order' and madly referencing themselves and not things (anymore). And this departure from 'realism' itself is not unlike the psychic disturbance described by Lacan.

Thus we note that the structure being built at the end of this novel is not the realist bridge between particulars ('It is a simple bridging problem, a problem of knocking together a bridge'), but rather a wall: 'Yet he writes to you, as I write to you, who are known above all men to select your words and set them in place and build your judgments as a mason builds a wall with bricks. Drowning, we write out of our separate fates. Save us. Your obedient servant, Elizabeth C. this 11 September 1603.' This wall is the barrier between radical irrationality, as found in the vertiginous semantic slippage into and amongst otherness, and a specific kind of realism signalled by linguistic stability ('you select your words and set them in place and build your judgments as a mason builds a wall with bricks').

Coetzee's text rearticulates the ardent hope that literature can deliver others to us, and us to others, in an unreasonable, irrational, and eminently total manner, and yet it shows behind the dissolution of distance and of singular being, behind a successful poet(h)ics, a maddening slide beyond the ken of the mind, a journey across a bridge that leads into a horrible mystery that can only be intimated with trepidation. Dissatisfied with the rational because of its hegemonic dominance of mental activity, its monopoly on the definition of what it is that separates humans from humans and humans from animals, and the cruelty that follows in the wake of such a separation, *Elizabeth Costello* nonetheless draws no conclusion, ultimately, but only a wall, and in so doing forces upon us, the reader, a choice of rationality enabled by linguistic fixity and 'realism,' or madness brought about by too much Otherness. And yet both sides of the choice are problematic. If we have been disabused of the 'economic approach' as an adequate formula with which to understand all human behaviour, if Costello has punctured the illusion of the rational as somehow transcendent and pure, then she has also laid bare the logical consequences of embracing otherness absolutely.

What can we learn, then, from this text with regard to 'globalization' and poetics? What I will argue here is that the missing term is the political. Elizabeth Costello's cynicism can be traced, ultimately, to an observation she makes early on, one that we now need to revisit:

> There used to be a time when we knew. We used to believe that when the text said, 'on the table stood a glass of water,' there was indeed a table, and a glass of water on it, and we had only to look at the word-mirror of the text to see them. But all that has ended. The word-mirror is broken, irreparably, it seems. About what is really going on in the lecture hall your guess is as good as mine: men and men, men and apes, apes and men, apes and apes ... There used to be a time, we believe, when we could say who we were. Now we are just performers speaking our parts. The bottom has dropped out. (19)

This remarkable passage contains, indeed, nearly the entire trajectory of the novel, moving from an age when knowledge was sure, when rationality did its work, and, co-extensively, when literary language did its work, as well: when the text said something, it conjured up that thing in our minds and in our system of belief. Words mirrored things and projected them into our consciousness, as well. In short, literature could do its work because the reader was able to make the connections between words and images, particular events and actions and some intended significance. One could, in short, have a particularly realistic set of beliefs and assumptions underwrite one's choice-making.[11] But the breaking of the word-mirror has to be seen not only in the context of a rupturing of literary functionality, but also in the context of a spill-over effect from the text to the world, in general, and it is a world which itself contains too much alterity, a world in which the global intrudes and insists on being fully recognized as other. This is where the political comes into play, even if only in a tangential and perhaps unmention-able way. And it does so through an ontological crisis concerning not just the social, but also the species. In this crisis, realism itself seems to fall victim to unbridled otherness. Who are 'we' (to go back to the testi-mony delivered to the tribunal)?

It is this aspect of the novel, beyond the simultaneous dissolution of both rationality and art, that is most troubling. For Coetzee seems to be saying that the dissolution of the rational and the aesthetic occurs within a systemic meltdown that takes along with it the ethical and political. And all this is attributable in no small degree to the invasion of otherness, and the failure of the liberal imagination to make good on its aspiration to accommodate it. For as much as romantic liberal human-ists welcome the opportunity to share the planet, the novel suggests that without a foundation of reasonable belief to secure the project, we are at a loss to survive the tidal wave of difference, because it will have taken effective political action with it. The 'globe' will outdo us, not because of its mass or multiplicity, but because we have no workable political instrument with which to mediate and negotiate a settlement.

NOTES

I would like to thank Heather Houser for very useful discussions regarding Coetzee and Elizabeth Costello.

1 Gary Becker, The Economic Approach to Human Behavior (Chicago: University of Chicago Press, 1976). Gary Becker was the Nobel laureate for economic science in 1992.
2 Peter Abell, 'Sociological Theory and Rational Choice Theory,' in Social The-ory, ed. Bryan Turner (Oxford: Blackwell, 1996), 252–77.
3 Jon Elster, Nuts and Bolts for the Social Sciences (Cambridge: Cambridge Uni-versity Press, 1989).
4 J.M. Coetzee, Elizabeth Costello (New York: Viking, 2003), 1. All subsequent references are to this edition.

5 See Derek Attridge, *J.M. Coetzee and the Ethics of Reading* (Chicago and London: University of Chicago Press, 2004), 192–205, for a useful discussion of the role of realism in this novel, as well as for a fascinating account of Coetzee's use of Costello's speeches in his own lecturing.

6 '*Sensus communis*: Clarifications of a Kantian Concept,' http://home.concepts-ict.nl/~kimmerle/framebraemb.htm. For more on the subject of the imagination and community, see my essay 'Pre-emption, Perpetual War, and the Future of the Imagination,' *boundary 2* 33.1 (Spring 2006): 151–70.

7 I thank Regenia Gagnier for discussions on the Sublime and Beautiful.

8 See Paul de Man, *Allegories of Reading: Figural Language in Rousseau, Nietzsche, Rilke, and Proust* (New Haven: Yale University Press, 1979).

9 Paul West, *The Very Rich Hours of Count von Stauffenberg* (Woodstock, NY: The Overlook Press, 1989, ca. 1980).

10 Emmanuel Levinas, 'Enigma and Phenomenon,' in *Basic Philosophical Writings*, ed. Adriaan T. Peperzak, Simon Critchley, and Robert Bernasconi (Bloomington and Indianapolis: Indiana University Press, 1996), 67. The relation of this 'irreducible disturbance' and the issue of politics and responsibility is drawn in Judith Butler, *Giving an Account of Oneself* (New York: Fordham University Press, 2006), 83–101, and elsewhere.

11 See M.H. Abrams, *The Mirror and the Lamp: Romantic Theory and the Critical Tradition* (New York: Oxford Press, 1953). See also the work of Elster and of Paisley Livingston (for example, 'Intentionalism in Aesthetics,' *New Literary History* 29.4 [1989]: 831–46) on the idea of authorial choice and intentionality.

8 Planetary Longings: Sitting in the Light of the Great Solar TV

MARY LOUISE PRATT

In the summer of 2002, at the mercy of a dogmatically anti-carnivorous son, I found myself in a tiny 'hole in the wall' vegetarian restaurant in the city of Cuzco in Peru. It was a very simple place where a tasty, nourishing meal was served for pennies to an entirely Peruvian, mostly male clientele. The walls, I noticed, were decorated with painted space-age images of stars, suns, and flying saucers. Shortly after sitting down, we realized that the customers were all intently watching a TV screen mounted from the ceiling. It was broadcasting, not the national networks, but a series of videotapes from abroad documenting the visits of extraterrestrial beings over the history of the earth.

The little restaurant, it turned out, was run by a new religious sect of 'divine revelation' called Alfa y Omega (Alpha and Omega), whose two central symbols are the lamb of god and the flying saucer (see pp. 208–9). According to the pamphlet I bought, Alfa y Omega's doctrines are received in the form of telepathic messages communicated by 'un divino padre solar (extraterrestre) procedente de los lejanos soles Alfa y Omega en la galaxia de Trino del microcosmos o reino de los cielos' [a divine solar (extraterrestrial) father from the distant suns of Alpha and Omega in the Trino galaxy of the microcosm or kingdom of the heavens].[1] These 'doctrinas para el tercer milenio' [doctrines for the third millennium] are preserved in four thousand scrolls, which explain 'el origen, causa y destino de todas las cosas conocidas y desconocidas' [the origin, cause, and destiny of all things known and unknown]. '¿Ya ingresaste?' [Have you joined up?] the waiter asked me when he sold me the pamphlet. 'Not yet,' I replied.

Like other post- and neo-Christian spiritual movements today, Alfa y Omega emphasizes, not belief or faith, but knowledge and understand-

Publicity material from Alfa y Omega, distributed in Cuzco, Peru (2002). Courtesy Asociación Filosófica, Científica y Cultural Alfa y Omega, Lima, Peru (www.alfayomega.com.pe).

ing. Like them, it is strongly anti-materialist. In its writings, Alfa y Omega refers to capitalism as 'la extraña ley del oro' [the strange law of gold] and announces 'un nuevo reinado de la verdad, la justicia y la igualdad con cielo nuevo, tierra nueva y conocimiento nuevo' [a new kingdom of truth, justice, and equality with a new heaven, a new earth, and new knowledge]. Its signifying machines are elaborate and operate in the micro and the macro. For example, the pamphlets on sale in the restaurant describe a moral calculus which evaluates a person's state of virtue by assigning points of darkness and light according to the number of molecules in the bodies of the people whom one has hindered or helped. Adoption of orphans is an act that gains many points of light. Then there is the Gran Televisión Solar, the Great Solar Television, a huge screen in the sky which sometime in the future will display everyone's sins 'en la presencia de toda la humanidad' [in the presence of all humanity]. The aspects of all this I want to underscore are, first, the emphasis on knowledge rather than belief, and, second, the global and planetary optic. The extraterrestrial, it seems, is mainly there as a point from which to define the terrestrial and the human in planetary terms.

Alfa y Omega was founded by a self-taught man from the Andean province of Ancash, Peru. It is one of many new philosophical-religious-cosmological formations that have appeared in the context of expansionist and predatory neo-liberal capitalism, the new empire. Like others of its kind, Alfa y Omega offers forms of signification that, on the one hand, reject materialism, consumerism, and the failed narrative of development, and, on the other, construct a global and planetary imaginary, a vision that interpellates 'all of humanity' – visibilized, hypothetically, by the Great Solar TV.

Such formations, it seems to me, respond to some particularly grotesque and systematic peculiarities of the reorganizing of the world by neo-liberalism. I refer, in particular, to a central contradiction: the idea of a global marketplace by which neo-liberalism legitimates itself is completely at odds with the dramatic polarization of wealth that its 'structural adjustments' actually produce. Neo-liberal policies exacerbate economic inequality, concentrating economic power in the hands of ever smaller numbers of people, and relentlessly immiserating everyone else. One result are vast zones of exclusion inhabited by millions of socially organized people who are and know themselves to be utterly dispensable to the global order of production and consumption.[2] All over the planet, then, large sectors of organized humanity live conscious of their redundancy to a global economic order which is able to make them aware of its existence, and their superfluity. People recognize themselves as expelled from the narratives of futurity the order offers, with little hope of entering or re-entering. This expulsion from history has been accompanied by rapid pauperization, ecological devastation, and a destruction of lifeways unprecedented in human history. My impression is that such a situation has not existed before now, certainly not on this planetary scale.

One result of this expulsion and immiseration is despair, arising both from material lack and from the semantic vacuum left by the collapse of narratives of progress. The UN reports a rise worldwide in individual and collective suicide, and there are whole societies that analysts say appear to be destroying themselves. The anthropologist James Ferguson refers ironically to a new form of cosmopolitanism in which more and more people across the globe speak of the place where they live as a place where there is nothing, where nothing happens, where you would never want to live. Everything of value is elsewhere.[3]

The crisis of futurity is probably most intense among the young, who often find that even the prospect of founding a household has passed out of reach. The brilliant Chilean novelist Diamela Eltit recently explored these conditions in her 2002 novel entitled *Mano de obra* [Workforce], whose protagonists are a group of young people who live together and work at a supermarket.[4] In a pitiless, often clinical language, Eltit evokes the despair, ruthless exploitation, obscene excesses and scarcities, and dehumanization that accompany life under unfettered commodity capitalism. In the supermarket, we witness the mercantilization of the *res publica*. The idea of rationality as a principle in opposition to chaos becomes a joke. In a brilliant novelistic manoeuvre, Eltit develops a corresponding domestic sphere for her characters. It is a multi-sexual, post-family heterotopia in which the characters struggle to create sustainable living arrangements despite their poverty and vulnerability. Their efforts dissolve into cruelty, isolation, and psychological breakdown. The characters are incapacitated by the levels of submission imposed by their economic insecurity. They become incapable of generating alternatives. Eventually, they lose their jobs, and, expelled even from exploitation, they end up reaffirming the magic power of white male authoritarianism – a dénouement with horrible resonance in post-dictatorship Chile. Expelled from their rented house, they enter the semantic vacuum of the street. They can be made superfluous (and super-fluid); they cannot, however, be made to disappear.

What I referred to above as zones of exclusion extend to vast regions of the globe, both rural regions and the vast impoverished settlements that mushroom around cities.[5] Such zones and their inhabitants are brought into view in the metropole on an occasional basis, and always in the codes of the abject, by epidemics, genocidal warfare, or 'natural' disasters like the tsunami that struck coastal southeast Asia in December 2004. The codes of abjection elide the fact that these are social spaces where life is being *lived otherwise*. Where identities cannot be organized around agricultural cycles, salaried work, consumption, communal lifeways, or personal projects like upward mobility, life has to be lived, organized, and understood by other means. People generate ways of life, values, knowledges and wisdoms, pleasures, meanings, hopes, forms of transcendence, relatively independent of the ideologies of the market. Alpha and Omega is one example; Zapatismo and other new forms of indigenous activism are another. In other words, behind the falsely inclusive smokescreen of the market, neo-liberalism creates vast human dramas that cannot be understood or even perceived from within neo-liberalism's own coordinates.[6] Like Eltit's young protagonists, marginalized citizens fall off the maps of markets, while continuing, in huge numbers, to exist and make their lives. These dramas of expulsion and exclusion involve an unprecedented scale of human suffering. They also give rise to knowledges, subjectivities, practices, agencies, and epistemes – that are not necessarily adapted to markets, and not necessarily functional for capitalism.

It is not for nothing, then, that the founder of Alpha and Omega identifies himself as a *futurologo*, a 'futurologue.' The inhabitants of zones of exclusion face a constant crisis of futurity. Narratives of modernization and progress no longer correspond either to their realities or to their hopes. Traditional or local knowledges are often attached to ways of life under siege like subsistence agricultural life with all the collective genius that makes it possible. Under the dictates of the global economic administrators (the World Bank and the IMF), state-based education systems dissolve or are vocationalized, expelling speculative, philosophical, or civic thought along with the critical, analytical, historical knowledges that enable subjects to locate themselves historically and ethically.[7] Hence perhaps the emphasis in the new religions, or at least some of them, on knowledge and understanding, rather than belief and obedience. Alpha and Omega, for instance, emphasizes 'Philosophical thoughts' in its doctrinal writings: 'La sabiduría,' its pamphlets say, 'es un don divino: cultivarla y perfeccionarla es nuestro deber' [Knowledge is a divine gift: cultivating and perfecting it is our duty]. 'Un hombre ignorante es un muerto caminante' [An ignorant man is a walking corpse]. 'Un público ilustrado en el conocimiento de dios jamás será engañado' [A public enlightened in the knowledge of god will never be deceived]. 'Un intellectual de mala conciencia hace más daño que cien ignorantes [One corrupt intellectual does more harm than a hundred ignoramuses].

In Latin America, the new religious or neo-religious formations, whose depoliticizing tendencies make intellectuals despair, produce new reflexive and self-reflexive subjects, knowledges, and agencies in the spaces that traditional cosmoses no longer occupy, and that secular humanism and civic interpellation no longer reach, or never did. They have been accompanied in minimally literate sectors by a proliferation of equally depoliticizing self-help literature.[8] In some respects, these new knowledges and forms of subjectivity are functional for capitalism – critics cite their ability to rationalize self-exploitation, for instance – but in others, the new knowledges point to ways of being and living that contradict the dictates of the market and consumer values. My aim is neither to idealize nor to trivialize or homogenize these formations, but only to recognize that they are there and that they arise from a semantic vacuum that neo-liberal restructuring creates but cannot resolve.[9]

So, new knowledges and imaginaries begin to form in the zones of exclusion produced by structural adjustment. This phenomenon finds an echo, it seems to me, in a curious textual trope that began, I think, to appear in Latin American fiction during the 1990s. In a number of novels of that decade, one encounters elaborate allegorical structures of signification which the protagonist of the novel recognizes as such, but is unable to decipher. For example, in another novel by Diamela Eltit, published in 1994 and entitled *Los vigilantes* [The Vigilantes], the obsessive and maladapted child of the narrator spends his days alone in a room creating elaborate structures with a set of dishes. The narrator recognizes these structures as laden with meaning, although they are indecipherable to her. She writes the child's absent father:

Los juegos que realiza tu hijo me resultan cada vez más impenetrables y no comprendo ya qué lugar ocupan los objetos y qué relación guardan con su cuerpo. Las vasijas están rigurosamente dispuestas en el centro de su cuarto formando una figura de la cual no entiendo su principio ni menos su final.

[The games your son plays are more and more impenetrable to me, and I no longer understand what role the objects play and what relation they have with his body. The containers are rigorously laid out in the centre of his room forming a figure whose beginning and end I cannot comprehend.][10]

The structures in question seem to suggest the key to a possible future, which, however, will not be hers. Expelled from their home by hostile neighbours, the mother and son end up by the riverside with the rest of the homeless citizenry, howling at the moon in the frigid night.

Salón de belleza [Beauty Parlour], a novel published in 1994 by the Mexican-Peruvian Mario Bellatín, tells the story of a beauty parlour that is gradually converted by its transvestite owner into a hospice for moribund sufferers of a mysterious plague, which is obviously AIDS. The protagonist adorns his salon with large aquariums, inside which the multiple varieties of fish create parallel social and reproductive orders that are clearly rule-governed, but incomprehensible to the narrator. The forms of predatory violence among males, females, and babies are particularly mysterious to him.[11] Allegorical tropes like these abound in the work of the anti-aesthetic Argentine novelist César Aira. In a text published in 2000 and entitled *La villa* [The Neighbourhood], for instance, a huge poor neighbourhood blanketing the outskirts of Buenos Aires lies at the centre of the story. It is governed by a coherent and self-regulating spatial, social, semiotic, and economic order, the workings of which are opaque, however, to the middle-class protagonists.[12] A notable feature, then, of the Latin American narrative of the '90s, these dynamic, allegorical formations exemplify what systems analysts call autopoiesis, that is, to quote Maturana and Varela, 'the generative process whereby everything that lives realizes its mode of being.'[13]

Planetary Imaginings: Towards a 'Global Human'?

Is it plausible to hypothesize a link between literary images of indecipherable embedded orders, on the one hand, and the telepathic scrolls of Alpha and Omega, on the other? In one case, the elements are extraterrestrial and decipherable (transcendent), and in the other, terrestrial and indecipherable (immanent). Both can be read as instances of autopoiesis and perhaps as figures of imagined alternative hegemonies. In my hypothesis, Alpha and Omega's telepathic scrolls and Eltit's artifices of dishes are enacting an emergent contemporary stage of the crisis of ethics and epistemology that has for a long time now been bumping us up against the limits of Western secular humanism.

Among humanism's most conspicuous and intractable limits are the structures of otherness, without which modernity remains indecipherable to itself. These realize themselves in familiar hierarchies of privilege and inequality, and in continuous claims for inclusion. The challenge, according to the Caribbean thinker Sylvia Wynter, is to find a 'new semantic charter,' a wholesale rewriting of knowledge that will inaugurate a new phase of 'the global human.'[14]

The efforts to overcome modernism's exclusions have been diverse and constant, and by no means confined to the academy. As Wynter observes, the social and identitarian movements that so disconcerted Left and Right in the 1980s arose out of modernity's institutionalized exclusions, and the Left's failure to address them. The so-called new social movements produced their own knowledges, desires, meanings, agents – intellectuals, artists, critics, and politicians. They attacked inequalities by converting differences into motors of autopoiesis aiming at egalitarian coexistence. These knowledges were, and still are, heresies seeking to become orthodoxies. A paradigmatic case, and protagonist, has been transnational feminism, a planetary work in progress. The new protagonism of indigenous peoples in several parts of the world is a more recent example.

From other sites of reflection, however, this autopoiesis from exclusion is denounced as parochial, balkanizing, self-centred. The only way to move forward, say these critics, is to leave behind the divisive wounds of the past, and meet together again beneath the sign of the European Enlightenment. In a recent essay called 'Finding Our Way back to the Enlightenment,' for instance, the progressive American intellectual Tomás de Zengotita argues that 'the only basis for a coherent ideology capable of uniting progressive forces in this critical hour' is Enlightenment humanism.[15] For de Zengotita the necessary basis for remaking the world is

an identification with humanity in its totality and with each human being. In its secular form this identification is rooted in the ideals of enlightened humanism, ideals articulated by Locke, Rousseau and Kant and put in play historically by the Bill of Rights and the Declaration of the Rights of Man. However miserably partisans of these principles failed to fulfill them in practice, the principles themselves are unambiguous, and they all depend on that fundamental identification of each of us with all of us, with the sheer human being abstracted in the idea from concrete contexts of history and tradition. (36)

We must, de Zengotita insists, face the possibility that 'the modern western tradition has a genuine claim – a superior claim – on the allegiance of humanity after all.' His final advice is that his readers stop reading Foucault and pick up Voltaire.

I cite de Zengotita, not as an idiosyncratic voice, but as a representative of an eloquent and vociferous current in the contemporary debate about values, defined by its rejection of that universally derided, and difficult to locate, villain, 'identity politics,' and by its call for a return to Enlightenment universalism. In these two demands, politically Left and Right versions of this current coincide.

As attractive and convincing as a reauthorization of the Enlightenment – or a turn from Foucault to Voltaire – may be, it is easy to anticipate the response of historically excluded groups. For the few who have attained a voice in the debate, the idea of what Fred Moten has called a 'voluntary de-racialization' of the democratic project, or of a voluntary re-neutralization of the category of gender, is unacceptable. It would lead directly to the loss of the few spaces tenuously won.[16]

How to exit this impasse? How, in other words, to move towards Wynter's global human? It seems to me that this conflict, which is intensifying in the United States as democracy erodes, is shaped by a pair of misunderstandings that can perhaps be clarified. The first has to do with the historicity of that eternally derided snark, identity politics. The so-called identity groups accused of fragmenting the struggle for the common good do not, we know, come from nowhere, but from historical denials of access to that common good. Critics in de Zengotita's line understand these exclusions as ills from the past that are to be atoned for in the present. But this is not the case. The ills of the past acquire significance only because the exclusions continue in the present, especially in political and social spheres. Contemporary social and identitarian movements arise, I would argue, only after excluded groups have made long and persistent efforts to achieve inclusion and access, especially access to the political process. The movements form only when attempts to achieve access to political process by established means have failed. Continued denial of access in the present explains subordinated groups' disinterest in a renewed Enlightenment narrative. The exclusions are not 'behind us.'

The second misunderstanding has to do with what I have come to call the monopolism of Enlightenment metropolitan thought, whose remedy is – I think – of all things, ethnographic. The proposal to reauthorize Enlightenment forms of knowledge and value as the best alternative for everyone seems to depend, to a degree, on a kind of ethnographic, empirical error. The error lies in assuming that the European Enlightenment has a monopoly on the forms and values it prescribes, as if they or anything like them have never come into being anywhere else in human geography and history. But do we really think that the powers of rationality were recognized only once, and in France? Or that, though slavery has existed in many places, the idea of freedom has only one genealogy? That the city is a modern invention, or a European one? Or the State? That cosmopolitanism has been unique to the modern West? That the idea of humankind has only this single point of origin?

We could consider here, for example, the principle of the common good. In empirical terms, it is simply erroneous to think of the idea of the common good as a unique invention of the European Enlightenment. This is just not the case. The common good is and has been a functioning principle of human groups all over the planet for time immemorial. Not necessarily all of them – no need to speak of universals here – but lots of them. The common good, in other words, has more than a single narrative of origins. Far more. It is easy to recognize that the West has never had a monopoly on greed, genocide, enslavement, exploitation, authoritarianism, heterosexism, religious violence, patriarchy, hierarchy, injustice. In exactly the same way, the West has not had a monopoly on empirical science, rationality, principles of equality, liberty, justice, law, the idea of the human, the rule of law, the responsibility of the strong towards the weak, the right of all to security and well-being. Elements like these have, and have had, plural existences and genealogies throughout the panorama of human societies.

Tellingly, de Zengotita acknowledges this possibility once in his essay. Like a crack between planks, a tiny parenthesis admits a shaft of light. Insisting on the possibility that the modern Western tradition has 'a genuine claim on the allegiance of humanity' (37), he adds, '(there may be other sources for these principles).' But the parenthesis takes him nowhere. This is symptomatic of an academic debate, where viewing these principles as unique features of the Western Enlightenment receives unquestioned acceptance, still. In fact, it remains an established convention even of debates that critique the 'colonial, expansionist logic' of Enlightenment universalism.[17] Since the monopolism of values is a shared ground for both sides in the debate, it is difficult not to see in it a parallel with the self-destructive, self-blinding monopolism of capitalism itself, at least as cultural theorists so often imagine it.

The monopolism of Enlightenment thought disqualifies it as a base for global consensus. It is impossible to neutralize differences for the sake of re-entering a palace of ethnocentrism, androcentrism, and obstinate coloniality. We have passed this way before.

Ethnography is the West's repository of non-European knowledges, one of many mechanisms that produce knowledge which belies Enlightenment monopolism. But ethnography is also an institution of the Enlightenment: through a preordained gesture, the knowledge that belies the monopoly is sealed off by one of ethnography's founding suppositions: the denial of equivalence between the ethnographer's knowledge and that of the people s/he is studying. That denial of equivalence was, of course, the foundational gesture for the regime of knowledge we know as ethnography. And yet equivalencies (or inter-sections and resonances) are the very condition of possibility of the work of ethnographers and emissaries, translators, and traitors. That is where it all starts, and, indeed, ethnography has lately been remaking itself in response to this contradiction. Perhaps a revolutionized cul-tural anthropology could become a source for the 'new semantic char-ter' Wynter called for. Such a knowledge field would be an instance of the phenomenon of cultural mediation, practised in one way or another by all human groups that have contact with other groups.

Once one thinks past the idea of a Western monopoly on certain val-ues, ideas, and knowledge, a straightforward alternative appears: dis-solve the narrative of the Enlightenment into a broader planetary account of what Wynter calls the global human; or else absorb it into a full-blown human history whose elements – not necessarily universals – have been invented and reinvented in more times and places than we will ever know. What de Zengotita recognizes as ideals of Enlighten-ment humanism, including the idea of 'humanity in its totality,' would be expected to turn up in many places not subsumed into the epic of the Occident. This may appear as an idealist proposal, but it is not; nor is it a naïve reaffirmation of innate human goodness, nor an inversion of the civilization-barbarism polarity, nor a re-homogenization of the species. Above all, it is not a universalist proposal, but rather one that tries to solve problems caused by universalism.

Intersection and Resonance

When one lets go of the common-sense idea of a metropolitan monop-oly on the values associated with the Enlightenment, one can begin looking for points of intersection and resonance across societies and histories. This step towards a global (not universal) human is something that the cybernetic revolution and geographic mobility make much more possible now than ever before. To offer a single very simple example from the contemporary global scenario: struggles over the privatization of water. Pretty much every time privatization of water is proposed, people, whether in Collingwood, Ontario, or Cochabamba, Bolivia, defend the idea of water as a common good that belongs equally to everyone. The force of this idea on the world stage right now lies precisely in the fact that, in purely ethnographic terms, it has many genealogies. It has originated on who knows how many different occasions in the course of the history and geography of human groups. In today's global scenario, the idea of water as a common good exists as a point of intersection of such multiple genealogies, and these have the capacity to resonate with and reinforce each other.

As this example suggests, a planetary optic requires a concept of the human that is superordinate to that of the Enlightenment and of capitalism. This idea is heretical to a doctrine that most Western intellectuals have installed in our heads: namely, that the human was invented by humanism. But here again we must repeat the question: what reason is there to think that the idea of the human ('an identification with humanity in its totality and with each human being') would have been invented only once? It is not in the slightest necessary to be occidental or occidentalized to conceive of humanity or the human in totalizing or globalizing or universalizing terms. Humanity can be totalized from anywhere, as it was in the little restaurant in Cuzco. (Everyone will see themselves on the Great Global TV.) In this moment of enormous planetary change, whose hallmarks seem to be polarization, disposability, disequilibrium, and unpredictability, that fact is deeply consequential.

Can we now identify an emergent planetary optic that can be grounded anywhere and that creates historical possibilities not available before? Such an idea would join a growing gallery of objects, concepts, knowledges, and subjects born out of the conjuncture of changes that have been labelled globalization. Even people like myself who for a long time saw the term 'globalization' as a fake alibi for capitalism and empire, now recognize that a new phase in the existence of the planet does seem to be occurring, its outlines still in flux. When Jacques Chirac in 2002 promised a 'réponse planétaire' to the AIDS pandemic, he was speaking from a subject position that had become normalized only recently. Global objects proliferate around us, and they seem to be of all kinds and shapes: viruses (cybernetic and biologic), evangelical Christianity and Islam, satellite television and the cellphone, hip-hop and rock, transnational feminism, the sweatshop, the anti-sweatshop movement, ecology, the t-shirt and rubber flip-flops, the traffic in human organs and the drug trade, vampires, and migrant communities.

The methods for identifying such objects are so far not formalized. Many people think they witnessed the birth of a new planetary object on 15 February 2002, in the worldwide demonstration against the invasion of Iraq. Was this a series of separate demonstrations in a multitude of different places? Or was it a single demonstration of a planetary nature, archipelagal in form? Many think it was the latter, threaded together by the Internet, digital imagery, and the cellphone. Consider, for instance, the planetary humanism of the following lines from the great global pool of anti-war messages in circulation that day (translation mine):

No a la guerra. Porque este planeta, esta humanidad, necesita voces y argumentos que luchen por la paz, por unir a todos los pueblos en una sola causa común por erradicar definitivamente las injusticias, el hambre, las enfermedades, porque ello es el origen de mucho odio, de mucha violencia, y de una de las fuentes de alimentación del terrorismo.

[No to war. For this planet, this humanity, needs voices and arguments that struggle for peace, to unite all peoples in a single common cause to eradicate injustices, hunger, sicknesses, for all of these are the origin of much hatred, and violence, and the nourishers of terrorism.][18]

This message emanates – no surprise – from the Web site of Alfa y Omega, from its headquarters in the working-class suburb of Lince in Lima, Peru. But it is fascinating to recognize that, in 2002, the message could have originated in the Lancandon forest in Chiapas, in a sherpa community in Tibet, in a house under siege in Baghdad, a union shop in London, a study in Toronto. In the message, the reader, and the adherents of Alfa y Omega, are interpellated by a planetary discourse of the human that is secular, terrestrial, and futuristic.

The social and ecological impacts of the last three decades of neoliberal plunder are the beginning of something, but they are not an end point. The imbalances they have produced are too great to be sustainable. Beginning in the mid-1990s, institutions began to coalesce at the global or planetary level, creating tensions and counterweights against the crushing momentum of the WTO and the IMF. The World Economic Summit hosted originally in Davos has been deliberately counter-weighted by the World Social Summit in Porto Alegre. The World Bank will share the stage with a World Court. A set of experimental World Summits have taken place – on water in Kyoto, on racism in Durban, on sustainable development in Johannesburg. A world summit of indigenous peoples called by the UN in Vienna in 1993 led to a Permanent Forum on Indigenous Peoples, and the declaration of the years 1995–2004 as the Decade of Indigenous Peoples. Paralleling the UN Decade for Women (1975–84), this action reminds us of the founding role transnational feminism has played in working out planetary practices. Beginning with the UN decade of women, the tenacious labours of global feminism have provided many of the templates for today's planetary endeavours. The US invasion of Iraq in 2002 crystallized a new and powerful transnational public opinion.

My aim here, however, is not to suggest a giant binary array of planetary good guys and bad guys. Rather, I wish to suggest a dynamic picture in which multi-faceted, multi-polar formations are taking form along planetary lines, improvised and unprecedented. None of these developments in and of themselves calls for hope: hopefulness remains what it always is, namely, a choice. If one does choose it, then in the midst of unparalleled perils, these kinds of planetary identification that can be articulated and recognized from any geographical, social, economic, or ethnic space, hold promise.

NOTES

This text is based on a paper presented in Spanish at a panel on 'Intellectuals, Gender and the State,' at the Latin American Studies Association meetings, Dallas, March 2003, and in English at the Canadian Learned Societies meetings in Halifax, May 2002. It appeared in Spanish as 'Los imaginarios planetarios,' in El salto de Minerva: intelectuales, género y estado en América Latina, ed. Mabel Moraña and Maria Rosa Oliveira Williams (Madrid: Iberoamericana, 2005), 269–82.

1 I am citing here the pamphlet Divina Revelación, Alfa y Omega, Divinas Leyes, El matrimonio, la familia, la educación y la moral (Lima: Peru, 2001). Translations are mine.

2 As I wrote these notes, in the first days of January 2005, world attention

was focused on the literally marginal coastlines of southern Asia, devastated ten days earlier by a huge tsunami wave, following an undersea earthquake. The victims, mainly subsistence fishermen and farmers, overwhelmingly exemplify the superfluity I am referring to here. Despite the ubiquitous presence of the radio, no effort was made to warn them of the likelihood of a tsunami. (The inhabitants of an American military base on Diego Garcia, on the other hand, were notified.) Even more telling, though at least 150,000 were killed and millions injured and left homeless, economists said the disaster would have no perceptible impact on the economies of any of the countries, because the economic power of these thousands of organized communities was so small.

3 Conference on Critical Cosmopolitanisms, University of California at Irvine, March 2003. Authorities in Lima recently closed a new freeway overpass in the city after an epidemic of suicides over many months by poor citizens. A taxi driver whom I asked why it was happening replied, 'Ya no aguantan su miseria' [They can no longer bear their misery].

4 Diamela Eltit, *Mano de obra* (Santiago: Seix Barral, 2002).

5 Among the regions of the world, inequality and immiseration have increased most in Latin America in the last three decades. Almost all Latin Americans experienced dramatic increases in economic vulnerability in these years, and today in many countries most of the population literally has nothing.

6 For additional reflections on this point, see M.L. Pratt, 'Why the Virgin of Zapopan Went to Los Angeles,' in *Images of Power: Iconography, Culture and the State in Latin Americar*, ed. Jens Andersman and William Rowe (New York: BergHahn Books, 2005).

7 In most Latin American countries, public university systems have been devastated by cuts directly imposed by IMG interventions. At the same time, private secular 'universities' have proliferated whose educational mission is purely instrumental and technocratic, and where there is no provision for research.

8 Along with self-help literature, the spread of evangelical Christianity has been one of the hallmarks of the neo-liberal era in Latin America and many parts of the world. For many reasons, I believe it should be regarded both as an instrument of, and a response to, the neo-liberal intervention.

9 I am following here the thought of political economist J.K. Gibson-Graham, notably in the important book *The End of Capitalism as We Knew It: A Feminist Critique of Political Economy* (Oxford: Blackwells, 1996). According to Gibson-Graham, capitalism tends to monopolize anti-capitalist thought, making it difficult for the observer to note the omnipresence of non-

capitalist practices and activities within 'capitalist' societies. Analysts, it is argued, must force themselves to attend to these phenomena, and to take them seriously, resisting the tendency to see capitalism as capable of explaining everything. See also Gibson-Graham's more recent book, *A Post-Capitalist Politics* (Minneapolis: University of Minnesota Press, 2006).

10 Diamela Eltit, *Los vigilantes* (Santiago: Sudamericana, 1994), 76.

11 Mario Bellatín, *Salón de belleza* (México: Tusquets, 1995).

12 César Aira, *La villa* (Buenos Aires: Emecé, 2001). These novels are discussed further in M.L. Pratt, 'Tres incendios y dos mujeres extraviadas: el imaginario novelístico frente al nuevo contrato social,' in *Espacio urbano, comunicación y violencia en América Latina*, ed. Mabel Moraña (Pittsburgh: Instituto Internacional de Literatura Iberoamericana, 2000), 91–106.

13 H. Maturana and F. Varela, *Autopoiesis and Cognition: The Realization of the Living* (Boston: D. Reidel, 1980).

14 Sylvia Wynter, 'The Ceremony Must Be Found: After Humanism,' *boundary 2* 12.3/13.1 (special issue on 'Humanism and the University') (Spring-Fall 1984): 22.

15 Tomás de Zengotita, 'Common Ground: Finding Our Way back to the Enlightenment,' *Harper´s* 306 (January 2003): 35–45.

16 I thank Fred Moten of the University of California at Irvine for his clarity on this point, at the Conference on Critical Cosmopolitanisms, held at UC Irvine, March 2003.

17 The term is used by Judith Butler, in Judith Butler, Ernesto Laclau, and Slavoj Žižek, *Contingency, Hegemony, Universality: Contemporary Dialogues on the Left* (London and New York: Verso, 2000), 13. This book, based on an e-mail exchange among the three thinkers, exemplifies the point I am making here. While the subject matters addressed might be expected to motivate an opening beyond the European Enlightenment corpus, the latter's monopoly on thought is unreflectively reproduced.

18 See www.Alfayomega.com.pe

9 Reframing Global/Local Poetics in the Post-imperial Pacific: Meditations on 'Displacement,' Indigeneity, and the Misrecognitions of US Area Studies

ROB WILSON

Displacing the US-Area Field Imaginary

Under 'displacement,' the *OED* tracks the quasi-materialist tangle of the English semantic record when it tells us that rulers, plants, waters, feelings of aggression, and day-labourers all can be *displaced*, that is, shifted, removed, deflected; in short, put out-of-place by some disruptive structural, biological, or tactical shift, as revealed in the *OED*'s macro-instance of creative destruction from 1880, 'the displacement of human labour ... through machinery.' Nowadays, with the more ethereal rise to power across the US academy of diaspora discourse, borderlands paradigms, and postcolonial dissemination models of split subjectivity, displacement has become a virtually normative concept/tactic by which to talk of, track, and organize the making of world literature, knowledge, community, and culture.

What Gayatri Spivak pedagogically embraces in her own transnational work as the 'practical structure of deconstruction as reversal-displacement'[1] had a far-reaching impact upon the postcolonial disciplinary regimes, area formations, and the fast-coming-unglued 'field imaginary' of the rapidly globalizing 1990s.[2] The multi-sited editors of *Dangerous Liaisons: Gender, Nation, and Postcolonial Perspectives* note that 'rearticulated notions of exile and diaspora' have become so commonplace by now in Anglo-American postcolonial discourse that 'displacement' is registered not just as a specific effect of post-independence history but, much more free-floatingly, is being used in many sites 'as a condition and a trope for cultural criticism itself.'[3]

To invoke a home-grown instance of contemporary anglo-globality, Homi Bhabha, working his way from the emergent and peripheral into the theory-dominant sector in Great Britain and North America,[4] serves as a synecdochical instance of a large-scale US move to install outer-national frameworks that positively value postcolonial displacement. Thus he writes in 'The World and the Home':

> Where the transmission of 'national' traditions was once the major theme of a world literature, perhaps we can now suggest that transnational histories of migrants, the colonized, or political refugees – these border and frontier conditions – may be the terrains of world literature. The center of such a study would neither be the 'sovereignty' of national cultures, nor the 'universalism' of human culture, but a focus on those 'freak displacements' [the quoted term is Nadine Gordimer's] emanating from postcolonial societies and reflected in its 'unhomely' writing.[5]

Bhabha urges this 'unhomely' mode of writing weird counter-English, even as he repetitively foregrounds the out-of-sync, off-centre, uncanny, and culturally doubled lives of postcolonial subjects not all quite as well-placed as himself – in the English Department at Harvard. He became chair-person of this department in 2004, via Chicago and also via Oxford, where he had trained in poststructural linguistics and in what Kuan-Hsing Chen calls 'diasporic opportunism' and the self-fashioning vocation of a perpetually textualized displacement.[6]

As another and stronger global sign of the trans-disciplinary shift warping the field-imaginary practices of the 1990s, diasporic discourse – for example, in the work of Paul Gilroy on the Black Atlantic or of Stuart Hall on ex-imperial England – registered various disjunctive, multi-sited, and transnational modes of what James Clifford calls the 'dwelling-in-displacement' for which prior nation-centred models of assimilation, citizenship, ethnicity, and settlement could not account. Clifford notes the effect on US and British cultural studies of this move to register diaspora, writing in his travelling-theory study *Routes* that 'diasporic language appears to be replacing, or at least supplementing, minority discourse.'[7]

In the more psychoanalytical mode of libidinal agonistics and mimetic aggression, displacement also registers, of course, the discursive shift of triangulated aggression away from a powerful father-figure towards a less powerful one, in order to mask retaliation, maintain sublimation, or occlude dissent.[8] Resisting free-floating homologies of travelling as some kind of de-nationalizing movement, Timothy Brennan argues the hidden geo-materiality of this subliminal agonistic shift and emphasizes its link to the rise and reign of postcolonial studies as a global fashion: such 'displacement,' he notes, 'far from being neutral, is designed precisely to force readers to remember the involuntary travel of deportation, migrations, economic lack, and war.'[9]

Diaspora discourse, commonly arising in dominant contexts like those inside the globalizing empire for capital/liberty that is the present US hegemony and its reign of neo-liberal banality and false binaries, can (ironically to be sure) help to loosen, diffuse, and thus weaken the languages of a coalitional counter-minority. In this way, it reflects an ever-more supple containment strategy of civilizational empire, embracing difference (as in the the fatal Disney-like embrace of Bambi, Lilo, or Fa Mulan) and thereby commodifying it. Ethnic citizens can now all too easily become recast as diasporics, with a double sense of 'rooted' belonging to countries here/there, but at the same time they also run the security 'homelands' risk of being reframed as 'un- or non-Americans, in a rehearsal of the logic of the Japanese internment.'[10] Displacement discourse does not, as such, simply signify the context-free sign of innovation, deconstruction, and difference, as we can begin to see here; for it can also be the agent of a field displacement, and, more importantly, it can reflect the large-scale geo-material realignment of US national power and the management of transnational and minority forces, developments that need to be distanced, placed in allegorical scarequotes as it were, and interrogated.

In this essay, I want to elaborate upon and discuss three large-scale displacements taking place in the postcolonial Pacific – (a) ecological, (b) financial, and (c) semiotic – concentrating more on the latter in the context of the former two. This will involve situating cultural texts overdetermined by 'displacement' within planetary and global/local contexts and showing how such texts implicate modes of semiotic displacement within the eminently material dynamics of ecological and financial imbalance, catastrophe, and unrest. I want thereby to challenge the limits of over-loosely or over-flexibly installed, text-centred displacement models, which are transforming the postcolonial field imaginaries of Asia/Pacific study in productive, if uneven, ways. Later, by way of a field-situated conclusion, I will focus upon two scholarly works from Asia-Pacific and Pacific American studies that associate 'displacement' with contrasting registers and applications: Yunte Huang's counter-orientalist study of textual mimicry and transcultural translation, *Transpacific Displacement: Ethnography, Translation, and Intertextual Travel in Twentieth-Century American Literature* (2002) and Houston Wood's more indigenous-centred study of rhetorical and political displacement, *Displacing Natives: The Rhetorical Production of Hawai'i* (1999). Both of these works are not just about displacement; rather, they activate it as a central trope in order to organize 'areas' and to configure frames of knowledge. Considered together, they show that, mired as we are in postcolonial newness and in the lurch towards affirming diasporic doubleness, we need a broader internationalist vision of external linkages and trans-area concepts than any pragmatic, merely nation-based or segregatively area-based vision of 'displacement' can now provide.[11]

While Chicano and Latin American subaltern studies are representative of the interlocking geopolitical and discursive shifts described above, Asian American and US Pacific studies have also reflected and impacted upon this field displacement; that is, upon the shift of focus, tools, interests, etc., that characterizes the transnationalizing field imaginary. As Arif Dirlik records in 'The Asia-Pacific in Asian-American Perspective' (1993), 'Asian American historiography, in recalling Asian Americans into the history of the United States, has made a significant contribution to US historiography by challenging its dominant paradigm of an expanding western frontier and showing that there was an eastern [trans-Pacific] frontier as well, with a significant Asian presence on its outposts.'[12] Outlining a strategic and place-based regional imaginary as well as the global/local dialectical optic with which my own work has been associated, Dirlik has argued that 'the struggle of Asian Americans against homogenization into a hegemonic culture is paradigmatic of Asia-Pacific as space of cultural production,' a focus that he then supplements with a shift towards indigenous and Fourth World concerns from the perspective of Pacific sites that further challenge the hegemony of US assimilation models.[13] More broadly, Dirlik, in his agonistic postcolonial approach to global studies over the past decade, has relentlessly opposed any glib concentration on diasporic models of trans-Pacific cultural production with a turn towards the place-based and community-building focus that had marked Asian American studies at its origin and that now drives many aspects of Pacific native cultural studies. This spatial turn, reacting to what Harry Harootunian has relentlessly critiqued as an appeal to larger units, regions, transnationality, globalization, and hyperspace, where diasporic flows of people are said to move across what are misrecognized as 'porous' borders, never sought – in my opinion – to lose sight of those 'vast deterritorializing force[s] of capital and labor' nor of the uneven developments, blasted allegories, and co-temporal 'everydayness' of global modernity.[14] Displacement remains a primary force driving global capitalism, a force registered in our anxious transitioning to transnational or post-area field mappings, as when Fredric Jameson urges that 'the extraordinary demographic displacements of mass migrant workers and of global tourists [are occurring] to a degree unparalleled in human history.'[15] But if displacement confronts us as a widespread effect and if new models of field-displacement study are receiving widespread currency, even after the border-guarding civilizational binaries that are returning with a vengeance post-9/11 – see the work of David Palumbo-Liu (2002) on the anti-minority consequences of 9/11 in the United States – what we need to ponder here is Cicero's *cui bono* question: *who or what is being displaced* ('to whose advantage')? As my opening *OED* semantics suggest, a range of subjects human and otherwise can be displaced, even more so given the rise of technologies of simulation and the multi-media of cross-border flow. Thus, signs, texts, peoples, labourers, islands, indigenous peoples, narratives, disciplinary fields all can be 'displaced.' Needless to say, not all of these displacements are equivalent in their historical emergence and geopolitical impact, nor should they all be given the same interpretive weight or disciplinary efficacy and focus. Some modes of displacement do need to be studied and (in a Gramscian 'organic' sense) connected to, whereas some (like those stressing the ever-reversible signs, ludic nihilism, and fungible borders of de-situated language-games) would be better subordinated or ignored.[16]

Mapping Indigenous Displacements in Tuvalu, Tonga, and Hawai'i: Semiotic, Ecological, and Geo-Material Entanglements

The global/local dialectics of the indigenously entangled yet transnationalizing Pacific region continue to work themselves out with near-hallucinatory consequences of geopolitical displacement that dwarf even the out-sized stage sets of ethnicized war in *Lara Croft: Tomb Raider* (2001) or of the Tolkien wars and quests set in the fantasmatic sublimity of a New Zealand shorn of its Maori subjects and historical grievances. To evoke an extreme example, at the same time that Tuvalu Island is sinking into the Pacific Ocean due to various factors of global warming and planetary flow, the tiny Polynesian government was granted the domain Internet name *extension.tv*, which it later sold to a Californian media company for fifty million dollars. So, if the global mediascape wryly empowers this ex-British island site with Internet royalties for

the next twelve years, the global ecoscape brings its place-based existence as local culture to near disappearance and forces its eleven thousand citizens to relocate their 'ethnoscape' lock, stock, and barrel to
New Zealand to survive.[17] Thus, Tuvalu still exists as Web site and global chat room and can maintain a virtual trans-Pacific existence to talk
about its global-local plight in cyberspace,[18] but its nine coral atolls go
under water and its culture is set offshore. Geography and genealogy
are fractured as such, as Pacific islander identity is forever cast into
diaspora and motion. The displacement of Tuvalu has been a particular
US concern since the unilateral Guano Islands Act of 1856 legalized the
extra-territorial extraction of bird droppings for industrial and military
uses in some seventy sites located in the Pacific, including Kiribati,
Tuvalu, and the Cook Islands, a global feat that 'presaged American
colonial presence in the central and south Pacific.'[19] Still, as we learn
from the CIA publications factbook now on-line as public culture,
Tuvalu's 'transnational issues' are at this point tame, or at least becoming invisible, for under 'Disputes – international,' Washington registers
'none.'[20]

The Pacific island of Tonga has fared no less perilously than Tuvalu,
due to its recent attempt to globalize government revenues, an attempt
amplified by selling passports to cash-ready Asians, especially those
anxious about Hong Kong's reversion to China in 1997. It was not,
however, Tonga's land or its cultural sovereignty but rather its investment dollars that disappeared into 'a mysterious company that has
now vanished,' as BBC News put it in October 2001.[21] Tonga, on the
uneven global playing field, was in fact an agent in its own financial
displacement. The singular South Pacific kingdom launched a compensatory lawsuit in San Francisco, hoping to recover some of the $26 mil-
lion it had lost in investment schemes directed by Jesse Bogdonoff, the
Bank of America employee who talked the Tongan king into investing
his kingdom's low-interest account into his own Wellness Technologies
along with an insurance-buyout company in Nevada called Millennium Asset Management and a dot.com start-up (since dot.gone into
bankruptcy). Instead of investing to repair local Tongan highways, the
diasporic king (living in an up-scale San Francisco suburb in Silicon
Valley near the Hearst family) played the Internet frontier under the
tutelage of his court jester and soon squandered the tiny ex-British
kingdom's surplus budget in offshore speculation.

Thinking about filing a counter-suit for character assassination, the
discredited US jester admitted that he had 'people in Tonga calling for

me to be thrown underground and cooked like a pig,' but blamed the lawsuit, not on residual primitivism, but on rival factions in the postcolonial government, and ascribed the loss to market forces.[22] Nothing of this failed globalization strategy bordering on opéra bouffe or Pacific Rim disillusionment fatigue, would surprise the readers of Epeli Hau'ofa's *Tales of the Tikongs* (1983), in which Tiko's comic entropy, development failures, and reverse Protestant work-ethic are modelled on the author's native Tonga, where he had once served as the king's secretary. If the local can overthrow and comically reverse colonial and neo-colonial schemes of ex-primitive appropriation in Hau'ofa's satirical fiction, global offshore powers can gobble up local capital and dismantle trans-Pacific dreams of global aggrandizement, as happened thanks to the ebullient American businessman 'who impressed the Tongan king so much that he issued a royal decree proclaiming him official court jester' (BBC News).

In a related Pacific-specific context bespeaking narrative appropriation and virtualization via an offshore poetics of island space and indigenous history, and in a kind of semiotic displacement, globally minded Hollywood producers plan to make a mega-budgeted biopic about the life of Native Hawaiian king Kamehameha I. This has become globally feasible with the rise of wrestling idol Dwayne 'The Rock' Johnson from the Aloha State to star in its lead role like some taro-stomping Angelina Jolie. One of the film's producers assured skeptics from Hawai'i that 'the goal of everyone in the project is to tell an epic story and hopefully capture it from a historically correct viewpoint.'[23] The de-worlded space of Native Hawaiians may still exist, to be sure, but the narrative resources and temporal arrangements of indigenous history, place, and myth can be altered to serve the genre needs and blockbuster economies of global spectacle, with multicultural wrestlers playing the identity-angst of indigenous kings. Or worse.

Indigenous culture in contemporary Hawai'i, a multicultural plantation community, Elvis Presley as a model citizen, CIA-trained social workers of glowing blackness, and disruptive outer-space aliens can all be made to coexist in the hyperbolic Hollywood fantasy of a watercolour-drenched Hawai'i, 'with inflections pidgin-true enough for local audiences but suitable for the mass market.'[24] In Disney's $80 million global/local cartoon *Lilo and Stitch* (2002), a broken family of bad-mouthed and ex-bullying Hawaiian sisters capaciously learn to accommodate their cultural frames of hula dancing, wave surfing ('it's the Hawaiian roller-coaster ride'), plate lunching, waitressing, and practising 'ohana' ('In Ohana, nobody is left out, nobody gets forgotten,' runs Nani's refrain) to include a motley array of aliens and visitors. By the film's oh so tourist-friendly end, the extended Hawaiian family will move beyond charges of contemporary dysfunctionality to adopt a genetically mutated and Elvis-loving blue dog from outer space who – like any colonist of extractive rapacity and crazed needs – is 'built to destroy,' along with a black ex-CIA social worker, and a bounty-hunting couple from outer space (or is it the Soviet Union?) turned into pleasure-loving and island-gallivanting, Aloha-shirted tourists.

In this way, science-fiction fantasies of genetic mutation fuse with an ugly-duckling fairy-tale plot and retro-atmospherics from *Dumbo* (1941) to create a backwater space of multicultural fusion and indigenous accommodation, as signalled by Tia Carrere (a Filipina actress from Hawai'i of *Wayne's World* fame who learned the song from her local aunt) singing Queen Liliuokalani's *mele* '*Aloha Oe*' – or good-bye – to Hawai'i's extended-family values.[25] Disney's writers and producers aimed through song, pidgin inflections, and plot to give 'a real sense of authenticity' to the setting, and for *Honolulu Advertiser* writer Michael Tsai, they succeeded with their 'hand-drawn tale of Hawaiian keiki Lilo and *hanai* [adopted] extra-terrestrial Stitch true to eye, ear and spirit' of Hawaiian culture and local modes.[26] If so, Hawaiian culture turns into pastiche, parody, joke, and myth; as story consultant Malia Jones, a surfer and model from Hawai'i, applauds the resulting global/local retrofitted mix: 'You can hardly see Hawai'i on a globe it's so tiny, but it's also unique and special. When you watch this film, you think, "How bizarre, but at the same time, how real."'[27]

Geography and genealogy are thus – in all good liberal conscience – simulated, mimed, and mined for local colour, as an ex-primitive identity gets cast into mixture and fusion. Thus, the racial tensions of settler colonialism give way to the feel-good resolutions and off-beat sentiments of small-kids cartoons: history is all in the postcolonial family, and much can be forgotten or papered over with sentimentality, pop-cultural kitsch, and song. (Let us not forget that Elvis's ties to Hawai'i consist in a prior tourist-fantasy movie, *Blue Hawaii*, and in his lesser-known funding of the Arizona Memorial at Pearl Harbor.) This is, then, what I am calling and (in this context) lamenting as semiotic displacement, and I would argue that the US field imaginary of transnational cultural studies needs to contest its quasi-orientalist workings.

Nothing surprises much anymore in these semiotic distortions and intertextual ready-mades of global-local poetics and *faux* indigeneity. If a plantation-town eatery can be called Mulan Wok in *Lilo and Stitch*, this is less a sign of 'local authenticity,' as claimed by moviemakers or the film's vaunted 'Hawaiianess,' than director-writer Chris Sander's winking allusion to his prior work of Asia/Pacific animation and global spectacle, *Mulan* (1998). With Chinese myth ending up here as a plate lunch in post-plantation Hawai'i (even as Duke Kahanamoku ends up as a poster for the cartoon characters in their quest for place, community, family, and a sense of belonging to 'the ohana'), we can only ratify Yunte Huang's claim that 'the journey of Mulan's transpacific migration that leads to her ultimate Americanization is now, like some kind of Pacific Bambi-woman, all but complete.'[28]

Extending the pleasure of the movie experience, two interactive computer games were soon released by Disney Interactive Inc. to amplify the Hawaiian fantasy: in one of these, 'Lilo & Stitch, Hawaiian Adventure,' children from six to eleven can track the storyline and 'help Lilo tame Stitch and teach him the value of "Ohana" – the Hawaiian word for family.' In another video game accompanying the range of Saturday-morning television shows based on this film and now seen around the world from Seoul and Los Angeles to Sao Paulo, 'Lilo & Stitch, Trouble in Paradise,' players zoom through spirit-haunted landscapes and act as the main characters, for 'as Lilo, players can bash objects and cast Voodoo spells' or as Stitch they can bash, spit, spin, or roll attack. They can play earthy Hawaiian role models or act out more complicated tasks like 'keeping tourists happy at a luau,' in other words.[29]

The 'infantilization' of Native Hawaiians has long worked alongside white fantasies of Hawaiian sexuality and cultural excess to serve the growth of the post-plantation tourist industry. Sally Engle Merry tracks this discourse of colonial ambivalence bequeathed by missionary-era anthropology: 'Even as Hawaiians were denigrated as inferior, sensual, and lazy, their music, dance, crafts and foods were admired and appropriated for tourism.'[30] All this to say that a children's movie like the seemingly harmless *Lilo and Stitch* cannot be separated from the larger poetics of cultural tourism and its tactics of cosmo-cultural or multicultural appropriation befitting the current discursive forms of our postcolonial era. Another Hawai'i-calls summer film called *Blue Crush* (2002) updates the sun-sex-and-savage sizzle fantasy of 'going native' that drove *Gidget Goes Hawaiian* (1961), pushing it in the post-feminist direction of the Anglo-blonde fantasy that suits the materialistic culture of global surfing consumption. Of course, in a politically correct twist, the natives and locals remain sullen, grieving, and hostile, crying, 'Hey, no use this beach, it *kapu* to the likes of you' to the incoming Californians, who just want to conquer the North Shore waves, have some romantic fun, and get famous ('kapu' means 'forbidden' in Hawaiian).

Such global productions increasingly circulate the local culture of much-filmed sites of erotic and exotic allure like Hawai'i, sending it offshore and worldwide. They resolve the tensions of imperial history and global imbalance into mongrel fantasy, soft spectacle, and present-serving myth. Given the reach and impact of an 'increasingly globalized popular culture,' we have to wonder – with Paul Gilroy – if such works are not engaged in creating 'racialized signs' of cultural difference and – with all the liberal goodwill of a corporate muticulturalism gone cosmopolitical – in spreading 'commodified exotica' under the myth of authenticity.[31] Solidarities evoked around blood or land, crucial to the sovereignty claims and ontology of native peoples in the Pacific, are thus superseded by the pop-culture community of Elvis Presley music, beach-going, and the pleasures of multicultural mixture.[32]

Full of a residual animism that settler colonialism has not yet fully *displaced* or marketed, the Hawaiian islands may be 'the most superstitious place in the world' (or at least in the United States). As ex-local Annie Nakao has written,[33] tracing the impact of Japanese *obake*, or ghost stories, and the uncanny hold of native Hawaiian lore – about the volcano goddess Pele, for example – upon Hawaiians (even driving the contradictions of a mixed-heritage novelist like John Dominis Holt in *Waimea Summer* [1975]), Hawaiian spiritually is ripe for New Age appropriation and for co-option by yogic or travel literature hybridity. While economically remote or irrelevant to global production, the offshore Pacific – however alternative its vision of 'Oceania' or of natives, places, and flows – has long served as a testing space for global fantasy and for the transnational reach of 'Americanization' stories, where nuclear weapons, imperial wars, contact phobias, cultural mutations, and (nowadays) the multicultural hyperbole of transnational community can work themselves out with romantic dreaminess, narrative immunity, and the ridiculous, postcolonial sublimity of historical oblivion.[34]

'Small countries' like these, as Édouard Glissant affirmed of islandnations like Martinique and its creative sur-Caribbean future of regenerative *créolité*, 'are part of the disorientation of the world,' impacted and creolized as they are into a 'contrastive poetics' as 'part of a global process' and of concurrent global/local discourse.[35] The sites and languages of Caliban have had to deal with the imposing tactics of an Anglo-global–minded Prospero for over five hundred years now, as

Roberto Retamar – taking the Cuban Afro-Caribbean angle of a situated poetics and a decolonizing geopolitics – has long observed of those Black Atlantic island cultures where 'the political is a destiny.'[36] If all these large-scale trans-Pacific displacements of the indigenous community – ecological, financial, semiotic, and cultural – demand from us the situated scrutiny and large-scale resistance of de-orientalizing tactics, it is because the 'uncanny' Pacific of transnational globalization remains haunted by historical injustice, social unevenness, and racial phobias coming back from the postcolonial future.[37] In other words, in these works, the Pacific yet again becomes a service-industry site and a racialized fantasy of what William Randolph Hearst boasted has been for centuries and should long remain (after the attack at Pearl Harbor aggravated the US quest for global hegemony and liberal humanism in the region) 'the white man's Pacific.'

In John Houston's close-to-war-propaganda film *Across the Pacific* (1942), the Pacific was portrayed as a deceptively romantic, uncanny, and ultimately phobic space full of inscrutable oriental forces – and their subversive white allies – harbouring imperial designs as they gather around to undermine the US hegemony over the Panama Canal just before the attack on Pearl Harbor. A huge strategizing white man, a Japanese spy and karate-expert double agent, is played by a breathless haiku-reciting Sydney Greenstreet. Even an Asian American *'nisei'* character from California is thus shown to be part of the international takeover move by the Japanese axis, and all this has to be decoded and stopped by the counter-espionage Humphrey Bogart character and his hotel-owning Chinese ally, who thwarts the Japanese air attack just in time in a kind of lone-gun, stealthy, and pragmatic bit-by-bit way. Such films helped to provide the perceptual apparatus to reclaim, fantasize over, and integrate the Pacific as an American-dominated space: 'For the Americans, the abstractness of their recapture of the Pacific islands made "cinema direction" a necessity – hence the importance of the camera crews committed to the [Pacific] campaign.'[38]

When William Randoph Hearst proclaimed that 'the Pacific is the white man's ocean,' it was in response to the Pearl Harbor air attack, and his aim was to spread and ratify American military, commercial, and media hegemony over the region by vanquishing 'the Yellow Peril' and enlisting Pacific islander support in their own Occidentalist displacement.[39] Houston's movie works to provide a US geopolitical rationale and, even more so, what Virilio calls the 'perceptual arsenal,' to keep the Pacific white. This phobic Pacific as space of peril and threat is recognizable in an array of war-era poems by Robinson Jeffers, as in 'The Eye,' which shows an ocean full of blood, scum, and filth, and the 'world-quarrel of westering / and eastering man, the bloody migrations, greed of power, clash of faiths.' It also appears in Robert Frost's West Coast poem 'Once by the Pacific,' where the ocean grows apocalyptic with yellow peril forces and where God's Jehovah-like wrath is inscribed in the trans-Pacific sky and water: 'The clouds were low and hairy in the skies, / Like locks blown forward in the gleam of eyes.' In his white-republic diatribe, *The Land of Gold: Reality versus Fiction* (1855), Hinton Rowan Helper portrayed this phobic version of the trans-Pacific as a mongrelizing site of swarming immigrants like 'the solemn Chinamen, tattooed [Pacific] islander, and slovenly Chilean' coming in across the ocean from alien sites of bad blood and cheap labour, thus creating a 'copper Pacific' every bit as threatening politically as the Black Atlantic of chattel slavery and miscegenation. 'Our population was already too heterogeneous,' Helper writes of everyday life in the free-soil American state of California, 'before the Chinese came; but now another adventitious ingredient has been added; and I should not wonder at all, if the copper of the Pacific yet becomes as great a subject of discord and dissension as the ebony of the Atlantic.'[40] Exclusion acts would soon be activated to try to keep this ever-coppering Pacific white, and to ensure that US Pacific coastal states like California remained the exclusive domain of so-called 'native' white labour.

Globalization discourse nowadays inscribes a very different trans-Pacific geopolitical scene or 'global cultural economy,' one maximally full of motion and chaotic mixture and amplified interconnection of the United States to Asia and the Pacific. This globalization discourse 'implies concurrence,' to evoke Glissant again, and would push the liberalizing globe towards some utopian transnational fusion. It would thus recuperate the Asian dimension of the trans-Pacific synthesis dreamed of in Whitman's 'Facing West from California's Shores' (1860), when 'the house of maternity' in Asian civilizations and wisdom-traditions would meet hard-headed European technologies, 'the circle almost circled,' Columbus or Emerson settling down to meditate in Bombay. This achieved globality implies, however, wholeness, completion, or fusion-culture. But, even back then, Whitman-the-post-imperial-American was haunted by lack, by incompletion, by the feeling that something is missing in the grand global journey of translated-empire from Atlantic origins to Pacific telos: 'But where is what I started for so long ago? And why is it yet unfound?' Thus, the poem ends on a note of cross-cultural failure. The seamlessness of globalization across the Pacific is threatened by a new-world order of anxieties, disrupted space-time coordinates, and everyday fears, and perhaps it is best to keep this war-era and Cold War–era Pacific of clashing imperalisms and racial antagonisms in mind as we push to map an array of uncanny forces and emergent forms that give the lie to the end-of-history triumph in marketization.

Framing Displacements in the US Trans-Pacific Field Imaginary: Towards a Critical Vision of the Worlded Pacific

For Yunte Huang, working on the transnationalized field imaginary of *Transpacific Displacement* (2002), 'displacement' is less a flow or removal of peoples or commodities than a textual effect of American modernism/postmodernism, as meanings migrate, mimicking and transforming both the objects of representation and the agents of intertextual creation. 'Transpacific' is thus given quite an affirmative intertextual meaning that defamiliarizes the orientalist vocabulary of East/West domineering exchange to which we have grown accustomed through the work of Said, Miyoshi, Palumbo-Liu, Fabian et al. 'Transpacific' becomes less a policed and nation-regulated 'border' site of exclusion and containment than a fluid, trans-oceanic, borderless zone of textual crossing and cultural mixing. The new field imaginary of Asian/American studies cutting across area studies certainly needs to attune itself to such intertextual dynamics and semiotic flows, but not, perhaps, exclusively so. As Huang summarizes his key methodological turn: 'What I call *transpacific displacement* is a historical process of textual migration of cultural meanings, meanings that include linguistic traits, poetics, philosophical ideas, myths, stories, and so on. And such displacement is driven in particular by the writers' desire to appropriate, capture, mimic, parody, or revise the Other's signifying practices in an effort to describe the Other'.[41]

As if activating some Emersonian principle of textual-ontological surprise, meanings migrate in bi-directional and unpredictable ways. Texts become sites of appropriate mimicry and ethnographic approximation, part homage and part piracy. Trans-lingual poetics becomes for Huang (following the experimental ethnography modes of Clifford, Greenblatt et al.) a mode of travelling and of doing minor or unofficial ethnography. The trans-Pacific routes of meaning recall those of the transatlantic diaspora, although neither slavery nor even the transnational horizon of

Chinese/US labour needs and people-flows (or blockages and exclusion acts) is ever fully an issue here. But Far East tourism and aesthetic
ethnography are at issue, since we are dealing more with the needs and
with the language tactics of the high-literary subject of modernism.
Trans-Pacific flow becomes centred around the Chinese-language-influ-
enced imagism of 'data collectors / writer-at-home,'[42] meaning ethnography teams like Ernest Fenellosa / Ezra Pound, Florence Ayscough /
Amy Lowell, Percival Lowell / Amy Lowell, and, later (more won-
drously), the mock-pidgenization of John Yau via 'further pidginizing
Charlie Chan's [pop orientalist] pidginization and doubly ventriloquizing Imagism's ventriloquism' of the imagistic Orient.[43]

Given the orientalism of dominant US culture, at one extreme, and
the postcolonial dismantling tactics of writers like John Yau and translators of Chinese experimental poetics like Jeffrey Twitchell and Ping
Wang, at the other, Yunte Huang notes an important discursive and situational contrast: 'Imagism's linguistic mimicry should be understood
in the context of American pop culture's pidginization of Chinese, as in
the Charley Chan fiction of Earl Der Biggers from the 1920s and 30s. But
both the mimicry and pidgenization will be subject to counter-mocking
in the work of Asian writers and Asian American writers such as Lin
Yutang and John Yau.'[44] Thus, the damage done by US literary or pop
cultural orientalism can be rectified, mocked, and overturned in the
intertextual transformations and dialogues of later authors. A kind of
linguistic idealism, and an ontology of mutual dialogue, haunts this
study, as it does those transcultural models of cultural creativity that
give 'displacement' a text-centred aura and effect.

If the risk of Huang's vision of Chinese/American trans-Pacific displacement is a kind of renewed textualism and formalism, it remains,
however, that the focus on textual displacement allows us to see not just
how texts are ideological or geo-political effects but also how they can
become agents of dialogue and transformation. Huang's cross-cultural
and translational model would itself displace a more stable or overdetermined vision of orientalist exchange that sees the Pacific as a one-
way imperial route, a frontier of ever-expanding domination and sub-
lation. Even the translation of US empire does not proceed evenly like
that. Here, the Chinese language and various Chinese poetic modes
become agents of global transformation and transculturation, altering
American poetics and racial and cultural relationships in unstable and
helpful ways.

With the rise of multilingual and disruptive trans-Pacific poetry like that of Theresa Cha or John Yau, which preserves modes of 'foreign-ness' and cultural difference (in contrast to Maxine Hong Kingston, who is too monolingually American and normalizing in her language practices for Huang), we can open out the American literary canon and racial formation in trenchant new ways. As Huang concludes, affirm-ing mimetic uncanniness on postcolonial grounds, we can firstly have 'a reconception of American literature in the context of transnational-ism, a rewriting of its history as one rooted in transnationalism and committed to intercultural (transpacific, transatlantic, transcontinental) practices.'[45] Secondly, we can open or transnationalize the canon towards a more trenchantly multilingual American literature, 'ack-nowledging that the literature, as we know it, is a body of multilingual writings, consisting not only of works that have been and continue to be written in languages other than English but also of works that are inherently polyglot'.[46]

What Huang stresses, then, in *Transpacific Displacement* is the inter-cul-tural and transcultural dimension of cultural practices, as well as the multilingual and polyglot contexts of contact and creation. Geo-material conditions of coercion, radical inequality, conflict, even incommensura-bility of languages and codes should not, however, fall out of this new field-imaginary conception of the post-imperial 'contact zone.'[47] Other-wise, this new trans-Pacific is a utopian one that trails along with the uneven makings of transnational capitalism in the ex-imperial region of APEC, then and now. Textual displacement and translational concerns are necessary but not sufficient components of any transformed field imaginary in our diasporic moment, I would urge. Considered as a cen-tre-to-periphery or global-to-local effect, 'displacement' carries far more injurious geopolitical meanings, as I have tried to show through the 'allegorical' evocation of comparative Asia/Pacific instances.[48]

Displacement is given a very different range of geopolitical as well as textual meanings in Houston Wood's study *Displacing Natives* (1999), which centres on the post-contact rhetorical displacement of Native Hawaiians in various dominant US cultural genres: contact narratives, sun, sand, and sex movies, anti-conquest narratives of cultural redemp-tion, etc. Interior Pacific works are seldom taken seriously in the mod-els and works of Asian American studies, but they should be, if we are to hear the full challenge to diasporic and trans-Pacific models being posed by critical languages more attuned to indigenous struggles for sovereignty, for decolonization, and for emancipation from settler peo-ples and their narrative apparatus of land control, colonial disavowal, and semiotic domination. Contesting the US 'monorhetoric' of national, territorial, and semiotic displacement of the native with the foreign, Wood concentrates upon a whole 'polyrhetoric' of Hawaiian nativism which ranges from self-ethnography to modes of Internet sovereignty struggle, where ties to place and nation have received global/local resonance and renewed impact in cyberspace.

Displacing Natives tracks indigenous Hawai'i with wit and concern, noting how the 'rhetoric of demonization' was followed over the uneven and mutually entangled course of the nineteenth and twentieth centuries by an Anglo-American-centric 'rhetoric of preservation' that, in both historical instances and rhetorical tropes, worked effectively to displace the Hawaiian Natives and their prior local mythologies of place, indigenous community, and nation. The colourful chapter on the Hollywood movies of 'safe savagery' studies the tormented yet fanciful semiotics of imagining Hawai'i in uneven global/local contexts of contact, and measures it against the colonization-cum-tourist fantasy of what Fredric Jameson would call (miming the postmodernist logic of cultural commodification) 'Disneyfication.' When transnational cultural and postcolonial studies eventually turn to situate the Pacific in transnational frames of geopolitical displacement and global impossibility, Houston Wood's work will be there to elucidate indigeneity as global/ local plight.[49]

It remains that displacement can function as a rhetorical event and as sign-to-sign translation, as we know in the wake of the linguistically austere poetics of Paul de Man et al., but the contexts and impacts in which this sign-shifting removal and deflection of Hawaiian and Asian/Pacific voices and histories take place ultimately need to be understood in larger geopolitical contexts, and especially against the long, material durée of America's disavowed imperialism and postwar history of area-displacement. In order to open up a more transnationalized or decolonized vision of Asia/Pacific or Asian American area studies right now, one that is not too exclusively focused on American ethnic frameworks, geo-material concerns do need to be taken into account. If they are not, then the vision will be belated, frail, and irrelevant before it is even born. As Bob Dylan wrote in homage to the grassroots American leftism of his protest folksong mentor, Woody Guthrie, 'Hey, hey, Woody Guthrie, I wrote you this song / About the funny old world that's a-comin along / Well, it looks like it's dying and it's hardly been born.' This is what I would like to affirm about the invention of a more capacious, capable, decolonized, global, yet critical vision of the

Asia/Pacific field imaginary: it looks like it's dying, but its cultural poetics have hardly been born. For we cannot displace the geopolitics of the past until its injustices and imbalances have been recollected forward into the transnational future.

NOTES

1 See Gayatri Spivak, 'Explanation and Culture: Marginalia,' in *Out There: Marginalization and Contemporary Cultures*, ed. Russell Ferguson, Martha Gever, Trinh T. Minh-ha, and Cornell West (Cambridge: MIT Press, 1990), 377, on tactics of feminist displacement overcoming the opposition of public and private knowledge-spaces.

2 Opening a space for 'postnational' New Americanist work in a special issue of *boundary 2* devoted to transnational and minority-driven field transformations, Donald Pease used the quasi-Lacanian term 'field imaginary' to 'designate a location for the disciplinary unconscious ... Here abides the field's fundamental syntax – its tacit assumptions, convictions, primal words, and the charged relations binding them together' ('New Americanists: Revisionist Interventions into the Canon,' *boundary 2* 19 [1990]: 11–12). Professionalized into a specific discipline and its fundamental syntax, a given scholar would achieve recognition through modes of identification as modelled in this field imaginary, which is by no means stable nor total in its power over the subject. A new 'field imaginary' would produce altered fields and generate different disciplinary subjects more attuned to the post–Cold War contradictions and needs for 'transnational literacy' and minority or outer-national practices.

3 See Aamir Mufti and Ella Shohat, 'Introduction,' in *Dangerous Liaisons: Gender, Nation, and Postcolonial Perspectives*, ed. Anne McClintock, Aamir Mufti, and Ella Shohat (Minneapolis: University of Minneapolis Press, 1997), 2. Mufti and Shohat call attention to Caren Kaplan's *Questions of Travel: Postmodern Discourses of Displacement* (Durham, NC: Duke University Press, 1996) as a representative text on theory-travel, which performs 'an analysis and account of the role of "displacement" in contemporary criticism' (11n4).

4 Gayatri Spivak, *A Critique of Postcolonial Reason: Toward a History of the Vanishing Present* (Cambridge: Harvard University Press, 1999), 314. On the need for 'greater transnational literacy' across the humanities, see p. 399ff.

5 'Homi Bhabha, 'The World and the Home,' reprinted in McClintock et al., eds, *Dangerous Liaisons*, 449.

6 For situated area critiques of postcolonial displacement, see Ania Loomba, *Colonialism/Postcolonialism* (London: Routledge, 2000), 178–9; and Harry Harootunian, *History's Disquiet: Modernity, Cultural Practice, and the Question of Everyday Life* (New York: Columbia University Press, 2000), 50–1. Bhabha's vision of postcolonial discourse is organized around an over-extended concept of 'agential displacement' and the textually ludic contingencies of cultural and historical mixture ('hybridity'); displacement is thus not so much a trope as a structural condition. But as Aijaz Ahmad challenges, 'History does not consist of perpetual migration, so that the universality of "displacement" that Bhabha claims both as the general human condition and the desirable philosophical position is tenable neither as description of the world nor as generalized political possibility ... Most migrants tend to be poor and experience displacement not as cultural plenitude but as torment; what they seek is not displacement but, precisely, a *place* from where they may begin anew, with some sense of a stable future' ('The Politics of Literary Postcoloniality,' *Race & Class* 36 [1995]: 14–16). For Ahmad, this *'place'* of organic affiliation and existential situation is inside the anti-imperialist nationhood, global entanglement, and class formations of postcolonial India.

7 James Clifford, *Routes: Travel and Translation in the Late Twentieth Century* (Cambridge: Harvard University Press, 1997), 254–5.

8 *The New Fontana Dictionary of Modern Thought*, ed. Alan Bullock and Stephen Trombley (London: Harper Collins, 1999), 232.

9 Timothy Brennan, *At Home in the World: Cosmopolitanism Now* (Cambridge: Harvard University Press, 1997), 17, in a critique of 'America Abroad' spreading neo-liberal terms and frames.

10 On the re-territorialization of ethnic identity, race, and national space, see David Palumbo-Liu, 'Multiculturalism Now: Civilization, National Identity, and Difference before and after September 11,' *boundary 2* 29 (2002): 122.

11 On the shift from Cold War area studies of Asia towards interdisciplinary and politically situated and global/local versions of the US/Asia geopolity, see Bruce Cumings, 'Boundary Displacement: The State, the Foundations, and Area Studies during and after the Cold War,' in *Learning Places: The Afterlives of Area Studies*, ed. Masao Miyoshi and Harry Harootunian (Durham, NC: Duke University Press, 2002), 261–302.

12 In Arif Dirlik, ed., *What's in a Rim? Critical Perspectives on the Pacific Region Idea* (Boulder, CO: Westview, 1993), 319.

13 'Asia-Pacific in Asian-American Perspective,' 325. See also Evelyn Hu-deHart, ed., *Across the Pacific: Asian Americans and Globalization* (Philadel-

phia: Temple University Press, 1999) on the transnationalization of US ethnic Asian frames.

14 For a critique of this 'spatial turn' and the appeal to chronotopes of 'spatial-temporal relationship,' see Harry Harootunian, 'Some Thoughts on Comparability and the Space-Time Problem,' *boundary 2* 32.2 (2005): 23–52, and 'Tracking the Dinosaur: Area Studies in a Time of "Globalism,"' chapter 1 in Harootunian, *History's Disquiet*, on the need for a vision of 'co-temporality' and for theoretical auto-critique in any bounded 'area' like Japan, China, or the Pacific islands as such.

15 See Fredric Jameson, *Postmodernism, or, The Cultural Logic of Late Capitalism* (Durham, NC: Duke University Press, 1992), 363.

16 For a hard-hitting critique of the irrelevance of much American Studies multicultural work and ethnic- and gender-based critiques to the state formation of US global hegemony, see Paul Bové, 'Can American Studies Be Area Studies?' in Miyoshi and Harootunian, eds, *Learning Places*, 206–30. On the manifest insufficiency of using nation-based frames in the era of capitalist globalization and the will to neo-liberal empire, see also Donald E. Pease and Robyn Wiegman, eds, *The Futures of American Studies* (Durham, NC: Duke University Press, 2002).

17 NPR news, 15 November 2001.

18 See: http://www.tuvalu.tv/nuke.

19 This practice was not stopped until 1983 when the United States signed treaties with Pacific Island nations relinquishing rights to islands, keys, and rocks claimed under the Guano Act. See Brij V. Lal and Kate Fortune, eds, *The Pacific Islands: An Encylopedia* (Honolulu: University of Hawaii Press, 2000), 239.

20 See: http://www.cia.gov/cia/publications/factbook/geos/tv.html.

21 See 'Tonga's Jester Has Last Laugh,' BBC Asia-Pacific News, 6 October 2001. According to this report, Tonga's King Taufaahau Tupou IV made this Bank of America account investment because the 'government would only spend it on building roads.'

22 See Andrew Quinn, 'Laughing All the Way to the Bank,' Reuters News Service, San Francisco, 6 June 2002.

23 *San Jose Mercury News*, 28 June 2002, p. A2

24 On Disney's quest to Hawaiianize and localize this tale originally slated to be set in Kansas, see Michael Tsai, '"Lilo & Stitch" Creators Get the Details Right,' *Honolulu Advertiser*, 20 June 2002.

25 'I've felt very free to inject some Hawaiianisms into the film,' the non-Hawaiian Carrere has remarked, merging indigenous Hawaiian into all-purpose localism, as signalled by her use of Pidgin English as sign of

Hawaiianess. Producer Clark Spencer similarly revealed that Jason Scott Lee (as David Kawena) and Carrere (playing big sister Nani) were cast into leading roles because 'we wanted to get some Hawaiian voices in the film because [the film] takes place in Hawaii.' See: http://members.fortunecity.com/backtodisney/LiloAndStitch.html.

26 See Tsai, '"Lilo & Stitch" Creators Get the Details Right.' As Kamehameha Schools Chorus director Lynell Bright says (in the same article) in praise of the film's two Hawaiian songs (which she conducted), 'With these songs, the exposure to the Hawaiian language will be worldwide.'

27 Malia Jones, quoted in Tsai, '"Lilo & Stitch" Creators Get the Details Right.'

28 On Disney's distortions of Fa Mulan into an icon of individual success and US pop feminism, see Yunte Huang, *Transpacific Displacement: Ethnography, Translation, and Intertextual Travel in Twentieth-Century American Literature* (Berkeley: University of California Press, 2002), 162–3.

29 See Jinny Gudmundsen, '"Lilo & Stitch" Goes Interactive,' *San Jose Mercury News*, 1 August 2002, p. 2E.

30 Sally Engle Merry, *Colonizing Hawaii: The Cultural Power of Law* (Princeton: Princeton University Press, 2000), 130–1.

31 Paul Gilroy, *Against Race: Imagining Political Culture beyond the Color Line* (Cambridge: Harvard University Press, 2000), 13–21. Gilroy is addressing the 'planetary traffic in the imagery of blackness' (21), which in a Pacific context often shifts into a fantasy of indigenous and Asian otherness in American contact-zones of proximity, admiration, and mixture.

32 On tactics of native ontology and sovereignty emerging across the Pacific, see Linda Tuhiwai Smith, *Decolonizing Methodologies: Research and Indigenous Peoples* (London and New York: Zed Books, 1999).

33 See Annie Nakao, 'Restless Spirits Lurk Everywhere in Hawaii,' *San Francisco Chronicle*, 1 August 2002, p. D12, who draws an ecological imperative: 'But much of the island lore emanates [not just from immigrant Japanese but] from a native Hawaiian culture that respects its spiritual environment – not a bad way to live on the earth.' If this is animistic myth, it offers some alternative stories for an ethos of place.

34 For a 'Polyn-Asian'–based updating of 'how island paradises are produced for global consumption,' see Jonathan Gil Harris and Anna Neill, 'Hollywood's Pacific Junk: The Wreckage of Colonial History in *Six Days and Seven Nights* and *Rapa Nui*,' *UTS Review* 7 (November 2001): 68-85: 'Consequently, the South Pacific has been colonized by Hollywood as a site of cultural rather than capital production, within which U.S. commercial ambitions can be phantasmatically reimagined and replayed' (76).

35 Édouard Glissant, 'Introductions,' in *Caribbean Discourse: Selected Essays*,

trans. J. Michael Dash (Charlottesville: University Press of Virginia, 1989), 3. On Glissant's version of 'contrastive poetics' as creolized global/local survival tactic, see p. 173.

36 See the by-now classic formulations in Roberto Fernández Retamar, *Caliban and Other Essays*, trans. Edward Baker (Minneapolis: University of Minnesota Press, 1989), particularly chapter 1, 'Caliban: Notes towards a Discussion of Culture in Our America.' This vision of a politicized and situated geopolitics of culture builds upon José Marti's 'New World' vision of 'our' ongoing North/South American geopolitical imbalances, blockages, and global/local injustices. As Fredric Jameson describes the plight of aesthetics in his foreword to Retamar's work, in entangled small island sites of richly creolized culture like Cuba, 'the political is a destiny, where human beings are from the outset condemned to politics' and to the broader decolonizing struggles of Third World alliance and trans-local formations (viii).

37 For a fine study of indigenous resistance and of nativist strategies to challenge global tourism and its white mythologies and fantasy needs in the contemporary Pacific, see Paul Lyons, *American Pacificism: Oceania in the U.S. Imagination* (London and New York: Routledge, 2005).

38 Paul Virilio, *War and Cinema: The Logistics of Perception*, trans. Patrick Camiller (London: Verso, 1989), 95n. On the US war movies of John Houston, Anatole Litvak, and Frank Capra, made in an era when Nazi-based German cinema (via Joseph Goebbels) sought to overcome 'American superproductions' and undermine 'the American perceptual arsenal' of world cinema, see pp. 9–10.

39 On the civilizational antagonism posited between a Euro-American-oriented West Coast bonded to Greco-Roman grandeur and the perils of a modernizing Asia which Hearst and others propagated, see Gray Brechin, *Imperial San Francisco: Urban Power, Earthly Ruin* (Berkeley: University of California Press, 1999), 230ff.

40 The stereotypical racial sway of Helper's work is quoted and discussed in Robert G. Lee, *Orientals: Asian Americans in Popular Culture* (Philadelphia: Temple University Press, 1999), 49, 26.

41 Yunte Huang, *Transpacific Displacement*, 3.

42 Ibid., 16.

43 Ibid., 24.

44 Ibid., 115.

45 Ibid., 187.

46 Ibid.

47 See Mary Louise Pratt, *Imperial Eyes: Travel Writing and Transculturation* (London and New York: Routledge, 1992), 69.

48 On the move from a 'synecdochical model' of political identity to an 'allegorical' vision of geopolitical comparison, as informing a transnationalized
vision of cultural studies in a decentred or post-US frame, see Kristin Ross,
'The World Literature and Cultural Studies Program [at UC Santa Cruz],'
Critical Inquiry 19 (1993): 670–4.

49 For emerging diasporic-based work in US Pacific studies, see the forthcoming essay by April K. Henderson, 'Makin' Moves on Your Regional Imaginary: Hip Hopping the Discursive Fields of Ethnic Studies and Pacific
Islands Studies' and the special issue of *Contemporary Pacific* devoted to
forging a Native Pacific Cultural Studies working 'On the Edge' (vol. 13,
2001) of area studies and across national and disciplinary borders.

Bibliography

Abell, Peter. 'Sociological Theory and Rational Choice Theory,' In *Social Theory*. Ed. Bryan Turner. Oxford: Blackwell, 1996. 252–77.

Abrams, Meyer Howard. *The Mirror and the Lamp: Romantic Theory and the Critical Tradition*. New York: Oxford Press, 1953.

Affergan, Francis. *Exotisme et altérité*. Paris: Presses universitaires de France, 1987.

Agamben, Giorgio. *Homo Sacer: Sovereign Power and Bare Life*. Trans. Daniel Heller-Roazen. Stanford: Stanford University Press, 1998.

Ahmad, Aijaz. 'The Politics of Literary Postcoloniality.' *Race & Class* 36 (1995): 14–16.

Aira, César. *La villa*. Buenos Aires: Emecé, 2001.

Amselle, Jean-Loup. *Vers un multiculturalisme français: l'empire de la coutume*. Paris: Champs Flammarion, 1998.

Antelme, Robert. *L'Espèce humaine*. 1947. Paris: Gallimard, 1957.

– *Textes inédits sur 'L'Espèce humaine': essais et témoignages*. Ed. Daniel Dobbels. Paris: Gallimard, 1996.

Appadurai, Arjun. 'Disjuncture and Difference in the Global Cultural Economy.' *Public Culture* 2.2 (1990): 1–23.

– 'Global Ethnoscapes: Notes and Queries for a Transnational Anthropology.' In *Interventions: Anthropologies of the Present*. Ed. R.G. Fox. Santa Fe: School of American Research, 1991. 191–210.

– *Modernity at Large: Cultural Dimensions of Globalization*. Minneapolis: University of Minnesota Press, 1996.

Apter, Emily. *Continental Drift: From National Characters to Virtual Subjects*. Chicago: University of Chicago Press, 1999.

Aristotle. *Poetics*. Trans. Stephen Halliwell. Cambridge: Harvard University Press, 1999.

Arnaud, Jacqueline. *Recherches sur la littérature maghrébine de langue française: le cas de Kateb Yacine*. Lille: Atelier National Reproduction des Thèses, 1982.

Arnold, A. James. 'The Field: Regional vs Global Models.' *Francophone Postcolonial Studies* 1.2 (Autumn/Winter 2003): 7–10.

Ashcroft, Bill, Gareth Griffins, and Helen Tiffin. *The Empire Writes Back: Theory and Practice in Post-Colonial Literatures.* London: Routledge, 1989.

Attridge, Derek. *J.M. Coetzee and the Ethics of Reading.* Chicago and London: University of Chicago Press, 2004.

– *The Singularity of Literature.* London and New York: Routledge, 2004.

Augé, Marc. *Non-lieux: introduction à une anthropologie de la surmodernité.* Paris: Seuil, 1992.

Bachelard, Gaston. *La Poétique de la rêverie.* Paris: Presses universitaires de France, 1961.

– *La Poétique de l'espace.* Paris: Presses universitaires de France, 1957.

Badiou, Alain. *Manifeste pour la philosophie.* Paris: Seuil, 1987.

Baudrillard, Jean. *Paroxysm: Interviews with Philippe Petit.* Trans. Chris Turner. London and New York: Verso, 1998.

Bauman, Zygmunt. *Globalization: The Human Consequences.* New York: Columbia University Press, 1998.

– *The Individualist Society.* Cambridge: Polity Press, 2001.

– 'The Making and Unmaking of Strangers.' In *Debating Cultural Hybridity: Multi-Cultural Identities and the Politics of Anti-Racism.* Ed. Pnina Werbner and Tariq Modood. London: Zed Books, 1997.

– *Mortality, Immortality, and Other Life Strategies.* Cambridge: Polity Press, 1992.

Beaujour, Michel. *Miroirs d'encre: rhétorique de l'autoportrait.* Paris: Seuil, 1980.

Becker, Gary. *The Economic Approach to Human Behavior.* Chicago: University of Chicago Press, 1976.

Bellatín, Mario. *Salón de belleza.* México: Tusquets, 1995.

Bernabé, Jean. *Fondal-Natal: grammaire basilectale approchée des créoles guadeloupéens et martiniquais.* Paris: L'Harmattan, 1983.

Bernheimer, Charles, ed. *Comparative Literature in the Age of Multiculturalism.* Baltimore: Johns Hopkins University Press, 1994.

Bhabha, Homi, 'The Third Space.' In *Identity: Community, Culture, Difference.* Ed. J. Rutherford. London: Lawrence and Wishart, 1990. 207–21.

– 'The World and the Home.' In *Dangerous Liaisons: Gender, Nation, and Postcolonial Perspectives.* Ed. Anne McClintock, Amir Mufti, and Ella Shohat. Minneapolis: University of Minnesota Press, 1997. 445–55.

Bickerton, Derek. *Dynamics of Creole System.* Cambridge: Cambridge University Press, 1975.

Blanchot, Maurice. *L'Amitié.* Paris: Gallimard, 1971.

– *La Communauté inavouable.* Paris: Minuit, 1983.

– *Écrits politiques: guerre d'Algérie, mai 68 etc. (1958–1993)*. Paris: Lignes et manifestes/Léo Scheer, 2003.
– *L'Entretien infini*. Paris: Gallimard, 1969.
– *L'Espace littéraire*. Paris: Gallimard, 1955.
– *L'Instant de ma mort*. 1994. Paris: Gallimard, 2002.
– *La Part du feu*. Paris: Gallimard, 1949.
Bongie, Chris. 'Belated Liaisons: Writing between the Margins of Literary and Cultural Studies.' *Francophone Postcolonial Studies* 1.2 (2003): 11–24.
– 'Exiles on Main Stream: Valuing the Popularity of Postcolonial Literature.' *Postmodern Culture* 14.1 (September 2003).
Booth, Wayne. *The Company We Keep: An Ethics of Fiction*. Berkeley: University of California Press, 1998.
Bourdieu Pierre. *Contre feux: propos pour servir à la résistance contre l'invasion néo-libérale*. Paris: Liber / Raisons d'agir, 1998.
Bove, Paul. 'Can American Studies Be Area Studies?' In *Learning Places: The Afterlives of Area Studies*. Ed. Masao Miyoshi and H. Harootunian. Durham, NC: Duke University Press, 2002. 206–30.
Brechin, Gray. *Imperial San Francisco: Urban Power, Earthly Ruin*. Berkeley: University of California Press, 1999.
Brennan, Timothy. *At Home in the World: Cosmopolitanism Now*. Cambridge: Harvard University Press, 1997.
– 'World Music Does Not Exist.' *Discourse: Journal for Theoretical Studies in Media and Culture* 23.1 ('Imperial Disclosures II') (Winter 2001): 44–62.
Brij, V. Lal, and Kate Fortune, eds. *The Pacific Islands: An Encyclopedia*. Honolulu: University of Hawai'i Press, 2000.
Britton, Celia. *Edouard Glissant and Postcolonial Theory: Strategies of Language and Resistance*. Charlottesville and London: University Press of Virginia, 1999.
– *The Nouveau roman: Fiction, Theory, and Politics*. London: Macmillan, 1992.
Brown, Nicholas. 'The Eidaesthetic Itinerary: Notes on the Geopolitical Movement of the Literary Absolute.' *South Atlantic Quarterly* 100.3 (Summer 2001): 829–52.
Bruns, Gerald L. 'The Concepts of Art and Poetry in Emmanuel Levinas's Writings.' In *The Cambridge Companion to Emmanuel Levinas*. Ed. Simon Critchley and Robert Bernasconi. Cambridge: Cambridge University Press, 2002.
Bullock, Alan, and Stephen Trombley, eds. *The New Fontana Dictionary of Modern Thought*. London: HarperCollins, 1999.
Butler, Judith. *Giving an Account of Oneself*. New York: Fordham University Press, 2006.
– *Subjects of Desire: Hegelian Reflections in Twentieth-Century France*. New York: Columbia University Press, 1987.

Butler, Judith, Ernesto Laclau, and Slavoj Žižek. *Contingency, Hegemony, Universality: Contemporary Dialogues on the Left*. London: Verso, 2000.

Cailler, Bernadette. 'Totalité et infini, altérité et relation: d'Emmanuel Levinas à Édouard Glissant.' In *Poétiques d'Edouard Glissant*. Ed. Jacques Chevrier. Paris: Presses de l'universite de Paris-Sorbonne, 1999. 112–31.

Canclini, Nestor Garcia. *Consumers and Citizens: Globalization and Multicultural Conflicts*. Minneapolis: Minnesota University Press, 2001.

Cantor, Jay. *The Space Between, Literature and Politics*. Baltimore: Johns Hopkins University Press, 1981.

Carnegie, Charles V. *Postnationalism Prefigured: Caribbean Borderlands*. New Brunswick, NJ: Rutgers University Press, 2002.

– 'Reaching for the Border.' *Small Axe* 10.2 (March 2006): v–ix.

Casanova, Pascale. *La République mondiale des lettres*. Paris: Seuil, 1999.

Chastel, André, 'André Malraux: métamorphose de l'art.' *Critique* 478 (1987): 185–202.

Cheah, Pheng, and Bruce Robbins. *Cosmopolitics: Thinking and Feeling beyond the Nation*. Minneapolis: University of Minnesota Press, 1998.

Chraïbi, Driss. *Le Passé simple*. Paris: Denoël, 1954.

Clark, Timothy. *Derrida, Heidegger, Blanchot: Sources of Derrida's Notion and Practice of Literature*. Cambridge: Cambridge University Press, 1992.

– 'Singularity in Criticism.' *Cambridge Quarterly* 33.4 (2004): 395–8.

Clifford, James. *The Predicament of Culture: Twentieth Century Ethnography, Literature, Art*. Cambridge: Harvard University Press, 1988.

– *Routes: Travel and Translation in the Late Twentieth Century*. Cambridge: Harvard University Press, 1997.

– *Writing Culture: The Poetics and Politics of Ethnography*. Berkeley: University of California Press, 1986.

Coetzee, J.M. *Elizabeth Costello*. New York: Viking, 2003.

Cohen, Joshua, ed. *For Love of Country: Debating the Limits of Patriotism*. Boston: Beacon Press, 1996.

Comparative Literature 53.4 (Autumn 2001). Special issue on 'Globalization and the Humanities.'

Comparative Literature Studies 41.1 (2004). Special issue on 'Globalization and World Literature.'

Connolly, William. *The Augustinian Imperative: A Reflection on the Politics of Morality*. London: Sage, 1993.

– *Ethos of Pluralization*. Minneapolis: University of Minnesota Press, 1995.

Cooper, Frederick. *Colonialism in Question: Theory, Knowledge, History*. Berkeley: University of California Press, 2005.

Cooppan, Vilashini. 'World Literature and Global Theory: Comparative Literature for the New Millennium' *Symploke* 9.1–2 (2001): 15–43.

Corey, Paul. 'Totality and Ambivalence: Postmodern Responses to Globalization and the American Empire.' Unpublished article. 2004. (Web-archived.)

Critchley, Simon. *The Ethics of Deconstruction: Derrida and Levinas.* Oxford: Blackwell, 1992 (2nd edition, Edinburgh University Press, 1999).

– *Ethics, Politics, Subjectivity: Essays on Derrida, Levinas, and Contemporary French Thought.* London: Verso, 1999.

Crowley, Martin. *Duras, Writing, and the Ethical.* Oxford: Oxford University Press, 2001.

Cumings, Bruce. 'Boundary Displacement: The State, the Foundations, and Area Studies during and after the Cold War.' In *Learning Places: The Afterlives of Area Studies.* Ed. Masao Miyoshi and Harry Harootunian. Durham, NC: Duke University Press, 2002. 261–302.

Damrosch, David. *What Is World Literature?* Princeton: Princeton University Press, 2003.

Dash, J. Michael. 'Postcolonial Thought and the Francophone Caribbean.' In *Francophone Postcolonial Studies: A Critical Introduction.* Ed. Charles Forsdick and David Murphy. London: Arnold, 2003. 231–41.

Davis, Colin. 'Antelme, Renoir, Levinas, and the Shock of the Other.' *French Cultural Studies* 14 (2003): 41–51.

– *Ethical Issues in Twentieth-Century Fiction: Killing the Other.* Basingstoke: Macmillan, 2000.

Davis, T., and K. Womack. *Mapping the Ethical Turn: A Reader in Ethics, Culture, and Literary Theory.* Charlottesville: University of Virginia Press, 2001.

de Gaulle, Charles. 'Discours prononcé à Bayeux' (1946) and 'Allocution prononcée à l'occasion de l'ouverture de la conférence de Brazzaville' (1944). In *Discours et messages.* 5 vols. Paris: Plon, 1970. 2:5–11 and 1:370–3.

– *Mémoires de guerre.* 3 vols. Paris: Plon, 1959.

– *Mémoires d'espoir: le renouveau (1958–62), l'effort (1962 ...), allocutions et messages (1946–1969).* Paris: Plon, 1994.

de la Gorce, Paul Marie. 'De Gaulle et la décolonisation.' In *De Gaulle en son siècle 6: liberté et dignité des peuples.* Paris: Institut Charles de Gaulle / La Documentation française / Plon, 1992. 11–34

de Man, Paul. *Allegories of Reading: Figural Language in Rousseau, Nietzsche, Rilke, and Proust.* New Haven: Yale University Press, 1979.

de Saussure, Ferdinand. *Cours de linguistique générale.* Paris: Payot, 1968.

de Zengotita, Tomás, 'Common Ground: Finding Our Way back to the Enlightenment.' *Harper's* 306 (January 2003): 35–45.

Debord, Guy. *La Société du spectacle*. Paris: Champ Libre, 1967.

Deleuze, Gilles, and Félix Guattari. *Capitalisme et schizophrénie I: l'anti-Œdipe*. Paris: Minuit, 1972.

– *Kafka: pour une littérature mineure*. Paris: Minuit, 1975.

Derrida, Jacques. *Le Monolinguisme de l'autre, ou la prothèse de l'origine*. Paris: Galilée, 1996.

Diacritics 31.3 (Fall 2001). Special issue on 'Theory, Globalization, Cultural Studies, and the Remains of the University.'

Dimock, Wai Chee. 'Genre as World System: Epic and Novel on Four Continents.' *Narrative* 14.1 (January 2006): 85–101.

Dirlik, Arif, ed. *What's in a Rim? Critical Perspectives on the Pacific Region Idea*. Boulder, CO: Westview, 1993.

During, Simon, ed. *Cultural Studies Reader*. London: Routledge, 1999.

Durkheim, Émile. *Les Formes élémentaires de la vie religieuse: le système totémique en Australie*. 1912; Paris: Livre de poche, 1991.

Eckstein, Barbara. *The Language of Fiction in a World of Pain: Reading Politics as Paradox*. Philadelphia: Pennsylvania University Press, 1990.

Elster, Jon. *Nuts and Bolts for the Social Sciences*. Cambridge: Cambridge University Press, 1989.

Eltit, Diamela. *Mano de obra*. Santiago: Seix Barral, 2002.

– *Los vigilantes*. Santiago: Sudamericana, 1994.

Encyclopaedia of Islam. 2nd ed. Vol. 5. Leiden: Brill, 1986.

Engle Merry, Sally. *Colonizing Hawaii: The Cultural Power of Law*. Princeton: Princeton University Press, 2000.

Eskin, Michael. 'On Literature and Ethics.' *Poetics Today* 25.4 (Winter 2004): 573–94.

Finkielkraut, Alain. *La Mémoire vaine*. Paris: Gallimard, 1989.

Freadman, Richard. 'Ethics, Autobiography and the Will: Stephen Spender's *World within World*.' In *The Ethics in Literature*. Ed. Andrew Hadfield, Dominic Rainsford, and Tim Woods. London: Palgrave Macmillan, 1999.

Gallagher, Mary. 'L'assujettissement du sujet poétique antillais.' In *Sens et présence du sujet poétique français et francophone depuis 1980*. Ed. Michael Brophy and Mary Gallagher. Amsterdam and New York: Rodopi, 2006. 117–25.

– 'Contemporary French Caribbean Poetry, or the Poetics of Reference.' *Forum for Modern Language Studies* 40.4 (2004): 451–62.

– 'The *Créolité* Movement: Paradoxes of a French Caribbean Orthodoxy.' In *Creolization: History, Ethnography, Theory*. Ed. Charles Stewart. Walnut Creek, CA: Left Coast Press, 2007. 220–36.

– 'La poétique de la diversité dans les essais d'Édouard Glissant.' In *Horizons d'Édouard Glissant*. Biarritz: J & D Editions, 1992. 27–35.

Gerber, François. *Malraux–De Gaulle: la nation retrouvée*. Paris: L'Harmattan, 1996.
Gibson-Graham, J.K. *The End of Capitalism as We Knew It: A Feminist Critique of Political Economy*. Oxford: Blackwells, 1996.
– *A Post-Capitalist Politics*. Minneapolis: University of Minnesota Press, 2006.
Giddens, Anthony. *Consequences of Modernity*. Palo Alto: Stanford University Press, 1990.
Gikandi, Simon, 'Globalization and the Claims of Postcoloniality.' *South Atlantic Quarterly* 100.3 (Summer 2001): 627–58.
Gilroy, Paul. *Against Race: Imagining Political Culture beyond the Color Line*. Cambridge: Harvard University Press, 2000.
Glissant, Édouard. *La Cohée du Lamentin. Poétique V*. Paris: Gallimard, 2005.
– *Le Discours antillais*. Paris: Seuil, 1981. *Caribbean Discourse: Selected Essays*. Trans. J. Michael Dash. Charlottesville: University of Virginia Press, 1992.
– *L'Intention poétique*. Paris : Seuil, 1969.
– *Introduction à une poétique du divers*. Paris: Gallimard, 1996.
– *Une nouvelle région du monde. Ésthétique I*. Paris: Gallimard, 2006.
– *Poétique de la Relation*. Paris: Gallimard, 1990. *Poetics of Relation*. Trans. Betsy Wing. Ann Arbor: University of Michigan Press, 1997.
– *Le Quatrième Siècle*. Paris: Seuil, 1964.
– *Soleil de la conscience*. Paris: Seuil, 1956.
– *Tout-monde*. Paris: Gallimard, 1993.
– *Traité du tout-monde. Poétique IV*. Paris: Gallimard, 1997.
Hadfield, Andrew, Dominic Rainsford, and Tim Woods, eds. 'Introduction.' In *The Ethics in Literature*. London: Macmillan, 1999.
Hall, Stuart. 'Whose Heritage? Un-settling "The Heritage," Re-imagining the Post-nation.' *Third Text* 49 (Winter 1999–2000): 3–13.
Hallward, Peter. *Absolutely Postcolonial: Writing between the Singular and the Specific*. Manchester: Manchester University Press, 2001.
– 'Edouard Glissant between the Singular and the Specific.' *Yale Journal of Criticism* 11.2 (1998): 441–62.
Hannerz, Ulf. *Transnational Connections*. London: Routledge, 1996.
Hardt, Michael, and Antonio Negri. *Empire*. Cambridge: Harvard University Press, 2000.
Harootunian, Harry. *History's Disquiet: Modernity, Cultural Practice, and the Question of Everyday Life*. New York: Columbia University Press, 2000.
– 'Some Thoughts on Comparability and the Space-Time Problem.' *boundary 2* 32.2 (Summer 2005): 23–52.
Harrison, Nicholas. *Postcolonial Criticism: History, Theory, and the Work of Fiction*. Cambridge: Polity Press, 2003.
– 'Who Needs an Idea of the Literary.' *Paragraph* 28.2 (July 2005): 1–17.

Hartman, Geoffrey H. *The Fateful Question of Culture*. New York: Columbia University Press, 1997.

Harvey, David. *The Condition of Postmodernity.* Oxford: Blackwell Press, 1989.

Heidegger, Martin. *Being and Time*. Trans. John Macquarrie and Edward Robinson. 1962. Oxford: Basil Blackwell, 1988.

Hill, Leslie. *Apolcalyptic Desires*. London: Routledge: 1993.

– *Bataille, Klossowski, Blanchot: Writing at the Limit*. Oxford: Oxford University Press, 2001.

– *Blanchot: Extreme Contemporary*. London: Routledge, 1997.

– '"Distrust of Poetry": Levinas, Blanchot, Celan.' *Modern Language Notes* 120 (2005): 986–1007.

Hillis Miller, J. *The Ethics of Reading: Kant, de Man, Eliot, Trollope, James, and Benjamin*. New York: Columbia University Press, 1987.

Huang, Yunte. *Transpacific Displacement: Ethnography, Translation, and Intertextual Travel in Twentieth-Century American Literature*. Berkeley: University of California Press, 2002.

Hu-deHart, Evelyn, ed. *Across the Pacific: Asian Americans and Globalization*. Philadelphia: Temple University Press, 1999.

Huggan, Graham. *The Post-colonial Exotic: Marketing the Margins*. London: Routledge, 2001.

Hutnik, John 'Adorno at Womad: South Asian Crossovers and the Limits of Hybridity Talk.' In *Debating Cultural Hybridity: Multi-Cultural Identities and the Politics of Anti-Racism*. Ed. Pnina Werbner and Tariq Modood. London: Zed Books, 1997. 106–36.

Jameson, Fredric. 'Modernism and Its Repressed: Robbe-Grillet as Anti-colonialist.' *Diacritics* 6.2 (Summer 1976): 7–14.

– 'Notes on Globalization as a Philosophical Issue.' In *The Cultures of Globalization*. Ed. Fredric Jameson and Masao Miyoshi. Durham, NC: Duke University Press, 1998.

– *Postmodernism, or, The Cultural Logic of Late Capitalism*. Durham, NC: Duke University Press, 1992.

– *A Singular Modernity: Essay on the Ontology of the Present*. London: Verso, 2002.

– 'Transformations of the Image in Postmodernity.' In *The Cultural Turn: Selected Writings on the Postmodern 1983–1998*. London: Verso, 1998. 93–135.

Jameson, Fredric, and Masao Miyoshi, eds. *The Cultures of Globalization*. Durham, NC: Duke University Press, 1998.

Jay, Paul. 'Beyond Discipline? Globalization and the Future of English.' *PMLA* 116.1 (Special issue on 'Globalizing Literary Study') (January 2001): 32–47.

Jefferess, David, and Simon Gikandi. 'Postcolonialism's Ethical (Re-)Turn: An Interview with Simon Gikandi.' *Postcolonial Text* 2.1 (2006).

Kadra-Hadjadji, Houaria. *Contestation et révolte dans l'œuvre de Driss Chraïbi.* Algiers: ENAL, 1986.

Kaplan, Caren. *Questions of Travel: Postmodern Discourses of Displacement.* Durham, NC: Duke University Press: 1996.

Kaye, Jacqueline, and Abdelhamid Zoubir. *The Ambiguous Compromise: Language, Literature and National Identity in Algeria and Morocco.* London and New York: Routledge, 1990.

Keenan, Thomas. *Fables of Responsibility: Aberrations of Predicaments in Ethics and Politics.* Palo Alto, CA: Stanford University Press, 1997.

Kojève, Alexandre. *Introduction à la lecture de Hegel.* Ed. Raymond Queneau. 1947. Paris: Gallimard, 1968.

Krauss, Rosalind. 'The Ministry of Fate.' In *A New History of French Literature.* Ed. Denis Hollier. Cambridge, MA: Harvard University Press, 1989. 1000–6.

Krishnaswamy, Revathi. 'The Criticism of Culture and the Culture of Criticism: At the Intersection of Postcolonialism and Globalization Theory.' *Diacritics* 32.2 (Summer 2002): 106–28.

Kristeva, Julia. *Étrangers à nous-mêmes.* Paris: Fayard, 1989. *Strangers to Ourselves.* Trans. Leon S. Roudiez. New York: Columbia University Press, 1995.

– *Le Génie féminin I, Hannah Arendt* (Paris: Fayard, 1999); *II, La Folie: Mélanie Klein* (Paris: Fayard, 2000); *III, Colette* (Paris: Fayard, 2002).

– *Histoires d'amour.* Paris: Denoël, 1983. *Tales of Love.* Trans. Leon. S Roudiez. New York: Columbia University Press, 1987.

– *Les Nouvelles Maladies de l'âme.* Paris: Fayard, 1993. *New Maladies of the Soul.* Trans. R. Guberman. New York: Columbia University Press, 1995.

– *La Révolte intime: discours direct.* Paris: Fayard, 1997. *Intimate Revolt: The Powers and Limits of Psychoanalysis.* Trans. Jeanine Herman. New York: Columbia University Press, 2002.

– *Les Samouraï.* Paris: Fayard, 1990. *The Samurai.* Trans. Barbara Bray. New York: Columbia University Press, 1992.

– *Soleil noir: dépression et mélancolie.* Paris: Gallimard, 1987. *Black Sun: Depression and Melancholia.* Trans. Leon S. Roudiez. New York: Columbia University Press, 1989.

Laclau, Ernesto, and Chantal Mouffe. *Hegemony and Socialist Strategy: Towards a Radical Democaratic Politics.* London: Verso, 1985.

Lacoue-Labarthe, Philippe. 'Fidélités.' In *L'Animal autobiographique: autour de Jacques Derrida.* Ed. Marie-Louise Mallet. Paris: Galilée, 1999.

Larsen, Neil 'Theory-Risk: Reflections on Globalization Theory and the Crisis in Argentina.' *New Centennial Review* 3.2 (2003): 23–40.

Lee, Robert J. *Orientals: Asian Americans in Popular Culture.* Philadelphia: Temple University Press, 1999.

Lejeune, Philippe. *Le Pacte autobiographique*. Paris: Seuil, 1975.

Levinas, Emmanuel. *Autrement qu'être, ou au-delà de l'essence*. The Hague: Martinus Nijhoff, 1974.*Otherwise than Being, or Beyond Essence*. Trans. Alphonso Lingis. Pittsburgh: Duquesne University Press, 1981.

– *De l'existence à l'existant*. Paris: Vrin, 1986.

– 'Enigma and Phenomenon.' In *Basic Philosophical Writings*. Ed. Adriaan T. Peperzak, Simon Critchley, and Robert Bernasconi. Bloomington and Indianapolis: Indiana University Press, 1996.

– *Entre nous*. Paris: Grasset & Fasquelle, 1991.

– *Éthique et infini*. Paris: Fayard, 1982.

– *Hors sujet*. Paris: Fata Morgana, 1987. *Outside the Subject*. Trans. Michael B. Smith. Stanford: Stanford University Press, 1993.

– *Humanisme de l'autre homme*. Paris: Fata Morgana, 1972.

– *Les Imprévus de l'histoire*. Paris: Livre de poche, 1994.

– *Noms propres*. Paris: Fata Morgana, 1976. *Proper Names*. Trans. Michael B. Smith. Stanford: Stanford University Press, 1996.

– 'La Réalité et son ombre.' *Les Temps Modernes* 38 (1948): 771–89.

– *Sur Maurice Blanchot*. Paris: Fata Morgana, 1975.

– *Totalité et infini: un essai sur l'extériorité*. The Hague: Martinus Nijhoff, 1961. *Totality and Infinity: An Essay on Exteriority*. Trans. Alphonso Lingis. Pittsburgh: Duquesne University Press, 1969.

– *Transcendance et intelligibilité*. Paris: Labor et Fides, 1984.

Lionnet, Françoise, and Shu-mei Shih, eds. *Minor Transnationalisms*. Durham, NC: Duke University Press, 2003.

Livingston, Paisley. 'Intentionalism in Aesthetics.' *New Literary History* 29.4 (1989): 831–46.

Loomba, Ania. *Colonialism/Postcolonialism*. London: Routledge, 2000.

Lyotard, Jean-François. *Chambre sourde: l'antiesthétique de Malraux*. Paris: Galilée, 1998.

– 'Le Monstre a occupé mes décombres (D'une biographie de Malraux),' *Critique* 591–2 (1996): 628–45.

– *Signé Malraux*. Paris: Grasset & Fasquelle, 1996.

MacIntyre, Alisdair. *A Short History of Ethics*. New York, Macmillan, 1966.

Malraux, André. *Le Miroir des limbes I: antimémoires*. Paris: Gallimard/Folio, 1972.

– *Le Miroir des limbes II: la corde et la souris*. Paris: Gallimard/Folio, 1976.

– *Le Musée imaginaire*. Paris: Gallimard, 1965.

– *La Politique, la culture: discours, articles, entretiens (1925–1975)*. Ed. Janine Mossuz-Lavau. Paris: Gallimard, 1996.

– *La Tête d'obsidienne*. Paris: Gallimard, 1974.

Marx, Karl, and Friedrich Engels. 'The Communist Manifesto (1848).' In *Karl*

Marx: Selected Writings. Ed. David McLellan. Oxford: Oxford University Press, 1977.

Maturana, Humberto, and Francisco Varela. *Autopoiesis and Cognition: The Realization of the Living.* Boston: D. Reidel, 1980.

Merleau-Ponty, Maurice. *Phenomenology of Perception.* Trans. Colin Smith. New York: Humanities Press, 1962.

– *Signs.* Trans. Richard McCleary. Evanston, IL: Northwestern University Press, 1964.

Miyoshi, Masao. 'A Borderless World? From Colonialism to Transnationalism and the Decline of the Nation-State.' *Critical Inquiry* 19 (Summer 1993): 726–51.

Modern Language Quarterly 65.3 (2004). Special issue on 'Globalism and Theory.'

Moretti, Franco. *Atlas of the European Novel 1800–1900.* London and New York: Verso, 1998.

– 'Conjectures on World Literature.' *New Left Review* 1 (January/February 2000): 54–68.

Mosquera, Gerardo. 'Alien-Own/Own-Alien: Globalization and Cultural Difference.' *boundary 2* 29.3 (Fall 2002): 163–74.

Mossuz-Lavau, Janine. *André Malraux et le gaullisme.* 1970. Paris: Presses de la Fondation Nationale des Sciences Politiques, 1982.

Murray, Stephen O., ed. *Islamic Homosexualities: Culture, History, and Literature.* New York: New York University Press, 1997.

Nancy, Jean-Luc. 'La Communauté désœuvrée.' *Alea* 4 (February 1983): 11–49. Reprinted in extended form in *La Communauté désœuvrée.* 1986. Paris: Christian Bourgois, 1990. 9–105.

– *La Création du monde ou la mondialisation.* Paris: Galilée, 2002.

Nielsen, Greg. 'Bakhtin and Habermas: Toward a Transcultural Ethics.' *Theory and Society* 24 (1995): 803–35.

O, Rachid. *L'Enfant ébloui.* Paris: Gallimard, 1995.

– *Plusieurs vies.* Paris: Gallimard, 1996.

Palumbo-Liu, David. 'Multiculturalism Now: Civilization, National Identity, and Difference before and after September 11.' *boundary 2* 29.2 (Summer 2002): 109–28.

Pease, Donald. 'New Americanists: Revisionist Interventions into the Canon.' *boundary 2* 17.1 (Spring 1990): 1–37.

Pease, Donald E., and Robyn Wiegman, eds. *The Futures of American Studies.* Durham, NC: Duke University Press, 2002.

Pecora, Vincent P. 'Ethics, Politics, and the Middle Voice.' *Yale French Studies* 79 ('Literature and the Ethical Question') (1991): 203–30.

Pickering, Robert. 'Écrire sous l'occupation: les mauvaises pensées et autres de Valéry.' *Revue d'histoire littéraire de la France* 88.6 (Nov./Dec. 1988): 1076–95.

Picon, Gaëtan. *Malraux par lui-même*. Paris: Seuil, 1974.

PMLA 116.1 (January 2001). Special issue on 'Globalizing Literary Studies.'

Pratt, Mary Louise. *Imperial Eyes: Travel Writing and Transculturation*. London and New York: Routledge, 1992.

– 'Tres incendios y dos mujeres extraviadas: el imaginario novelístico frente al nuevo contrato social.' In *Espacio urbano, comunicación y violencia en América Latina*. Ed. Mabel Moraña. Pittsburgh: Instituto Internacional de Literatura Iberoamericana. 2000. 91–106.

– 'Why the Virgin of Zapopan Went to Los Angeles.' In *Images of Power*. Ed. Jens Andersman. Manchester: Manchester University Press, 2004.

Rabaté, Jean-Michel. 'Theory 911.' *PMLA* 118.2 (2003): 331–5.

Rancière, Jacques. 'Éclipse de la politique.' *Lignes* 8 (2002): 35–46.

– *Malaise dans l'esthétique*. Paris: Galilée, 2004.

– *La Parole muette: essai sur les contradictions de la littérature*. Paris: Hachette, 1998.

Rau, Sangeeta 'Ethical Encounters: Spivak, Alexander, and Kincaid.' *Cultural Studies* 17.1 (2003): 42–55.

Readings, Bill. *The University in Ruins*. Cambridge: Harvard University Press, 1996.

Redfield, Marc. 'Introduction.' *Diacritics* 31.3 ('Theory, Globalization, Cultural Studies, and the Remains of the University') (Fall 2001): 2–14.

Retamar, Roberto Fernandez. *Caliban and Other Essays*. Trans. Edward Baker. Minneapolis: University of Minnesota Press, 1989.

Robbins, Bruce. *Feeling Global: Internationalism in Distress*. New York and London: New York University Press, 1999.

Robbins, Jill. 'Aesthetic Totality and Ethical Infinity.' *L'Esprit créateur* 35.3 (1995): 66–79. Reprinted in *Emmanuel Levinas: Critical Assessments of Leading Philosophers*. Ed. Claire Elise Katz. Vol. 5. London: Routledge, 2005. 356–68.

– *Altered Reading: Levinas and Literature*. Chicago: University of Chicago Press, 1999.

Ross, Kristin. 'The World Literature and Cultural Studies Program.' *Critical Inquiry* 19.4 (1993): 666–76.

Russell, Bertrand. *Human Society in Ethics and Politics*. New York: Unwin Hyman, 1954.

Sartre, Jean-Paul. *L'Etre et le néant: essai d'ontologie phénoménologique*. Paris: Gallimard, 1943.

– *Qu'est-ce que la littérature?* Paris: Gallimard, 1948.

Sassens, Saskia. *Losing control? Sovereignty in an Age of Globalization*. New York: Columbia University Press, 1996.

Saussy, Haun. *Comparative Literature in an Age of Globalization*. Baltimore: Johns Hopkins University Press, 2006.

Schehr, Lawrence. *Alcibiades at the Door*. Stanford: Stanford University Press, 1995.

Schmitt, Arno, and Jehoeda Sofer, eds. *Sexuality and Eroticism among Males in Moslem Societies*. New York: The Haworth Press, 1992.

Segalen, Victor. *Essai sur l'exotisme: notes pour une esthétique du divers*. Paris: Fata Morgana, 1978.

Shaw, M., ed. *Politics and Globalization: Knowledge, Ethics, and Agency*. New York: Routdedge, 1995.

Smith, Nathaniel B. 'The Idea of the French Hexagon.' *French Historical Studies* 6.2 (1969): 139–55.

Sorkin, Adam. *Politics and the Muse*. Bowling Green, OH: Bowling Green State University, 1989.

South Atlantic Quarterly 100.3 (Summer 2001). Special issue on 'Anglophone Literatures and the Global.'

Spivak, Gayatri. *A Critique of Postcolonial Reason: Toward a History of the Vanishing Present*. Cambridge: Harvard University Press, 1999.

– *Death of a Discipline*. New York: Columbia University Press, 2003.

– 'Ethics and Politics in Tagore, Coetzee, and Certain Scenes of Reading.' *Diacritics* 32.3/4 (Fall 2002): 17–32.

– 'Explanation and Culture: Marginalia.' In *Out There: Marginalization and Contemporary Cultures*. Ed. Russell Ferguson, Martha Gever, Trinh T. Minh-ha, and Cornell West. Cambridge: MIT Press, 1990.

– 'Teaching for the Times.' In *Dangerous Liaisons: Gender, Nation, and Postcolonial Perspectives*. Ed. Anne McClintock, Amir Mufti, and Ella Shohat. Minneapolis: University of Minnesota Press, 1997. 468–90.

– 'World Systems and the Creole.' *Narrative* 14.1 (January 2006): 102–12.

Szeman, Imre. 'Culture and Globalization, or, The Humanities in Ruins.' *New Centennial Review* 3.2 (2003): 91–115.

– 'Imagining the Future: Globalization, Postmodernism, and Criticism.' Forthcoming in *Metaphors of Globalization: Mirrors, Magicians, and Mutinies*. Ed. Markus Kornprobst et al. London: Palgrave.

– *Zones of Instability: Literature, Postcolonialism, and the Nation*. Baltimore: Johns Hopkins University Press, 2003.

Taylor, Charles. *Sources of the Self: The Making of Modern Identity*. Cambridge: Harvard University Press, 1992.

Tuhiwai Smith, Linda. *Decolonizing Methodologies: Research and Indigenous Peoples*. London and New York: Zed Books, 1999.

Virilio, Paul. *War and Cinema: The Logistics of Perception*. Trans. Patrick Camiller. London: Verso, 1989.

von Hallberg, Robert, ed. *Politics and Poetic Value*. Chicago: University of Chicago Press, 1987.

Wallerstein, Immanuel. *The Modern World System: Capitalist Agriculture and the World Economy in the Sixteenth Century*. New York: Academic Press, 1974.

– 'The National and the Universal: Can There Be Such a Thing as World Culture?' In *Culture, Globalization, and the World System*. Ed. A.D. King. Minneapolis: University of Minnesota Press, 1997. 91–105.

Weber, Eugen, 'L'Hexagone.' In *Les Lieux de mémoire*. Ed. Pierre Nora. 3 vols. Paris: Gallimard/Quarto, 1997. 1:1171–90.

West, Paul. *The Very Rich Hours of Count von Stauffenberg*. Woodstock, NY: The Overlook Press, 1989, ca. 1980.

Wolton, Dominique. *L'Autre Mondialisation*. Paris: Flammarion, 2003.

Wood, Houston. *Displacing Natives: The Rhetorical Production of Hawai'i*. Boulder, CO: Rowman & Littlefield, 1999.

Woods, Tim. *The Poetics of the Limit: Ethics and Politics in Modern and Contemporary Poetry*. London: Palgrave, 2002.

Wright, J.W., and Everett Rowson, eds. *Homoeroticism in Classical Arabic Writing*. New York: Columbia University Press, 1997.

Wynter, Sylvia. 'The Ceremony Must Be Found: After Humanism.' *boundary 2* 12.3 and 13.1 ('Humanism and the University') (Spring-Fall 1984): 19–70.

Young, Robert. *Colonial Desire: Hybridity in Theory, Culture, Race*. London: Routledge, 1995.

– 'Ideologies of the Postcolonial.' *Interventions* 1.1 (1998/9): 4–8.

Young-Bruehl, Elizabeth, ed. *Global Cultures: A Transnational Short Fiction Reader*. Middletown, CT: Wesleyan University Press, 1994.

Notes on Contributors

Celia Britton is Professor of French and Francophone Literature at University College London. She has published widely on French Caribbean literature and thought, including *Édouard Glissant and Postcolonial Theory: Strategies of Language and Resistance* (1999), *Race and the Unconscious: Freudianism in French Caribbean Thought* (2002), and *The Sense of Community in French Caribbean Fiction* (2008).

Mary Gallagher is Associate Professor of French and Francophone Studies at University College Dublin. She has published on Caribbean writing in French, notably *La Créolité de Saint-John Perse* (Gallimard, 1998) and *Soundings in French Caribbean Writing since 1950* (Oxford University Press, 2002), and is currently working on a monograph on Lafcadio Hearn's Creole odyssey.

Julia Kristeva is Professor at the Institut universitaire de France and at the University of Paris 7 – Denis-Diderot and is a member of the Société Psychanalytique de Paris. She also teaches regularly at Columbia University and at the University of Toronto. Her most recent publications are *Seule une femme* (L'Aube, 2007) and *Cet incroyable besoin de croire* (Bayard, 2007).

David Palumbo-Liu is Professor of Comparative Literature at Stanford University. Author of *Asian/American: Historical Crossings of a Racial Frontier* (1999) and co-editor with Hans Ulrich Gumbrecht of *Streams of Cultural Capital: Transnational Cultural Studies* (1997), he is currently co-editing an interdisciplinary anthology, *World-Scale Ambitions*, reassessing world-systems analysis, and completing a monograph on otherness, ethics, globalization, and narrative.

Mary Louise Pratt is Silver Professor at New York University, where she teaches in the Departments of Social and Cultural Analysis, and Spanish and Portuguese. An expanded edition of her well-known book, *Imperial Eyes*, appeared in 2007. She has written numerous essays on Latin American literature and culture, and on neo-liberal forms of planetarity and empire, and is currently studying language and globalization.

Richard Serrano is Associate Professor of French and Comparative Literature at Rutgers University. He is the author of two books, *Neither a Borrower: Forging Traditions in French, Chinese and Arabic Poetry* (Legenda, 2002), and *Against the Postcolonial: Writers at the Ends of French Empire* (Lexington, 2005). He is currently working on two book projects, one exploring the relationship between the Qur'an and poetry, and the other on women and eighteenth-century Chinese and Korean poetry.

Douglas Smith is Senior Lecturer in French and Francophone Studies at University College Dublin. Author of a study on the French reception of Nietzsche (*Transvaluations: Nietzsche in France 1872–1972*), he also translated *On the Genealogy of Morals* and *The Birth of Tragedy* for Oxford World Classics. He has published articles on twentieth-century French literature, cinema, photography, and theory and is currently working on a cultural history of space in post-war France.

Rob Wilson is Professor of Literature at the University of California at Santa Cruz. *'Henry, Torn from the Stomach': Towards a Poetics of Conversion and Counter-Conversion in the Postcolonial US Empire* is forthcoming from Harvard University Press, and a collection of cultural criticism (co-edited with Christopher Connery), *The Worlding Project: Doing Cultural Studies in the Era of Globalization*, appeared with North Atlantic Books / New Pacific Press in 2007.

CULTURAL SPACES

Cultural Spaces explores the rapidly changing temporal, spatial, and theoretical boundaries of contemporary cultural studies. Culture has long been understood as the force that defines and delimits societies in fixed spaces. The recent intensification of globalizing processes, however, has meant that it is no longer possible – if it ever was – to imagine the world as a collection of autonomous, monadic spaces, whether these are imagined as localities, nations, regions within nations, or cultures demarcated by region or nation. One of the major challenges of studying contemporary culture is to understand the new relationships of culture to space that are produced today. The aim of this series is to publish bold new analyses and theories of the spaces of culture, as well as investigations of the historical construction of those cultural spaces that have influenced the shape of the contemporary world.

Series Editors:
Richard Cavell, University of British Columbia
Imre Szeman, McMaster University

Editorial Advisory Board:
Lauren Berlant, University of Chicago
Homi K. Bhabha, Harvard University
Hazel V. Carby, Yale University
Richard Day, Queen's University
Christopher Gittings, University of Western Ontario
Lawrence Grossberg, University of North Carolina
Mark Kingwell, University of Toronto
Heather Murray, University of Toronto
Elspeth Probyn, University of Sydney
Rinaldo Walcott, OISE/University of Toronto

Books in the Series:
Peter Ives, *Gramsci's Politics of Language: Engaging the Bakhtin Circle and the Frankfurt School*
Sarah Brophy, *Witnessing AIDS: Writing, Testimony, and the Work of Mourning*
Shane Gunster, *Capitalizing on Culture: Critical Theory for Cultural Studies*
Jasmin Habib, *Israel, Diaspora, and the Routes of National Belonging*
Serra Tinic, *On Location: Canada's Television Industry in a Global Market*
Evelyn Ruppert, *The Moral Economy of Cities: Shaping Good Citizens*
Mark Coté, Richard J.F. Day, and Greig de Peuter, eds., *Utopian Pedagogy: Radical Experiments against Neoliberal Globalization*
Michael McKinnie, *City Stages: Theatre and Urban Space in a Global City*
Mary Gallagher, ed., *World Writing: Poetics, Ethics, Globalization*